D0786668

Bloom's Modern Critical Views

African-American
  Poets: Volume 1
African-American
  Poets: Volume 2
Aldous Huxley
Alfred, Lord Tennyson
Alice Munro
Alice Walker
American Women
  Poets: 1650–1950
Amy Tan
Anton Chekhov
Arthur Miller
Asian-American
  Writers
August Wilson
The Bible
The Brontës
Carson McCullers
Charles Dickens
Christopher Marlowe
Contemporary Poets
Cormac McCarthy
C.S. Lewis
Dante Aligheri
David Mamet
Derek Walcott
Don DeLillo
Doris Lessing
Edgar Allan Poe
Émile Zola
Emily Dickinson
Ernest Hemingway
Eudora Welty
Eugene O'Neill
F. Scott Fitzgerald
Flannery O'Connor
Franz Kafka
Gabriel García
  Márquez
Geoffrey Chaucer
George Orwell
G.K. Chesterton

Gwendolyn Brooks
Hans Christian
  Andersen
Henry David Thoreau
Herman Melville
Hermann Hesse
H.G. Wells
Hispanic-American
  Writers
Homer
Honoré de Balzac
Jamaica Kincaid
James Joyce
Jane Austen
Jay Wright
J.D. Salinger
Jean-Paul Sartre
John Donne and the
  Metaphysical Poets
John Irving
John Keats
John Milton
John Steinbeck
José Saramago
Joseph Conrad
J.R.R. Tolkien
Julio Cortázar
Kate Chopin
Kurt Vonnegut
Langston Hughes
Leo Tolstoy
Marcel Proust
Margaret Atwood
Mark Twain
Mary Wollstonecraft
  Shelley
Maya Angelou
Miguel de Cervantes
Milan Kundera
Nathaniel Hawthorne
Native American
  Writers
Norman Mailer

Octavio Paz
Paul Auster
Philip Roth
Ralph Ellison
Ralph Waldo
  Emerson
Ray Bradbury
Richard Wright
Robert Browning
Robert Frost
Robert Hayden
Robert Louis
  Stevenson
The Romantic Poets
Salman Rushdie
Samuel Taylor
  Coleridge
Stephen Crane
Stephen King
Sylvia Plath
Tennessee Williams
Thomas Hardy
Thomas Pynchon
Tom Wolfe
Toni Morrison
Tony Kushner
Truman Capote
Walt Whitman
W.E.B. Du Bois
William Blake
William Faulkner
William Gaddis
William Shakespeare:
  Comedies
William Shakespeare:
  Histories
William Shakespeare:
  Romances
William Shakespeare:
  Tragedies
William Wordsworth
Zora Neale Hurston

Bloom's Modern Critical Views

THOMAS HARDY
New Edition

Edited and with an introduction by
Harold Bloom
Sterling Professor of the Humanities
Yale University

**BLOOM'S
LITERARY CRITICISM**
An imprint of Infobase Publishing

Bloom's Modern Critical Views: Thomas Hardy—New Edition

Copyright © 2010 by Infobase Publishing
Introduction © 2010 by Harold Bloom

Bloom's Literary Criticism
An imprint of Infobase Publishing
132 West 31st Street
New York NY 10001

Library of Congress Cataloging-in-Publication Data
Thomas Hardy / edited and with an introduction by Harold Bloom. — New ed.
    p. cm.—(Bloom's modern critical views)
Includes bibliographical references and index.
ISBN 978-1-60413-807-8 (acid-free paper) 1. Hardy, Thomas, 1840–1928—Criticism and interpretation. 2. English literature—History and criticism.
    I. Bloom, Harold.
PR4754.T46 2010
823'.8—dc22
                                        2009034816

Contributing editor: Pamela Loos
Cover designed by Alicia Post
Composition by IBT Global, Inc., Troy NY
Cover printed by IBT Global, Inc., Troy NY
Book printed and bound by IBT Global, Inc., Troy NY
Date printed: January 2010
Printed in the United States of America

10 9 8 7 6 5 4 3 2 1

Contents

Editor's Note

My introduction traces Hardy's embodiments of Schopenhauer's will to live in four major novels: *The Mayor of Casterbridge, The Return of the Native, Tess of the D'Urbervilles,* and *Jude the Obscure.* I also consider briefly the relation between Hardy's final poems and Shelley's.

An overview of Hardy's poetry is provided by Trevor Johnson, who emphasizes their rugged honesty, after which Simon Gatrell analyzes Henchard's character in *The Mayor of Casterbridge.*

The sexual allure of Hardy's Tess is faithfully observed by Peter Widdowson, while Robert Schweik finds in *Jude the Obscure* a curious balance of realism and expressionism.

Samuel Hynes deftly compares the style of old age in the poetry of Yeats and Hardy, after which Michael Irwin notes the running down of Hardy's vision of sexual love.

Verse and short story narratives in Hardy are contrasted by Douglas Dunn, while in the volume's final essay, William Kerrigan displays gusto in choosing some major Hardy lyrics for praise.

HAROLD BLOOM

Introduction

The Mayor of Casterbridge

For Arthur Schopenhauer, the will to live was the true thing in itself, not an interpretation but a rapacious, active, universal, and ultimately indifferent drive or desire. Schopenhauer's great work, *The World as Will and Representation*, had the same relation to and influence on many of the principal nineteenth- and early twentieth-century novelists that Freud's writings have in regard to many of this century's later, crucial masters of prose fiction. Zola, Maupassant, Turgenev, and Tolstoy join Thomas Hardy as Schopenhauer's nineteenth-century heirs, in a tradition that goes on through Proust, Conrad, and Thomas Mann to culminate in aspects of Borges and of Beckett. Since Schopenhauer (despite Freud's denials) was one of Freud's prime precursors, one could argue that aspects of Freud's influence on writers simply carry on from Schopenhauer's previous effect. Manifestly, the relation of Schopenhauer to Hardy is different in both kind and degree from the larger sense in which Schopenhauer was Freud's forerunner or Wittgenstein's. A poet-novelist like Hardy turns to a rhetorical speculator like Schopenhauer only because he finds something in his own temperament and sensibility confirmed and strengthened, and not at all as Lucretius turned to Epicurus or as Whitman was inspired by Emerson.

The true precursor for Hardy was Shelley, whose visionary skepticism permeates the novels as well as the poems and *The Dynasts*. There is some technical debt to George Eliot in the early novels, but Hardy in his depths was little more moved by her than by Wilkie Collins, from whom he also learned elements of craft. Shelley's tragic sense of eros is pervasive throughout Hardy and ultimately determines Hardy's understanding of his strongest

1

heroines: Bathsheba Everdene, Eustacia Vye, Marty South, Tess Durbeyfield, Sue Bridehead. Between desire and fulfillment in Shelley falls the shadow of the selfhood, a shadow that makes love and what might be called the means of love quite irreconcilable. What M.D. Zabel named as "the aesthetic of incongruity" in Hardy and ascribed to temperamental causes is in a profound way the result of attempting to transmute the procedures of *The Revolt of Islam* and *Epipsychidion* into the supposedly naturalistic novel.

J. Hillis Miller, when he worked more in the mode of a critic of consciousness like Georges Poulet than in the deconstruction of Paul de Man and Jacques Derrida, saw the fate of love in Hardy as being darkened always by a shadow cast by the lover's consciousness itself. Hugh Kenner, with a distaste for Hardy akin to (and perhaps derived from) T.S. Eliot's in *After Strange Gods*, suggested that Miller had created a kind of Proustian Hardy, who turns out to be a case rather than an artist. Hardy was certainly not an artist comparable to Henry James (who dismissed him as a mere imitator of George Eliot) or James Joyce, but the High Modernist shibboleths for testing the novel have now waned considerably, except for a few surviving high priests of modernism like Kenner. A better guide to Hardy's permanent strength as a novelist was his heir D.H. Lawrence, whose *The Rainbow* and *Women in Love* marvelously brought Hardy's legacy to an apotheosis. Lawrence, praising Hardy with a rebel son's ambivalence, associated him with Tolstoy as a tragic writer:

> And this is the quality Hardy shares with the great writers, Shakespeare or Sophocles or Tolstoi, this setting behind the small action of his protagonists the terrific action of unfathomed nature; setting a smaller system of morality, the one grasped and formulated by the human consciousness within the vast, uncomprehended and incomprehensible morality of nature or of life itself, surpassing human consciousness. The difference is, that whereas in Shakespeare or Sophocles the greater, uncomprehended morality, or fate, is actively transgressed and gives active punishment, in Hardy and Tolstoi the lesser, human morality, the mechanical system is actively transgressed, and holds, and punishes the protagonist, whilst the greater morality is only passively, negatively transgressed, it is represented merely as being present in background, in scenery, not taking any active part, having no direct connexion with the protagonist. Oedipus, Hamlet, Macbeth set themselves up against, or find themselves set up against, the unfathomed moral forces of nature, and out of this unfathomed force comes their death. Whereas

Anna Karenina, Eustacia, Tess, Sue, and Jude find themselves up against the established system of human government and morality, they cannot detach themselves, and are brought down. Their real tragedy is that they are unfaithful to the greater unwritten morality, which would have bidden Anna Karenina be patient and wait until she, by virtue of greater right, could take what she needed from society; would have bidden Vronsky detach himself from the system, become an individual, creating a new colony of morality with Anna; would have bidden Eustacia fight Clym for his own soul, and Tess take and claim her Angel, since she had the greater light; would have bidden Jude and Sue endure for very honour's sake, since one must bide by the best that one has known, and not succumb to the lesser good.

("Study of Thomas Hardy")

This seems to me powerful and just, because it catches what is most surprising and enduring in Hardy's novels—the sublime stature and aesthetic dignity of his crucial protagonists—while exposing also his great limitation, his denial of freedom to his best personages. Lawrence's prescription for what would have saved Eustacia and Clym, Tess and Angel, Sue and Jude is perhaps not as persuasive. He speaks of them as though they were Gudrun and Gerald and thus have failed to be Ursula and Birkin. It is Hardy's genius that they are what they had to be: as imperfect as their creator and his vision, as impure as his language and his plotting, and finally painful and memorable to us:

Note that, in this bitterness, delight,
Since the imperfect is so hot in us,
Lies in flawed words and stubborn sounds.

Of Hardy's major novels, *The Mayor of Casterbridge* is the least flawed and clearly the closest to tragic convention in Western literary tradition. If one hesitates to prefer it to *The Return of the Native*, *Tess*, or *Jude*, that may be because it is the least original and eccentric work of the four. Henchard is certainly the best articulated and most consistent of Hardy's male personages, but Lucetta is no Eustacia, and the amiable Elizabeth Jane does not compel much of the reader's interest. The book's glory, Henchard, is so massive a self-punisher that he can be said to leap over the psychic cosmos of Schopenhauer directly into that of Freud's great essay on the economics of masochism, with its grim new category of "moral masochism." In a surprising way, Hardy reverses, through Henchard, one of the principal *topoi* of Western tragedy, as set forth acutely by Northrop Frye:

> A strong element of demonic ritual in public punishments and similar mob amusements is exploited by tragic and ironic myth. Breaking on the wheel becomes Lear's wheel of fire; bear-baiting is an image for Gloucester and Macbeth, and for the crucified Prometheus the humiliation of exposure, the horror of being watched, is a greater misery than the pain. *Derkou theama* (behold the spectacle; get your staring over with) is his bitterest cry. The inability of Milton's blind Samson to stare back is his greatest torment, and one which forces him to scream at Delilah, in one of the most terrible passages of all tragic drama, that he will tear her to pieces if she touches him.

For Henchard "the humiliation of exposure" becomes a terrible passion, until at last he makes an exhibition of himself during a royal visit. Perhaps he can revert to what Frye calls "the horror of being watched" only when he knows that the gesture involved will be his last. Hence his will, which may be the most powerful prose passage that Hardy ever wrote:

> They stood in silence while he ran into the cottage; returning in a moment with a crumpled scrap of paper. On it there was pencilled as follows:—
>
> "Michael Henchard's Will
>
> "That Elizabeth-Jane Farfrae be not told of my death, or made to grieve on account of me.
> "& that I be not bury'd in consecrated ground.
> "& that no sexton be asked to toll the bell.
> "& that nobody is wished to see my dead body.
> "& that no murners walk behind me at my funeral.
> "& that no flours be planted on my grave.
> "& that no man remember me.
> "To this I put my name.
>
> "Michael Henchard."

That dark testament is the essence of Henchard. It is notorious that "tragedy" becomes a very problematical form in the European Enlightenment and afterwards. Romanticism, which has been our continuous modernism from the mid-1740s to the present moment, did not return the tragic hero to us, though from Richardson's Clarissa Harlowe until now we have received many resurgences of the tragic heroine. Hardy and Ibsen can be judged to have come closest to reviving the tragic hero, in contradistinction to the hero-villain who, throughout romantic tradition, limns his nightpiece and judges it to have been his best. Henchard, despite his blind strength and his terrible errors, is no villain, and as readers we suffer with him, unrelievedly, because our sympathy for him is unimpeded.

Unfortunately, the suffering becomes altogether *too* unrelieved, as it does again with Jude Fawley. Rereading *The Mayor of Casterbridge* is less painful than rereading *Jude the Obscure*, since at least we do not have to contemplate little Father Time hanging the other urchins and himself, but it is still very painful indeed. Whether or not tragedy should possess some catharsis, we resent the imposition of too much pathos on us, and we need some gesture of purification if only to keep us away from our own defensive ironies. Henchard, alas, *accomplishes nothing*, for himself or for others. Ahab, a great hero-villain, goes down fighting his implacable fate, the whiteness of the whale, but Henchard is a self-destroyer to no purpose. And yet we are vastly moved by him and know that we should be. Why?

The novel's full title is *The Life and Death of the Mayor of Casterbridge: A Story of a Man of Character*. As Robert Louis Stevenson said in a note to Hardy, "Henchard is a great fellow," which implies that he is a great personality rather than a man of character. This is, in fact, how Hardy represents Henchard, and the critic R.H. Hutton was right to be puzzled by Hardy's title, in a review published in *The Spectator* on June 5, 1886:

> Mr. Hardy has not given us any more powerful study than that of Michael Henchard. Why he should especially term his hero in his title-page a "man of character," we do not clearly understand. Properly speaking, character is the stamp graven on a man, and character therefore, like anything which can be graven, and which, when graven, remains, is a word much more applicable to that which has fixity and permanence, than to that which is fitful and changeful, and which impresses a totally different image of itself on the wax of plastic circumstance at one time, from that which it impresses on a similarly plastic surface at another time. To keep strictly to the associations from which the word "character" is derived, a man of character ought to suggest a man of steady and unvarying character, a man who conveys very much the same conception of his own qualities under one set of circumstances, which he conveys under

another. This is true of many men, and they might be called men of character *par excellence*. But the essence of Michael Henchard is that he is a man of large nature and depth of passion, who is yet subject to the most fitful influences, who can do in one mood acts of which he will never cease to repent in almost all his other moods, whose temper of heart changes many times even during the execution of the same purpose, though the same ardour, the same pride, the same wrathful magnanimity, the same inability to carry out in cool blood the angry resolve of the mood of revenge or scorn, the same hasty unreasonableness, and the same disposition to swing back to an equally hasty reasonableness, distinguish him throughout. In one very good sense, the great deficiency of Michael Henchard might be said to be in "character." It might well be said that with a little more character, with a little more fixity of mind, with a little more power of recovering *himself* when he was losing his balance, his would have been a nature of gigantic mould; whereas, as Mr. Hardy's novel is meant to show, it was a nature which ran mostly to waste. But, of course, in the larger and wider sense of the word "character," that sense which has less reference to the permanent definition of the stamp, and more reference to the confidence with which the varying moods may be anticipated, it is not inadmissible to call Michael Henchard a "man of character." Still, the words on the title-page rather mislead. One looks for the picture of a man of much more constancy of purpose, and much less tragic mobility of mood, than Michael Henchard. None the less, the picture is a very vivid one, and almost magnificent in its fullness of expression. The largeness of his nature, the unreasonable generosity and suddenness of his friendships, the depth of his self-humiliation for what was evil in him, the eagerness of his craving for sympathy, the vehemence of his impulses both for good and evil, the curious dash of stoicism in a nature so eager for sympathy, and of fortitude in one so moody and restless,—all these are lineaments which, mingled together as Mr. Hardy has mingled them, produce a curiously strong impression of reality, as well as of homely grandeur.

One can summarize Hutton's point by saying that Henchard is stronger in pathos than in ethos, and yet ethos is the daimon, character is fate, and Hardy specifically sets out to show that Henchard's character is his fate. The strength of Hardy's irony is that it is also life's irony and will become Sigmund Freud's irony: Henchard's destiny demonstrates that there are no accidents, meaning that nothing happens to one that is not already oneself. Henchard stares out at the night as though he were staring at an adversary, but there is nothing out there. There is only the self turned against the self, only the drive, beyond the pleasure principle, to death.

The pre-Socratic aphorism that character is fate seems to have been picked up by Hardy from George Eliot's *The Mill on the Floss*, where it is attributed to Novalis. But Hardy need not have gleaned it from anywhere in particular. Everyone in Hardy's novels is overdetermined by his or her past, because for Hardy, as for Freud, everything that is dreadful has already happened, and there never can be anything absolutely new. Such a speculation belies the very word *novel* and certainly was no aid to Hardy's inventiveness. Nothing that happens to Henchard surprises us. His fate is redeemed from dreariness only by its aesthetic dignity, which returns us to the problematical question of Hardy's relation to tragedy as a literary form.

Henchard is burdened neither with wisdom nor with knowledge; he is a man of will and of action, with little capacity for reflection but with a spirit perpetually open and generous toward others. J. Hillis Miller sees him as being governed erotically by mediated desire, but since Miller sees this as the iron law in Hardy's erotic universe, it loses any particular force as an observation on Henchard. I would prefer to say that Henchard, more even than most men and like all women in Hardy, is hungry for love, desperate for some company in the void of existence. D.H. Lawrence read the tragedy of Hardy's figures not as the consequence of mediated desire but as the fate of any desire that will not be bounded by convention and community.

This is the tragedy of Hardy, always the same: the tragedy of those who, more or less pioneers, have died in the wilderness, whither they had escaped for free action, after having left the walled security, and the comparative imprisonment, of the established convention. This is the theme of novel after novel: remain quite within the convention, and you are good, safe, and happy in the long run, though you never have the vivid pang of sympathy on your side: or, on the other hand, be passionate, individual, wilful, you will find the security of the convention a walled prison, you will escape, and you will die, either of your own lack of strength to bear the isolation and the exposure, or by direct revenge from the community, or from both. This is the tragedy, and only this: it is nothing more metaphysical than the division of a man against himself in such a way: first, that he is a member of the community, and must, upon his honour, in no way move to disintegrate the community, either in its moral or its practical form; second, that the convention of the community is a prison to his natural, individual desire, a desire that compels him, whether he feel justified or not, to break the bounds of the community, lands him outside the pale, there to stand alone, and say: "I was right, my desire was real and inevitable; if I was to be myself I must fulfil it, convention or no convention," or else, there to stand alone, doubting, and saying: "Was I right, was I wrong? If I was wrong, oh, let me die!"—in which case he courts death.

The growth and the development of this tragedy, the deeper and deeper realisation of this division and this problem, the coming towards some conclusion, is the one theme of the Wessex novels.

("Study of Thomas Hardy")

This is general enough to be just but not quite specific enough for the self-destructive Henchard. Also not sufficiently specific is the sympathetic judgment of Irving Howe, who speaks of "Henchard's personal struggle—the struggle of a splendid animal trying to escape a trap and thereby entangling itself all the more." I find more precise the dark musings of Sigmund Freud, Hardy's contemporary, who might be thinking of Michael Henchard when he meditates on "The Economic Problem in Masochism":

The third form of masochism, the moral type, is chiefly remarkable for having loosened its connection with what we recognize to be sexuality. To all other masochistic sufferings there still clings the condition that it should be administered by the loved person; it is endured at his command; in the moral type of masochism this limitation has been dropped. It is the suffering itself that matters; whether the sentence is cast by a loved or by an indifferent person is of no importance; it may even be caused by impersonal forces or circumstances, but the true masochist always holds out his cheek wherever he sees a chance of receiving a blow.

The origins of "moral masochism" are in an unconscious sense of guilt, a need for punishment that transcends actual culpability. Even Henchard's original and grotesque "crime," his drunken exploit in wifeselling does not so much engender in him remorse at the consciousness of wrongdoing but rather helps engulf him in the "guilt" of the moral masochist. That means Henchard knows his guilt not as affect or emotion but as a negation, as the nullification of his desires and his ambitions. In a more than Freudian sense, Henchard's primal ambivalence is directed against himself, against the authority principle in his own self.

If *The Mayor of Casterbridge* is a less original book than *Tess* or *Jude*, it is also a more persuasive and universal vision than Hardy achieved elsewhere.

Miguel de Unamuno, defining the tragic sense of life, remarked that: "The chiefest sanctity of a temple is that it is a place to which men go to weep in common. A *miserere* sung in common by a multitude tormented by destiny has as much value as a philosophy." That is not tragedy as Aristotle defined it, but it is tragedy as Thomas Hardy wrote it.

The Return of the Native

I first read *The Return of the Native* when I was about fifteen and had reread it in whole or in part several times through the years before rereading it now. What I had remembered most vividly then I am likely to remember again: Eustacia, Venn the red man, the heath. I had almost forgotten Clym, and his mother, and Thomasin, and Wildeve and probably will forget them again. Clym, in particular, is a weak failure in characterization and nearly sinks the novel; indeed ought to capsize any novel whatsoever. Yet *The Return of the Native* survives him, even though its chief glory, the sexually enchanting Eustacia Vye, does not. Her suicide is so much the waste of a marvelous woman (or representation of a woman, if you insist on being a formalist) that the reader finds Clym even more intolerable than he is and is likely not to forgive Hardy, except that Hardy clearly suffers the loss quite as much as any reader does.

Eustacia underwent a singular transformation during the novel's composition, from a daimonic sort of female Byron, or Byronic witchlike creature, to the grandly beautiful, discontented, and human—all too human but hardly blameworthy—heroine, who may be the most desirable woman in all of nineteenth-century British fiction. "A powerful personality uncurbed by any institutional attachment or by submission to any objective beliefs; unhampered by any ideas"—it would be a good description of Eustacia but is actually Hardy himself through the eyes of T.S. Eliot in *After Strange Gods*, where Hardy is chastised for not believing in original sin and deplored also because "at times his style touches sublimity without ever having passed through the stage of being good."

Here is Eustacia in the early "Queen of Night" chapter:

> She was in person full-limbed and somewhat heavy; without ruddiness, as without pallor; and soft to the touch as a cloud. To see her hair was to fancy that a whole winter did not contain darkness enough to form its shadow: it closed over her forehead like nightfall extinguishing the western glow.
>
> Her nerves extended into those tresses, and her temper could always be softened by stroking them down. When her hair was brushed she would instantly sink into stillness and look like the

Sphinx. If, in passing under one of the Egdon banks, any of its thick skeins were caught, as they sometimes were, by a prickly tuft of the large *Ulex Europaeus*—which will act as a sort of hairbrush—she would go back a few steps, and pass against it a second time.

She had Pagan eyes, full of nocturnal mysteries, and their light, as it came and went, and came again, was partially hampered by their oppressive lids and lashes; and of these the under lid was much fuller than it usually is with English women. This enabled her to indulge in reverie without seeming to do so: she might have been believed capable of sleeping without closing them up. Assuming that the souls of men and women were visible essences, you could fancy the colour of Eustacia's soul to be flame-like. The sparks from it that rose into her dark pupils gave the same impression.

Hardy's Eustacia may owe something to Walter Pater's *The Renaissance*, published five years before *The Return of the Native*, since in some ways she makes a third with Pater's evocations of the Botticelli Venus and Leonardo's Mona Lisa, visions of antithetical female sexuality. Eustacia's flamelike quality precisely recalls Pater's ecstasy of passion in the "Conclusion" to *The Renaissance*, and the epigraph to *The Return of the Native* could well have been:

This at least of flame-like our life has, that it is but the concurrence, renewed from moment to moment, of forces parting sooner or later on their ways.

This at least of flamelike Eustacia's life has, that the concurrence of forces parts sooner rather than later. But then this most beautiful of Hardy's women is also the most doom-eager, the color of her soul being flamelike. The heath brings her only Wildeve and Clym, but Paris doubtless would have brought her scarce better, since as Queen of Night she attracts the constancy and the kindness of sorrow.

If Clym and Wildeve are bad actors, and they are, what about Egdon Heath? On this, critics are perpetually divided, some finding the landscape sublime, while others protest that its representation is bathetic. I myself am divided, since clearly it is both and sometimes simultaneously so! Though Eustacia hates it fiercely, it is nearly as Shelleyan as she is and rather less natural than presumably it ought to be. That it is more overwritten than overgrown is palpable:

To recline on a stump of thorn in the central valley of Egdon, between afternoon and night, as now, where the eye could reach nothing of the world outside the summits and shoulders of heathland which filled the whole circumference of its glance, and to know that everything around and underneath had been from prehistoric times as unaltered as the stars overhead, gave ballast to the mind adrift on change, and harassed by the irrepressible New. The great inviolate place had an ancient permanence which the sea cannot claim. Who can say of a particular sea that it is old? Distilled by the sun, kneaded by the moon, it is renewed in a year, in a day, or in an hour. The sea changed, the fields changed, the rivers, the villages, and the people changed, yet Egdon remained. Those surfaces were neither so steep as to be destructible by weather, nor so flat as to be the victims of floods and deposits. With the exception of an aged highway, and a still more aged barrow presently to be referred to—themselves almost crystallized to natural products by long continuance—even the trifling irregularities were not caused by pickaxe, plough, or spade, but remained as the very finger-touches of the last geological change.

Even Melville cannot always handle this heightened mode; Hardy rarely can, although he attempts it often. And yet we do remember Egdon Heath, years after reading the novel, possibly because something about it wounds us even as it wounds Eustacia. We remember also Diggory Venn, not as the prosperous burgher he becomes, but as we first encounter him, permeated by the red ochre of his picturesque trade:

The decayed officer, by degrees, came up alongside his fellow-wayfarer, and wished him good evening. The reddleman turned his head and replied in sad and occupied tones. He was young, and his face, if not exactly handsome, approached so near to handsome that nobody would have contradicted an assertion that it really was so in its natural colour. His eye, which glared so strangely through his stain, was in itself attractive—keen as that of a bird of prey, and blue as autumn mist. He had neither whisker nor moustache, which allowed the soft curves of the lower part of his face to be apparent. His lips were thin, and though, as it seemed, compressed by thought, there was a pleasant twitch at their corners now and then. He was clothed throughout in a tight-fitting suit of corduroy, excellent in quality, not much worn, and well-chosen for its purpose; but deprived of its original colour by his trade. It showed to advantage the good shape of his figure. A certain well-to-do air about the man suggested that he was not poor for his degree. The natural query of an observer would have been, Why should such a promising being as this have hidden his prepossessing exterior by adopting that singular occupation?

Hardy had intended Venn to disappear mysteriously forever from Egdon Heath, instead of marrying Thomasin but yielded to the anxiety of giving the contemporary reader something cheerful and normative at the end of his austere and dark novel. He ought to have kept to his intent, but perhaps it does not matter. The heath endures, the red man either vanishes or is transmogrified into a husband and a burgher. Though we see Clym rather uselessly preaching to all comers as the book closes, our spirits are elsewhere, with the wild image of longing that no longer haunts the heath, Hardy's lost Queen of Night.

Tess of the d'Urbervilles

Of all the novels of Hardy, *Tess of the d'Urbervilles* now appeals to the widest audience. The book's popularity with the common reader has displaced the earlier ascendancy of *The Return of the Native*. It can even be asserted that Hardy's novel has proved to be prophetic of a sensibility by no means fully emergent in 1891. More than a century later, the book sometimes seems to have moments of vision that are contemporary with us. These tend to come from Hardy's intimate sympathy with his heroine, a sympathy that verges on paternal love. It is curious that Hardy is more involved with Tess than with Jude Fawley in *Jude the Obscure*, even though Jude is closer to being Hardy's surrogate than any other male figure in the novels.

J. Hillis Miller, in the most advanced critical study yet attempted of *Tess*, reads it as "a story about repetition," but by "repetition" Miller appears to mean a linked chain of interpretations. A compulsion to interpret may be the reader's share and may be Hardy's own stance toward his own novel (and perhaps even extends to Angel Clare's role in the book) but seems to me fairly irrelevant to Tess herself. Since the novel is a story about Tess, I cannot regard it as being "about" repetition or even one that concerns a difference in repetitions. Hardy's more profound ironies are neither classical nor romantic, but biblical, as Miller himself discerns. Classical irony turns on contrasts between what is said and what is meant, while romantic irony inhabits the gap between expectation and fulfillment. But biblical irony appears whenever giant incongruities clash, which happens when Yahweh, who is incommensurate, is closely juxtaposed to men and women and their vain imaginings.

When Yahweh devours roast calf under the terebinths at Mamre, or when Jacob wrestles with a nameless one among the Elohim at Penuel, then we are confronted by an irony neither classical nor romantic.

Hardy, like his master Shelley, is an unbeliever who remains within the literary context of the Bible, and again like Shelley he derives his mode of prophetic irony from the Bible. A striking instance (noted by Hillis Miller) comes in chapter 11:

> In the meantime Alec d'Urberville had pushed on up the slope to clear his genuine doubt as to the quarter of The Chase they were in. He had, in fact, ridden quite at random for over an hour, taking any turning that came to hand in order to prolong companionship with her, and giving far more attention to Tess's moonlit person than to any wayside object. A little rest for the jaded animal being desirable, he did not hasten his search for landmarks. A clamber over the hill into the adjoining vale brought him to the fence of a highway whose contours he recognized, which settled the question of their whereabouts. D'Urberville thereupon turned back; but by this time the moon had quite gone down, and partly on account of the fog The Chase was wrapped in thick darkness, although morning was not far off. He was obliged to advance with outstretched hands to avoid contact with the boughs, and discovered that to hit the exact spot from which he had started was at first entirely beyond him. Roaming up and down, round and round, he at length heard a slight movement of the horse close at hand; and the sleeve of his overcoat unexpectedly caught his foot.
>
> "Tess!" said d'Urberville.
>
> There was no answer. The obscurity was now so great that he could see absolutely nothing but a pale nebulousness at his feet, which represented the white muslin figure he had left upon the dead leaves. Everything else was blackness alike. D'Urberville stooped; and heard a gentle regular breathing. He knelt and bent lower, till her breath warmed his face, and in a moment his cheek was in contact with hers. She was sleeping soundly, and upon her eyelashes there lingered tears.
>
> Darkness and silence ruled everywhere around. Above them rose the primeval yews and oaks of The Chase, in which were poised gentle roosting birds in their last nap; and about them stole the hopping rabbits and hares. But, might some say, where was Tess's guardian angel? Where was the providence of her simple faith? Perhaps, like that other god of whom the ironical Tishbite

spoke, he was talking, or he was pursuing, or he was in a journey, or he was sleeping and not to be awaked.

Why it was that upon this beautiful feminine tissue, sensitive as gossamer, and practically blank as snow as yet, there should have been traced such a coarse pattern as it was doomed to receive; why so often the coarse appropriates the finer thus, the wrong man the woman, the wrong woman the man, many thousand years of analytical philosophy have failed to explain to our sense of order. One may, indeed, admit the possibility of a retribution lurking in the present catastrophe. Doubtless some of Tess d'Urberville's mailed ancestors rollicking home from a fray had dealt the same measure even more ruthlessly towards peasant girls of their time. But though to visit the sins of the fathers upon the children may be a morality good enough for divinities, it is scorned by average human nature; and it therefore does not mend the matter.

As Tess's own people down in those retreats are never tired of saying among each other in their fatalistic way: "It was to be." There lay the pity of it. An immeasurable social chasm was to divide our heroine's personality thereafter from that previous self of hers who stepped from her mother's door to try her fortune at Trantridge poultry-farm.

The ironical Tishbite is the savage Elijah the prophet, who mocks the priests of Baal, urging them: "Cry aloud: for he is a god; either he is talking, or he is pursuing, or he is in a journey, or peradventure he sleepeth, and must be awaked." Elijah's irony depends on the incommensurateness of Yahweh and the human—all too human—Baal. Hardy's irony cannot be what Hillis Miller deconstructively wishes it to be when he rather remarkably suggests that Tess herself is "like the prophets of Baal," nor does it seem right to call Yahweh's declaration that He is a jealous (or zealous) God "the divine lust for vengeance," as Miller does. Yahweh, after all, has just given the Second Commandment against making graven images or idols, such as the Baal whom Elijah mocks. Hardy associates Alec's "violation" of Tess with a destruction of pastoral innocence, which he scarcely sees as Baal worship or idolatry. His emphasis is precisely that no mode of religion, revealed or natural, could defend Tess from an overdetermined system in which the only thing-in-itself is the rapacious will to live, a will that itself is, as it were, the curse of Yahweh on the hungry generations.

Repetition in *Tess* is repetition as Schopenhauer saw it, which is little different from how Hardy and Freud subsequently saw it. What is repeated, compulsively, is a unitary desire that is rapacious, indifferent, and universal.

The pleasures of repetition in Hardy's Tess are not interpretive and perspectival, and so engendered by difference, but are actually masochistic, in the erotogenic sense, and so ensue from the necessity of similarity. Hardy's pragmatic version of the aesthetic vision in this novel is essentially sadomasochistic, and the sufferings of poor Tess give an equivocal pleasure of repetition to the reader. The book's extraordinary popularity partly results from its exquisitely subtle and deeply sympathetic unfolding of the torments of Tess, a pure woman because a pure nature and doomed to suffer merely because she is so much a natural woman. The poet Lionel Johnson, whose early book (1895) on Hardy still seems to me unsurpassed, brought to the reading of Tess a spirit that was antithetically both Shelleyan and Roman Catholic:

> As a girl of generous thought and sentiment, rich in beauty, rich in the natural joys of life, she is brought into collision with the harshness of life.... The world was very strong; her conscience was blinded and bewildered; she did some things nobly, and some despairingly: but there is nothing, not even in studies of criminal anthropology or of morbid pathology, to suggest that she was wholly an irresponsible victim of her own temperament, and of adverse circumstances.... She went through fire and water, and made no true use of them: she is pitiable, but not admirable.

Johnson is very clear-sighted but perhaps too much the Catholic moralist. To the common reader, Tess is both pitiable and admirable, as Hardy wanted her to be. Is it admirable, though, that, by identifying with her, the reader takes a masochistic pleasure in her suffering? Aesthetically, I would reply yes, but the question remains a disturbing one. When the black flag goes slowly up the staff and we know that the beautiful Tess has been executed, do we reside in Hardy's final ironies, or do we experience a pleasure of repetition that leaves us void of interpretive zeal, yet replete with the gratification of a drive beyond the pleasure principle?

Jude the Obscure

Thomas Hardy lived to be eighty-seven and a half years old, and his long life (1840–1928) comprised two separate literary careers, as a late Victorian novelist (1871–1897) and as a poet who defies temporal placement (1898–1928). The critical reaction to his final novels, The Well-Beloved and Jude the Obscure, ostensibly motivated Hardy's abandonment of prose fiction, but he always had thought of himself as a poet and by 1897 was financially secure enough to center himself on his poetry. He is—with Housman, Yeats, D.H. Lawrence, Wilfred Owen, and Geoffrey Hill—one of the half-dozen or so major poets of the British Isles in the century just past. In regard to his prose works, he can be judged to be one of the crucial novelists of the final three decades of the nineteenth century, the bridge connecting George Eliot and the Brontës to Lawrence's novels in the earlier twentieth century.

T.S. Eliot, who continues to enjoy a high critical reputation despite being almost always wrong, attacked Hardy in a dreadful polemic, *After Strange Gods,* where the novelist-poet is stigmatized as not believing in original sin, which turns out to be an aesthetic criterion, since Hardy's style "touches sublimity without ever having passed through the stage of being good." This inaccurate wisecrack is prompted by Eliot's severe summary of the post-Protestant Hardy: "A powerful personality uncurbed by any institutional attachment or by submission to any objective beliefs; unhampered by any ideas." Eliot's institutional attachment was to the Anglo-Catholic Church: his "objective beliefs" were Christianity, royalism, and what he called "classicism" and his "ideas" excluded Freud and Marx.

Hardy, as High Romantic as Shelley and the Brontës, or as Lawrence and Yeats, cannot be judged by neo-Christian ideology. The best books on him remain, in my judgment, Lionel Johnson's early *The Art of Thomas Hardy,* and D.H. Lawrence's outrageous *Study of Thomas Hardy and Other Essays*—which is mostly about Hardy's impact on Lawrence. Michael Millgate's remains the best biography, but since Hardy burned letters and concealed relationships, we still do not know enough to fully integrate the work and the life. Both of Hardy's marriages evidently did not fulfill him, and his lifelong attraction to women much younger than himself has an Ibsenite and Yeatsian aura to it. There is a dark intensity, in the novels and poems alike, that has marked sado-masochistic overtones.

Hardy's personal greatness as a novelist is enhanced (and enabled) by his freedom from T.S. Eliot's attachments and submissions. The agnostic Hardy was Schopenhauerian before he read Schopenhauer and found a name for the will to live that destroys the protagonists of his novels. Hardy's women and men are driven by the tragic forces that are incarnated in Sophocles's Electra, Shakespeare's Lear and Macbeth, and Tolstoy's Anna Karenina. Henry James, who regarded Hardy as a poor imitator of George Eliot, was as mistaken as T.S. Eliot was after him.

What matters most, in Hardy's women and men, is their tragic dignity, though their author denies them the ultimate freedom of choice. Hardy's chief limitation, as a novelist, is his sense that the will is overdetermined, as it is in Schopenhauer. What saves Hardy's novels is that pragmatically he cannot maintain the detachment he seeks in regard to his central personages.

Yeats, very much in Pater's tradition, said that: "We begin to live when we conceive of life as tragedy." Hardy would not have remarked that, but he believed it, and exemplifies it in his novels. *The Mayor of Casterbridge, Tess of the d'Urbervilles*, and *Jude the Obscure* are novelistic tragedies, closer to Shakespeare than to George Eliot. *Tess* in particular has something of the universal appeal of Shakespearean tragedy, though the sadomasochistic gratification of the audience/readership is again an equivocal element in Hardy's aesthetic power. And yet who would have it otherwise? *Tess* is the most beautiful of Hardy's pastoral visions, and the tragic Tess is the most disturbing of all his heroines, because the most desirable.

Alone among Hardy's novels, *Jude the Obscure* has three strong figures, all triumphs of representation: Sue, Jude, Arabella. Unfortunately, it also has little Father Time, Hardy's most memorable disaster in representation. Even more unfortunately, it is a book in which Hardy's drive to go on telling stories gives way to his precursor Shelley's despair that there is one story and one story only, the triumph of life over human integrity. As the most Shelleyan of Hardy's novels (except perhaps for *The Well-Beloved*, which precedes it in initial composition, though not in revision and publication), *Jude the Obscure* has a complex and perhaps crippling relation to *Epipsychidion*. Sue Bridehead is more Shelleyan than even Shelley's Emilia in that poem and would have been better off married to Shelley than to Jude Fawley, which is not to say that poor Shelley could have survived the union any better than the unhappy Jude.

D. H. Lawrence, inevitably, was Sue's most articulate critic:

> Her female spirit did not wed with the male spirit: she could not prophesy. Her spirit submitted to the male spirit, owned the priority of the male spirit, wished to become the male spirit.

Sue needs no defense, least of all in the present day when she has become prevalent, a subtle rebel against any dialectic of power founded wholly on mere gender. Yet, within the novel, Sue is less a rebel than she is Jude's Shelleyan epipsyche, his twin sister (actually his cousin) and counterpart. She can live neither with Jude nor without him, and their love is both narcissistic and incestuous, Hardy's metaphor for the will to live at its most destructive, because in Jude and Sue it destroys the most transcendent beings Hardy had ever imagined.

It will not suffice to call *Jude the Obscure* a tragedy, since what is most tragic in Jude and Sue is their Shelleyan transcendence. When Shelley attempted tragedy in *The Cenci*, he succeeded only by diverting the form into a lament for the descent of Beatrice Cenci to her father's level. But Jude and Sue cannot be said to descend, any more than Eustacia, Henchard, and Tess descend. The will to live in Hardy's cosmos is too terrible and too incessant for us to speak of it as debasing its subjects or victims. In a world dominated by drive, a spirit like Jude's is condemned to die whispering the Jobean lament: "Let the day perish wherein I was born." *Jude the Obscure* is Hardy's book of Job and, like Job, is too dark for tragedy, while, unlike Job, it is just the reverse of theodicy, being Hardy's ultimate declaration that the ways of the immanent will toward man are unjustifiable.

Few interchanges in literature are at once so pathetic and so charming as the intricate, Shelleyan dances of scruple and desire intertwined that involve Sue and Jude:

> He laughed. "Never mind," he said. "So that I am near you, I am comparatively happy. It is more than this earthly wretch called Me deserves—you spirit, you disembodied creature, you dear, sweet, tantalizing phantom—hardly flesh at all; so that when I put my arms round you, I almost expect them to pass through you as through air! Forgive me for being gross, as you call it! Remember that our calling ourselves cousins when really strangers was a snare. The enmity of our parents gave a piquancy to you in my eyes that was intenser ever than the novelty of ordinary new acquaintance."
>
> "Say those pretty lines, then, from Shelley's 'Epipsychidion' as if they meant me," she solicited, slanting up closer to him as they stood. "Don't you know them?"
>
> "I know hardly any poetry," he replied, mournfully.
>
> "Don't you?" These are some of them:
> "'There was a Being whom my spirit oft
> Met on its visioned wanderings far aloft.
> . . . .
> A seraph of Heaven, too gentle to be human,
> Veiling beneath that radiant form of woman . . .'"
>
> "Oh, it is too flattering, so I won't go on! But say it's me!—say it's me!"
>
> "It *is* you, dear; exactly like you!"
>
> "Now I forgive you! And you shall kiss me just once there—not very long." She put the tip of her finger gingerly to her cheek, and he did as commanded. "You do care for me very much, don't you, in spite of my not—you know?"
>
> "Yes, sweet!" he said, with a sigh, and bade her good-night.

It is Sue, right enough, and it is disaster. The true epigraph to *Jude the Obscure* comes at the climax of *Epipsychidion*:

In one another's substance finding food,

Like flames too pure and light and unimbued
To nourish their bright lives with baser prey,
Which point to Heaven and cannot pass away:
One hope within two wills, one will beneath
Two overshadowing minds, one life, one death,
One Heaven, one Hell, one immortality,
And one annihilation.

That "one will beneath" the "two overshadowing minds" of Sue and
Jude is the immanent will of Thomas Hardy, and it indeed does become "one
annihilation."

Poetry

Only a poet challenges a poet as poet, and so only a poet makes a poet. To the
poet-in-a-poet, a poem is always *the other man*, the precursor, and so a poem
is always a person, always the father of one's second birth. To live, the poet
must *misinterpret* the father, by the crucial act of misprision, which is the
rewriting of the father.

But who, what is the poetic father? The voice of the other, of the daimon,
is always speaking in one; the voice that cannot die because already it has survived death—*the dead poet lives in one.* In the last phase of strong poets, they
attempt to join the undying *by living in the dead poets* who are already alive in
them. This late return of the dead recalls us, as readers, to a recognition of the
original motive for the catastrophe of poetic incarnation. Vico, who identified the origins of poetry with the impulse toward divination (to foretell, but
also to become a god by foretelling), implicitly understood (as did Emerson
and Wordsworth) that a poem is written to escape dying. Literally, poems are
refusals of mortality. Every poem therefore has two makers: the precursor and
the ephebe's rejected mortality.

A poet, I argue in consequence, is not so much a person speaking to others as a person rebelling against being spoken to by a dead being (the precursor) outrageously more alive than he or she. Poets dare not regard themselves
as being *late*, yet cannot accept a substitute for the first vision they reflectively
judge to have been their precursor's also. Perhaps this is why the poet-in-a-
poet *cannot marry*, whatever the person-in-a-poet chooses to have done.

Poetic influence, in the sense I give to it, has almost nothing to do with
the verbal resemblances between one poet and another. Hardy, on the surface, scarcely resembles Shelley, his prime precursor, but then Browning, who
resembles Shelley even less, was yet more fully Shelley's ephebe than even
Hardy was. The same observation can be made of Swinburne and of Yeats in
relation to Shelley. What Blake called the spiritual form, at once the aboriginal

poetical self and the true subject, is what the ephebe is so dangerously obliged to the precursor for even possessing. Poets need not *look* like their precursors, and the anxiety of influence more frequently than not is quite distinct from the anxiety of style. Since poetic influence is necessarily misprision, a taking or doing amiss of one's burden, it is to be expected that such a process of malformation and misinterpretation will, at the very least, produce deviations in style between strong poets. Let us remember always Emerson's insistence as to what it is that makes a poem:

> For it is not metres, but a metre-making argument, that makes a poem,—a thought so passionate and alive, that, like the spirit of a plant or an animal, it has an architecture of its own, and adorns nature with a new thing. The thought and the form are equal in the order of time, but in the order of genesis the thought is prior to the form. The poet has a new thought: he has a whole new experience to unfold; he will tell us how it was with him, and all men will be the richer in his fortune. For, the experience of each new age requires a new confession, and the world seems always waiting for its poet.
>
> ("The Poet")

Emerson would not acknowledge that meter-making arguments themselves were subject to the tyrannies of inheritance, but that they are so subject is the saddest truth I know about poets and poetry. In Hardy's best poems, the central meter-making argument is what might be called a skeptical lament for the hopeless incongruity of ends and means in all human acts. Love and the means of love cannot be brought together, and the truest name for the human condition is simply that it is loss:

> And brightest things that are theirs. . . .
> Ah, no; the years, the years;
> Down their carved names the rain-drop ploughs.

These are the closing lines of "During Wind and Rain," as good a poem as our century has given us. The poem, like so many others, is a grandchild of the "Ode to the West Wind," as much as Stevens's "The Course of a Particular" or any number of major lyrics by Yeats. A carrion eater, old style, would challenge my observations, and to such a challenge I could offer, in its own terms, only the first appearance of the refrain:

> Ah, no; the years O!
> How the sick leaves reel down in throngs!

But such terms can be ignored. Poetic influence, between strong poets, works in the depths, as all love antithetically works. At the center of Hardy's verse, whether in the early *Wessex Poems* or the late *Winter Words*, is this vision:

And much I grieved to think how power and will
In opposition rule our mortal day—
And why God made irreconcilable
Good and the means of good; and for despair
I half disdained mine eye's desire to fill
With the spent vision of the times that were
And scarce have ceased to be—

Shelley's *Triumph of Life* can give us also the heroic motto for the major characters in Hardy's novels: "For in the battle Life and they did wage, / She remained conqueror." The motto would serve as well for the superb volume *Winter Words in Various Moods and Metres*, published on October 2 in 1928, the year that Hardy died on January 11. Hardy had hoped to publish the book on June 2, 1930, which would have been his ninetieth birthday. Though a few poems in the book go back as far as the 1860s, most were written after the appearance of Hardy's volume of lyrics *Human Shows* in 1925. A few books of twentieth-century verse in English compare with *Winter Words* in greatness, but very few. Though the collection is diverse and has no central design, its emergent theme is a counterpoise to the burden of poetic incarnation and might be called the return of the dead, who haunt Hardy as he faces toward death.

In his early poem "Shelley's Skylark" (1887), Hardy, writing rather in the style of his fellow Shelleyan Browning, speaks of his ancestor's "ecstatic heights in thought and rhyme." Recent critics who admire Shelley are not particularly fond of "To a Skylark," and it is rather too ecstatic for most varieties of modern sensibility, but we can surmise why it so moved Hardy:

We look before and after,
    And pine for what is not—
Our sincerest laughter
    With some pain is fraught—
Our sweetest songs are those that tell of saddest thought.
Yet if we could scorn
    Hate and pride and fear;
If we were things born
    Not to shed a tear,
I know not how thy joy we ever should come near.

The thought here, as elsewhere in Shelley, is not so simple as it may seem. Our divided consciousness, keeping us from being able to unperplex joy from pain and ruining the presentness of the moment, at least brings us an aesthetic gain. But even if we lacked our range of negative affections, even if grief were not our birthright, the pure joy of the lark's song would still surpass us. We may think of Shelleyan ladies like Marty South and even more Sue Bridehead, who seems to have emerged from the *Epipsychidion*. Or perhaps we may remember Angel Clare as a kind of parody of Shelley himself. Hardy's Shelley is very close to the most central of Shelleys, the visionary skeptic, whose head and whose heart could never be reconciled, for they both told truths, but contrary truths. In *Prometheus Unbound*, we are told that in our life the shadow cast by love is always ruin, which is the head's report, but the heart in Shelley goes on saying that if there is to be coherence at all, it must come through Eros.

Winter Words, as befits a man going into his later eighties, is more in ruin's shadow than in love's realm. The last poem, written in 1927, is called "He Resolves to Say No More" and follows directly on "We Are Getting to The End," which may be the bleakest sonnet in the language. Both poems explicitly reject any vision of hope and are set against the Shelleyan rational meliorism of *Prometheus Unbound*. "We are getting to the end of visioning / The impossible within this universe," Hardy flatly insists, and he recalls Shelley's vision of rolling time backward, only to dismiss it as the doctrine of Shelley's Ahasuerus: "(Magians who drive the midnight quill / With brain aglow / Can see it so)." Behind this rejection is the mystery of misprision, of deep poetic influence in its final phase, which I have called *apophrades* or the return of the dead. Hovering everywhere in *Winter Words*, though far less explicitly than it hovers in *The Dynasts*, is Shelley's *Hellas*. The peculiar strength and achievement of *Winter Words* is not that we are compelled to remember Shelley when we read in it, but rather that it makes us read much of Shelley as though Hardy were Shelley's ancestor, the dark father whom the revolutionary idealist failed to cast out.

Nearly every poem in *Winter Words* has a poignance unusual even in Hardy, but I am moved most by "He Never Expected Much," the poet's reflection on his eighty-sixth birthday, where his dialogue with the "World" attains a resolution:

> "I do not promise overmuch,
>   Child; overmuch;
> Just neutral-tinted haps and such,"
>   You said to minds like mine.
> Wise warning for your credit's sake!

Which I for one failed not to take,
And hence could stem such strain and ache
   As each year might assign.

The "neutral-tinted haps," so supremely hard to get into poems, are the staple of Hardy's achievement in verse and contrast both to Wordsworth's "sober coloring" and Shelley's "deep autumnal tone." All through *Winter Words* the attentive reader will hear a chastened return of High Romantic Idealism but muted into Hardy's tonality. Where Yeats malformed both himself and his High Romantic fathers Blake and Shelley in the violences of *Last Poems and Plays*, Hardy more effectively subdued the questing temperaments of his fathers Shelley and Browning in *Winter Words*. The wrestling with the great dead is subtler in Hardy and kinder both to him and to the fathers.

TREVOR JOHNSON

Hardy's Poetry: A General Survey

> ... The characteristic of all great poetry—the general perfectly reduced to
> the particular.
>
> —Hardy in conversation with Elliott Felkin in 1919

Hardy always thought of himself as a poet first and foremost. He was not
above making disparaging remarks about the fiction which brought him his
bread and butter, dismissing it once as a 'mechanical trade'. He wrote poetry
intermittently for seventy years or so although virtually none of it saw print
until he was nearly sixty. The *Complete Poems* contains 947 poems and the
late Philip Larkin boldly asserted that it was ' . . . many times over the best
body of poetic work this century has so far to show', backing his judgement
by including 28, his largest single allocation, in his *Oxford Book of Twentieth
Century Verse*. Dame Helen Gardner, in her *New Oxford Book of Verse* also
chose 22, thereby placing Hardy on a level with the very greatest English
poets of the last five centuries. The most recent large conspectual anthology, John Wain's *Oxford Library of English Poetry* (1987) gives Hardy similar
prominence. There are three complete editions of his verse and more than
twenty selections have been made from it. So much cannot be said of any of
his contemporaries, or more than a few of his predecessors.

Yet all this represents an astonishing shift in opinion from 1898 when
Wessex Poems was saluted as including 'the most astounding balderdash that ever

From *A Critical Introduction to the Poems of Thomas Hardy*, pp. 36–54. © 1991 by Henry
Anthony Trevor Johnson.

found its way into a book of verse', while the view propounded by F. R. Leavis, and echoed by R. P. Blackmur among others, that Hardy had by what might be called happy accident produced a mere handful of great poems, was widely current until quite recently. Although, as Hardy drily observed, part of the initial reaction could be ascribed to 'his having taken the liberty to adopt another vehicle of expression than prose-fiction without consulting [the critics]', there were other reasons, not altogether insubstantial, why even well-disposed readers found a good deal to puzzle and provoke them in Hardy's verse. If time has dispersed some of the obstacles, others remain in place. Partly by examining them and partly by taking into account Hardy's own pronouncements about what he was trying to do in his poetry, we may find our way towards a standpoint from which more detailed consideration of individual poems may begin.

To begin with, as even his denigrators have always admitted, Hardy's is a singular genius; his verse has a stern, stubborn individuality which, for all its evident integrity, can be forbidding. It is difficult to imitate and has rarely been successfully parodied. Though seldom obscure, it is both exceptionally varied and exceptionally idiosyncratic in form, while it displays as wide a range of subjects as any English poet's work before or since. But just about the last epithet anyone would be likely to apply to it is *charming*, and it is very seldom that Hardy offers us anything as immediately winning as *Weathers* (512/ALL/H/*) which over a dozen composers have set to music and which appears in innumerable school anthologies, often as the sole example of Hardy's work! It begins

> This is the weather the cuckoo likes,
>   And so do I;
> When showers betumble the chestnut spikes,
>   And nestlings fly:
> And the little brown nightingale bills his best,
> And they sit outside at 'The Travellers' Rest',
> And maids come forth sprig-muslin drest,
> And citizens dream of the south and west,
>   And so do I.

What could be more engaging than the lilting rhythms (the stanza form is indeed Elizabethan in origin), the sharp-eyed observation of springtime—'showers *betumble* the chestnut *spikes*'—the shared enjoyment of life's simpler pleasures, even the impudent, six-times-repeated initial *And*, which we have all been taught never to begin a sentence with? Nothing, except perhaps the Shakespeare of *Love's Labour's Lost* who, in one of the play's concluding lyrics, also brings on the cuckoo to tell of spring

When shepherds pipe on oaten straws,
And merry larks are ploughmens clocks
When turtles tread and rooks and daws,
And maidens bleach their summer smocks:

Shakespeare was country bred too; the acute vision, the gaiety, the sparkling imagery, the easy mastery of form they also share. Yet neither stanza can be called typical of its author, though we may well wish that both had written more in this vein.

The truth is that much of Hardy's characteristic strength, and something of his characteristic weakness too, derives from his steady refusal to write one kind of poetry—the kind well exemplified by the first verse of *Weathers*—to the exclusion of another. For just as Shakespeare goes on to tell of *Winter* (notice the *Ands*),

When icicles hang by the wall,
And Dick the shepherd blows his nail:
And Tom bears logs into the hall,
And milk comes frozen home in pail
When blood is nipt and ways be foul,

so Hardy, in verse 2 of *Weathers*, goes on,

This is the weather the shepherd shuns,
    And so do I;
When beeches drip in browns and duns,
    And thresh and ply;
And hill-hid tides throb, throe on throe,
And meadow rivulets overflow,
And drops on gate-bars hang in a row,
And rooks in families homeward go,
    And so do I.

The catalogue of winter's discomforts—the sodden landscape, the icy winds, the black, lumbering birds—makes a bleak contrast with the first stanza, which is, of course, much more agreeable to contemplate. But, as Coleridge, with whose critical opinions Hardy was well acquainted, once said, one of the most widespread errors is the confusion of what is 'agreeable' with what is 'beautiful'. So, in his *Apology to Late Lyrics and Earlier* Hardy quotes Wordsworth's Preface to *The Lyrical Ballads* (jointly written by him and Coleridge) to the effect that most readers assume that 'by the act of writing in verse' poets undertake to confine themselves to ' . . . certain [i.e. pleasing and innocuous] classes of ideas and expressions.' Such readers think poetry is meant to cheer us up, and would take Browning at his breeziest (in, say, 'God's in his Heaven, // All's right with the world!') as a touchstone of what poetry's mission should be. To them Hardy might well seem a crusty old curmudgeon, glumly intent on the mirier back-alleys of human existence, though such a view would have to be based upon superficial reading, something Hardy often complained of. But Hardy is not so much concerned with subject matter as with attitudes. He cites next in his *Apology* two phrases from one of his favourite poems, Wordsworth's *Ode: Intimations of Immortality from Recollections of Early Childhood*. He says, and this is absolutely crucial to his poetic creed, that

> It must be obvious to open intelligences that . . . disallowance of 'obstinate questionings' and 'blank misgivings' (ll. 146 & 149 of the *Ode*) tends to a paralysed intellectual stalemate . . . the present author's alleged . . . 'pessimism' is, in truth, only such 'questionings' in the exploration of reality.

Hardy thereupon quotes from his own *In Tenebris II* (137/C/D/ W/H/*) the line

> If a way to the Better there be, it exacts a full look at the Worst.

Since 1945 it is easier for us to agree with him, no doubt.

Hardy's references to Coleridge, Wordsworth, to the German poet Heine, and his contention that ' . . . the real function of poetry [is] the application of ideas to life' (which is Hardy's précis of remarks made by Matthew Arnold, whom he thought the best critic of his time, *on* Wordsworth,) all show how firmly he took his stand within the English poetic tradition. Yet many, both at the outset of his poetic career and since, have seen him as an iconoclast, someone who 'dispensed with tradition in his most ambitious verse' as J. C. Ransom disparagingly put it in an influential essay. Hardy certainly did not think he had done any such thing; indeed, in conversation with the young Robert Graves, then much in thrall to *vers libre* theories, he firmly observed, 'All we can do is to write on the old themes and in the old styles and try to do a little better than those who went before us.' He was playing down his own innovations somewhat perhaps but there can be no possible doubt that he saw himself as working within that great continuum of English poets and their poems which we usually refer to as 'the tradition'.

But there has always been a diversity of views about the nature and the purposes of poetry, and the side Hardy took in this debate is made clear in his journal for 29 May 1887. He quotes from the minor eighteenth-century poet Thomson these lines

Thrice happy he who on the sunless side
Of a romantic mountain,
Sits coolly calm; while all the world without
Unsatisfied and sick, tosses at noon . . .

and comments 'Instance of a WRONG (i.e. *selfish*) philosophy in poetry.' Now although Hardy thought this wrong, the vast preponderance of Victorian readers, not to mention most critics and many poets, would have thought Thomson's idea—which is basically that poetry is a form of *escape*—absolutely right.

There is no shortage of evidence. F. T. Palgrave's *Golden Treasury* of 1861 was easily the most influential, as it was also the best-selling Victorian anthology. Hardy bought it when it first appeared or soon after. It was really a manifesto for Tennyson's view of poetry, however, for Tennyson made the final choice of the poems in it, and there can be little doubt he also determined the general tenor of the *Preface*. Here we learn that 'poetry gives pleasures more golden than gold, leading us in *higher and healthier* ways than those of the world.' (My italics). There is much more to the same purpose and the editors remorselessly carry this principle into practice. Presumably because (as they unblushingly inform us) ' . . . more thought than mastery of expression' was a disqualification, three poets whom Hardy particularly admired get very short shrift. Donne—the *only* poet whose influence Hardy specifically acknowledged—is totally excluded, while Sir Thomas Wyatt and George Herbert get just one poem each. Significantly, the Romantics as a group get more space than all the other poets, apart from Shakespeare, put together, albeit the mediocre Thomas Campbell's allocation of eleven is the same as Keats's. This is because they exhibit 'a bloom of feeling . . . unattained and perhaps unattainable by their predecessors.' A little earlier the very influential poet and essayist R. W. Emerson had announced in America that 'The poet cannot descend into the turbid present without injury to his rarest gifts . . . nothing is of any value [in poetry] except the transcendental.' Tennyson was one of his admirers, not surprisingly.

F. W. Bateson mordantly summed up this attitude to poetry as 'The quickest way out of Manchester' and nothing could be further removed from Hardy's theory and practice. Railway station waiting-rooms and third-class carriages, insects flying into his lamp, the skeleton of an old parasol, a second-hand suit, a pat of butter, lines from a Borough Minute Book, even a pair of new boots, in his old age a passing motor car: all are, for him, equally the stuff of poetry. Indeed he frequently starts with something tangible, and often not conventionally 'poetic' at all. Two notes from his Journals make his position plain. In 1877 he observed, 'There is enough beauty in what is left in life, after all the false romance has been extracted, to make a sweet pattern ... the art lies in making defects [in Nature] the basis of a hitherto unperceived beauty ... latent in them.' More succinctly, he noted in 1888, 'To find beauty in ugliness is the province of the poet.'

Keats, whom he revered and studied closely (even suggesting an emendation in the text of his poems) would have agreed. In his early verse, which Victorian readers admired most warmly, he could write

> Give me a golden pen and let me lean
> On heap'd-up flowers in regions far and clear ...

But he defines the poet's mission very differently in *The Fall of Hyperion*. There he says that 'The poet and the dreamer are distinct // Sheer opposites ...' and when he asks how the 'throne' of the highest poetry may be attained,

> 'None can usurp this height,' returned that shade,
> But those to whom the miseries of the world
> *Are* misery and will not let them rest ...

For Hardy then, though he could and did admire poetry which revealed, like Keats's *Ode to a Nightingale*,

> Charm'd magic casements, opening on the foam
> Of perilous seas, in faery lands forlorn.

it was also necessary to open a few windows on life as lived in Mixen Lane (the dreadful slum depicted in his novel *The Mayor of Casterbridge*).

The matter a poet chooses to depict is one thing; the method he employs to depict it another. Even if we concede that the strictures on Hardy's subjects were insubstantial, deriving from a simplistic notion of the purpose of poetry, we still have to face the fact that Hardy's treatment, his poetic style, has come in for a great deal of adverse comment, some of it from readers not unsympathetic to his aims. It may be as well to confess at once that this is where a blanket denial will not wash. Hardy *did* write some of the weakest lines (and a few of the more inept poems) that any major English poet has produced, and it is not enough to use, as some have, his 'playfulness' in exculpation. One can say, as some recent critics have said, that even Hardy at his worst is instantly recognisable as Hardy; one may even come to enjoy some of his eccentricities. But the fact that we grow fond of our pet mongrel does not turn it into a dog with a pedigree, capable of winning at Cruft's.

Some examples may substantiate my point. Hardy had a remarkable vocabulary but his sudden shifts from one *level* to another do not always come off. When he drops out of a dignified into a mundane diction, as in *The Levelled Churchyard* (127/0*)

> We late-lamented, resting here
> Are mixed to human jam . . .

the impact, albeit meant to shock, is merely ludicrous, like Harry Graham's *Ruthless Rhymes for Heartless Homes*. Brilliantly as he exploited and often extended the resources of metre he could stray into forms out of key with the mood of the poem. Thus a lyric of sad reflection, *The Dawn After the Dance* (182/C) inappropriately moves to a jingling, cantering rhythm throughout,

> I would be candid willingly, but dawn draws on so chillingly
> As to render further cheerlessness intolerable now . . .

Gilbert might have written it for Sullivan to set to music.

Then there are the occasions where it seems that Hardy simply cuts prose up into more or less regular lengths. Who, for example, would care to mark the line divisions in this fragment from *In the Servants' Quarters* (316/C/W.*): 'Man you too, aren't you one of these rough followers of the criminal; all hanging about to hear how he is going to bear examination in the hall?'? Also he has lines which seem asthmatic from the strain of getting everything in, like this one from *At Madame Tussaud's in Victorian Years* (4371W)

> Yet, gamuts that graced forty year's flight were not a small thing!

But these slips and fumbles do not amount to more than a minute proportion of Hardy's output. All his life he was fascinated by the technicalities of verse. A devoted experimentalist, he employed more distinctive stanza forms than any other English poet, sometimes writing 'skeleton' outlines in order to 'try out' new patterns. An occasional over-reaching is the price we have to pay for his many triumphs in harmonising the movement of his verse with the mood he wishes to convey. His *The Fallow Deer at the Lonely House* (551/C/D/G/H/*) perfectly exemplifies this gift in its second verse.

> We do not discern those eyes
>   Watching in the snow;
> Lit by lamps of rosy dyes
> We do not discern those eyes
> Wondering, aglow
> Four-footed, tip-toe.

Only a pedant would grumble that 'eyes' cannot be 'four-footed'. (All Hardy and Emma can see of the deer from inside the lighted room is their eyes.) The 'otherness' of the animal world outside, the blend of fear and curiosity—the deer poised to flee at the least sound or movement—is not only conveyed by the unerring choice of epithet for the closing four words, but also by the short lines in which the natural stressing of the words induces a tense, hesitant quality, best brought out by reading the poem aloud.

Perhaps a poem which displays good and bad side by side may be helpful. It is hard to imagine solitude better rendered than in *The Wanderer* (553/*)

> Sometimes outside the fence
>   Feet swing past,
> Clock-like, and then go hence,
>   Till at last
> There is a silence, dense
>   Deep and vast.

Here the rhythm is itself 'clock-like'; the emptiness of the night suggested by the strong pause after 'silence' with the double rhyme and heavy stresses on the concluding adjectives, 'dense', 'deep' and 'vast' (which are by no means synonymous). This poem also supplies instances of Hardy's original, sometimes odd, but always arresting use of language. Initially he describes the stars, conventionally enough, as 'The lights by which I sup // Glimmeringly . . . ' (a tramp is speaking). But he goes on to say, 'They wag as though they were // Panting for joy'. Well, do stars *wag*? Not, it must be admitted, in poetry before Hardy. Yet, as a matter of observable fact, they do, or appear to do so, however much 'Twinkle, twinkle, little star' obstructs this perception for most of us. Like Alice's Humpty Dumpty, Hardy was determined to be 'master' where words were concerned, which was not invariably a wise resolution. *The Wanderer* also reveals a much less persuasive Hardy. When his benighted narrator complains that there is

... no beseeming abode
I can try
For shelter, so abroad
    I must lie.

one feels that even a house-agent would wince at 'beseeming abode', even a schoolboy conscript feel that 'abode' isn't the ideal rhyme for 'abroad'!

Words, considered as things in themselves, were a minor passion of Hardy's. He prized his copy of the all-inclusive *New English Dictionary*, in the later volumes of which several words are exemplified largely from his works! And some of the words he employed do seem to have been exhumed from defunct dictionaries: *influent, largened, thuswise, meseemed, asile, typic, roomage, joyance, cohue* all come from a random dip into his *Complete Poems*. Though always an easy target for quibblers, the actual incidence of such words is very slight, and even when taken out of context, few need glossing. Still, archaic words are one thing, Hardy's own coinages quite another and a much more important aspect of his art. His most characteristic device is the compound epithet; hardly a page goes by without one or two. They are not invariably convincing. The lines from *Copying Architecture in an Old Minster* (369/W/C/*), 'Maybe they have met for a parle on some plan // To better ail-stricken mankind', not only suffer from the intrusively gallic 'parle' (i.e. parley) but 'ail-stricken' surely *sounds* far too much like the sequel to an Anglo-Saxon feast. However, Hardy's occasional linguistic misadventures are a small price to pay for what G. M. Young memorably called 'his ancient music ... this gnarled and wintry phrasing'. Nor is it always 'wintry' either. It can bestow on us such glowing turns of phrase as 'the foam-fingered sea', the 'Isle by the Race // Many-caverned, bald, wrinkled of face', 'mothy curfew-tide' and 'air-blue', and such delicate insights as 'cobweb-time', 'wind-thridded' and 'ripple-gleam'. I could continue but I do not wish to imply that Hardy's use of more conventional language is less effective. He can bring out lines as Miltonic in their assurance as these from a sonnet, *The Schreckhorn, with Thoughts of Leslie Stephen* (264/ALL/H)

And the eternal essence of his mind
Enter this silent adamantine shape,

Hardy has phrases like 'Oblivion's swallowing sea', in *The-To-Be-Forgotten* (110/C/*). which Shakespeare somehow omitted from his plays; he can write openings as lyrical as Herrick's; 'She was as fair as early day // Shining on meads unmown', though *The Satin Shoes* (334) does not long continue in this vein. With equal felicity, he can pick his verse bare of all but the very simplest words, as in *I Found Her Out There* (281/C/D/W/H/*)

> I found her out there
> On a slope few see,
> That falls westwardly
> To the salt-edged air,
> Where the ocean breaks
> On the purple strand,
> And the hurricane shakes
> The solid land.

Here the purity and restraint of the language need no comment, but it is worth noticing the dextrous use of sibilants (in all but the initial line) to prevent the clipped lines becoming abrupt. And, to take a single word, how much of the force of 'hurricane' derives from the framework of plain English around it, and how evocative of the smell and 'feel' of the sea is the solitary compound 'salt-edged' (a brilliant emendation for 'sharp-edged'). Indeed, all the *Poems of 1912–13* abound in miraculously apt phrasing, while frequently the most striking effects arise from Hardy's insistence on the *exact* word, at whatever risk of its being unexpected, for what he wishes to convey. For example, in *Beeny Cliff* (291/ALL/H/*) he writes, 'Still in all its chasmal beauty bulks old Beeny to the sky,', a line which, in 'chasmal' and 'bulks', contains two words few other poets would have employed. Yet these unfamiliar, even disconcerting, words, seen in context—the crucial stipulation—acquire inevitability. No others, however many alternatives are explored, quite fit. In this once much-vexed matter of his vocabulary then, Hardy is so often bang on target that a few ill-directed shafts seem insignificant. Furthermore, what at first glance may appear inept, can, on reflection and re-reading, become peculiarly apt. Most poets would be content with the line, from *The Wind's Prophecy* (440/C/D/W/*) as Hardy originally drafted it, 'Where the sun *rises*, mist-imbued' with its striking compound epithet. But Hardy, in search of a more sudden, startling quality for his sunrise, changed the commonplace verb 'rises' for 'ups it'. Sometimes, as perhaps here, one may argue whether the game was worth the candle, but Hardy always knew what he was about, and nearly always achieves his aim. His occasionally obsessive concern for verbal precision was indeed a facet of his general attitude to poetry and truth. He had little time for Pope's thesis, in his *An Essay on Criticism*, that in poetry,

> True wit is Nature to advantage dressed
> What oft was thought, but ne'er so well expressed.

There all the emphasis is on the skill with which the poet presents what he has to say: what the poem is *about*—its theme or subject—will be, Pope implies, of little importance as against its treatment. Hardy took the opposite view, siding with Wordsworth who exhorted the poet always to 'look steadily at his subject' and Matthew Arnold who echoes this in his insistence that poetry should 'strive ... to see the thing [i.e. the subject] as in itself it really is.' Put bluntly, it is *what* the poet says that matters most. Hardy often expressed his distaste for what he called 'poetic veneer' and dismissed it tartly as 'the art of saying nothing in mellifluous polysyllables'. To his friend Edmund Gosse he confided, 'For as long as I can remember my instinctive feeling has been to avoid the jewelled line in poetry as being effeminate.' He cites another friend's—Leslie Stephen's— dictum with warm approval, 'The ultimate aim of the poet should be to touch our hearts by showing his own, and not to exhibit his learning, his fine taste, or his skill.' Bearing all this in mind it is not at all surprising to find that Hardy's own definition was, 'The secret of poetry lies in seeing into the heart of a thing, which ... is realism in fact', a position he always defended vigorously, contending that there was such a thing as 'too much style' and arguing, in 1901, that,

> There is a latent music in the sincere utterance of deep emotion, however expressed, which fills the place of the actual word-music in rhythmic phraseology on thinner emotive subjects ... some verses ... apparently infringe all rules, and yet bring unreasoned convictions that they are poetry.

He also grounded his convictions on his experience as an architect, pointing out that the 'great Gothic Cathedrals' often display this 'art of cunning irregularity', from which he claimed to have derived the 'principle of spontaneity' and carried it into his verse.

Now there may very well be a smack of rationalisation about all this; most of us, after all, are attracted to those theories which square with our own practice. But there were good reasons why, beginning to write poetry abortively in the 1860s, and returning to it in the 1890s, Hardy should have rejected that reliance on ' ... finish ... clarity and unity' which Tennyson and Palgrave set up as criteria for admission to the pages of *The Golden Treasury*. Tennyson himself was, after all, the greatest exponent of the 'jewelled line' in English, becoming Poet Laureate in 1850. He had an impeccable ear and an endless supply of melodious phrases. Such *tours de force* as

> The moan of doves in immemorial elms,
> And murmuring of innumerable bees.

from *The Princess* (1853) were on everyone's lips in the later nineteenth century. Tennyson came to dominate the poetic landscape; a poet both great and various, it was impossible to ignore him. Hardy certainly did not ignore him, on the contrary he greatly admired him, just as Tennyson admired Hardy's novel *A Pair of Blue Eyes*. But, from the outset of his career Hardy was determined to 'go and do otherwise'. He could, of course, sometimes overdo his distrust of the Tennysonian line. No doubt Tennyson would have admired the opening of *In Front of the Landscape* (246/C/W/H/*) with its vivid picture of

> ... a headland of hoary aspect
> Gnawed by the tide,
> Frilled by the nimb of the morning ...

The tactile verb 'gnawed', the strikingly visual 'frilled by the nimb' are very much in his own line. But what would he have made of the 'faces' later on,

> Some as with slow-born tears that brinily trundled [down them]

This has impact; it is, if you think about it both apt and accurate, but it deliberately disperses all the expected associations of 'tears' as, say, crystals, dew-drops or pearls. On balance, in this poem, it works. But sometimes Hardy so cudgels the reader with his insistence on truth to fact as to knock the stuffing out of the poem. Thus, he starts a lyric in the Elizabethan manner, *The Memorial Brass 186—?* (4521W)

> Why do you weep there, O sweet lady,
> Why do you weep before that brass?—

and then immediately informs us, parenthetically, superfluously and to the optimum deflationary effect that,

> (I'm a mere student sketching the mediaeval.)

Not content with this display of the 'art of sinking' he reverts to his opening mode with

> Is some late death lined there, alas?—

only, driven by the exigencies of rhyme, to wrench the last line into

> Your father's? ... Well, all pay the debt that paid he!'

The next line, and this is very rare in Hardy, is actually impossible to scan.

'Young man, O must I tell!—My husbands.' *And under*

The italicised words simply cannot be made to fit the metre. The poem—an ironic anecdote of a kind to which Hardy was over-addicted anyway—may well have been meant to shock, but not, one feels, in quite this way!

But mis-hits do not play a large part in Hardy's 943 poems. Far more often than not he was right in his aims; far more often than not he demonstrably achieves them. Even Tennyson has no line more opulent than the one that opens *Beeny Cliff* (291/ALL/H/*),

O the opal and the sapphire of that wandering western sea

Here the use of jewels for the sea-colours; opal for the evanescent sunlit water, sapphire for the blue-black shadow below the cliff, the long roll of the line with its strong alliteration (O/opal, sapphire/sea, wandering/western) binding it together—Hardy is always first-class on the sea—combine to produce an unrivalled warmth and brilliance of effect. The unusual epithet 'wandering' (which Tennyson himself had used of the sea in *In Memoriam*) is also felicitous.

But the next line is a test case. It runs

And the woman riding high above with bright hair flapping free

Now the word 'flapping' is decidedly not the one that most Victorian poets would have chosen. Its associations are predominantly with washing on the line, or perhaps ungainly birds. Either 'flowing' or 'floating' would be far more glamorous and Hardy must have been especially tempted by 'floating' since, in *Some Recollections*, Emma, in telling of this very incident, had herself written of 'my hair floating in the wind'. But he remembered even better than she did, with an astonishing clarity and precision which he knew well to be one of his greatest assets as a poet. When he was 75 he noted, 'I have a faculty (possibly not uncommon) for burying an emotion in my heart or brain for forty years, and exhuming it at the end of that time as fresh as when interred.' This is something more than nostalgic recall; it is an ability to recreate, to re-explore the past as if it were still the present. In many of Hardy's finest poems Time is the enemy against which memory is the only shield. But if, for whatever reason, memory is distorted, to comfort, to ennoble or even in quest of the melodious, then the cause of truth and poetry is betrayed, and Time will have triumphed. So in *I Found Her Out There* (281/C/D/W/H/*) Emma is pictured gazing out at 'Dundagel's famed head'

> As a wind-tugged tress
> Flapped her cheek like a flail.

That, on the wild Atlantic coast of North Cornwall, is what happens. On those high cliffs the wind is never steady; it blows in unpredictable swirls and gusts (nearly causing the hero's death in *A Pair of Blue Eyes*) so that long, heavy, ringleted hair doesn't 'flow' or 'float' but does, in fact, flap! It may seem niggling to insist upon so apparently trivial a matter, but if, as Coleridge said, poetry is 'the best words in the best order' then no amount of care in choosing the best is too much. Moreover, the antagonism of Time and Memory are among the essential ingredients of Hardy's poetic art, from which his tireless quest for truth to the actual experience naturally stems. If we want poetry tailored to what readers are accustomed to, to what 'looks' or 'sounds' most beguiling, we must go elsewhere for it.

'Real poets', wrote the countryman John Clare in the year of Hardy's birth, 'must be truly honest men, // Tied to no mongrel laws on flattery's page.' Clare's supremely authentic pictures of the rural world were bowdlerised by his publisher who was horrified by such scenes as that of a field-mouse disturbed by reapers, bolting out 'With all her young ones hanging from her teats'. Similarly, Wilfrid Owen's terrible visions of war derive from his belief that ' . . . true poets must be truthful' and that 'the poetry is in the pity'. It is with men like these that Hardy belongs; those who refuse to pick over their experience and amend or select from it on any ground whatever, especially that of what is or is not pleasing to the conventionally minded reader. Hardy set himself to struggle against the expectations of a public addicted to *Golden Treasury* verse. That his struggles are sometimes ungainly, his vocabulary eccentric, his subject matter dreary and his irony somewhat too predictable cannot be denied. But we should not look for perfect balance in a rebellious intellect, and, even at his worst, Hardy's work was a salutary corrective. For, though it took W. B. Yeats half a lifetime to discover that, in poetry, 'there's more enterprise in walking naked' Hardy, one might say, had never done anything else. This is the quality Hardy shared with Wordsworth and it is perfectly summed up by Matthew Arnold in his essay on the older poet. '[Wordsworth's] expression may often be called bald . . . but it is bald as the bare mountain tops are bald, with a baldness full of grandeur'.

If, in conclusion, I say very little about Hardy's 'thought' it is because I think it is seldom feasible or desirable to siphon it off from the poems in which it is suspended. Many ingenious and some ingenuous attempts have been made to pigeon-hole Hardy's ideas. He has been labelled 'Nietzchean', 'Schopenhauerian', 'monistic materialist', 'determinist' and 'scientific human-ist' at various times, which to me suggests some inherent elusiveness in the subject of the labels. Hardy was unusually well read in both ancient and mod-ern philosophy, subscribing to the esoteric journal *Mind*. He even found room in his late, light-hearted *Drinking Song* (896/C/*)—a potted verse-history of philosophy—for Einstein 'with a notion ... // That there's no time, no space, no motion'. Browning's once-vaunted 'philosophy' he unkindly dismissed as 'worthy of a dissenting grocer,' and he bemoaned the fact that 'in their later writings [Wordsworth and Tennyson] ... fall into the error of recording their convictions' (as opposed to their 'impressions'). In 1917 an article about his work prompted him to this riposte:

> Many critics treat my works of art as if they were a scientific system
> of philosophy, although I have repeatedly stated that the views in
> them are *seemings*, provisional impressions only, used for artistic
> purposes. ...

This summing-up is perfectly compatible with the fact that a good few of Hardy's poems exhibit very similar 'impressions'. Mere repetition does not validate an idea; only the vital force of the poem expressing it can hope to do that, and often only then just for the moment of reading. Hardy would have thought it absurd to say, as Shelley did, that 'Poets are the ... unacknowl-edged legislators of the world', much as he admired Shelley's poetry.

Nevertheless, to say that Hardy was not and did not wish to seem a systematic thinker is not to deny him many valuable insights into the human condition. His attitude to his own poetry may strike us as modest, even hum-ble. He told his second wife that 'He had written his poems entirely because he liked doing them, without any ulterior thought; because he wanted to say the things they contained ...', and, though he could drive a hard bargain where his novels were concerned, he actually offered to pay for the publica-tion of *Wessex Poems* in 1898 and made it a condition of his will that his *Collected Poems* should be sold at a price within reach of the 'poorer reader', a condition still honoured today by Macmillan.

Remarkably, one might even say paradoxically, this modest estimate of his own importance goes with what is arguably one of the most protean tal-ents of any English poet; there is almost nothing in the range of human experience from which Hardy cannot fashion a poem. It is this openness, this immense receptivity, which he never lost, that enables him so often to sur-prise us—even in run-of-the-mill poems—with some new perception, some sudden apprehension of the force and value of life, and led Edward Thomas to say (reviewing *Time's Laughingstocks*), 'This book contains ninety-nine reasons for not living. Yet it is not a book of despair. It is a book of sincerity.' Thomas saw more clearly than most of his contemporaries that it was just this sincerity which prevented Hardy from systematising life, which he saw as inherently mysterious, according to any set of preconceptions whatever. As Middleton Murry put it, memorably, in an essay on Hardy's poetry, 'The great poet remembers both rose and thorn, and it is beyond his power to remember them otherwise than as together.' Hardy's was an austere concept of the poet's task; always to tell the whole truth, never to edit experience, never to accept facile answers. But he left a distinctive legacy to his successors, many of whom, Edward Thomas, Siegfried Sassoon, W. H. Auden, C. Day Lewis, Dylan Thomas and Philip Larkin among them; have warmly acknowledged their debt to him. In October 1919 Sassoon came to Max Gate and presented Hardy with a unique tribute which moved him very deeply. It was a beautifully bound manuscript volume in which 43 poets, including the Laureate Bridges, Kipling, Yeats, De la Mare, D. H. Lawrence, Robert Graves, Edmund Blunden and Sassoon himself had each inscribed one of their own poems. Typically, Hardy wrote to thank each of them in his own hand and individually. The poems were not written about Hardy, of course, though subsequently several good ones have been, notably by De la Mare, Sassoon, Blunden and Day Lewis. Yet noise is quite as appropriate as the lines written by Wordsworth in his *A Poet's Epitaph*, with which I end this chapter.

> In common things that round us lie
> Some random truths he can impart,—
> The harvest of a quiet eye
> That broods and sleeps on his own heart.
>   From *Lyrical Ballads with Other Poems*, 1800

SIMON GATRELL

The Mayor of Casterbridge:
The Fate of Michael Henchard's Character

In editions read today the title-page of the novel always identified as *The Mayor of Casterbridge* in fact reads *The Life and Death of the Mayor of Casterbridge: A Story of a Man of Character*. This is a complex announcement, almost every substantive element of which rewards inspection, but it is perhaps more appropriate to begin further back historically, for, as with other novels, Hardy only gradually came to this fully-fledged description of his fiction. The earliest version of the title, written at the head of the holograph manuscript and used for both English and American serializations in 1886, was simply *The Mayor of Casterbridge*. There are also two intermediate versions to consider. When Hardy revised the text of the novel for the English first edition towards the end of 1886, he decided to provide a more elaborate title: *The Mayor of Casterbridge: The Life and Death of a Man of Character*. Contemporary reviewers found material in this statement on which they could base a critical discussion of the novel, and in one of those characteristic responses to the fooleries of critics to which Hardy found himself throughout his life only too prone, he reduced this version when the novel was first reprinted in 1887 in one volume to *The Mayor of Casterbridge: A Story of a Man of Character*. It remained thus for Osgood, MacIlvaine's collected edition, and Hardy only reintroduced the 'Life and Death' element, in

From *Thomas Hardy and the Proper Study of Mankind*, pp. 68–96, 188–90. © 1993 by Simon Gatrell.

the form we now know it, in 1902 when Macmillan printed a new title-page for their issue of an impression of the Osgood plates.

To return, then, to the earliest, simplest title. The first question it provokes is why *The Mayor of Casterbridge*, not *Michael Henchard*? Why is Henchard's function more important than his name? The force of this question is intensified when it is remembered that he is mayor for less than half of the novel. A partial reason for the choice is probably to be found in one aspect of the novel's supporting structure of reference and allusion—classical and medieval theories of tragedy (almost purely Aristotelian, as Dale Kramer points out),[1] which demand that the tragic hero shall be a man of high social status, for whom the wheel of fortune will turn downwards. One of the novel's major topics is the nature and function of the town of Casterbridge (as the early title also suggests), and the mayor of the town is its first citizen under the crown. Although in England appointment or election to an important but temporary office does not for the most part entitle the holder to use the title for the rest of his or her life, nevertheless to have been mayor provides sufficient social status for the operation of the rules of tragedy in Henchard's rapid and inexorable decline from that status and what it implies.

Conformation with the conventions of tragedy is, however, a superficial justification for Hardy's apparent concentration on Henchard's office; the name mayor means more to Henchard than it would to most others entitled to use it. To explore a little further it is useful first to go back eight years to *The Return of the Native*, Hardy's first attempt at an overtly tragic novel. The chapter entitled 'Queen of Night', the seventh of the first book, is the narrator's major attempt at defining Eustacia Vye, the tragic centre of the novel. Like the whole novel (and *The Mayor of Casterbridge*) the chapter is a chaos of references and allusions, but the tendency of the whole is expressed in the first paragraph:

> Eustacia Vye was the raw material of a divinity. On Olympus she would have done well with a little preparation. She had the passions and instincts which make a model goddess, that is, those which make not quite a model woman. Had it been possible for the earth and mankind to be entirely in her grasp for a while, had she handled the distaff, the spindle, and the shears at her own free will, few in the world would have noticed the change of government. There would have been the same inequality of lot, the same heaping up of favours here, of contumely there, the same generosity before justice, the same perpetual dilemmas, the same captious alternation of caresses and blows as we endure now. (p. 63)

By raising this image of Eustacia ruling the world, Hardy deliberately draws attention to his insight that it is in part frustration at her lack of power in any area of life save the sexual, at her lack even of the possibility of ever obtaining such power, which drives Eustacia to the actions that lead ultimately to her death. Hardy intensifies this frustration by placing her in an environment where even her sexual energy and authority have an extremely limited range of potential subjects to subdue and control.[2]

In some interesting *ways The Mayor of Casterbridge* can be seen as a sequel to *The Return of the Native*, and in the current context it may profitably be suggested that if, in the preceding quotation, feminine nouns and pronouns were changed to masculine, and 'Eustacia Vye' to 'Michael Henchard', the passage would (in isolation) remain effective. The essential difference between the two characters is that, being a man, Henchard has the freedom and the opportunity, as he certainly has the desire, to attain power, to achieve a certain amount of control over a small section of earth and mankind. On the other hand, when we first see him he faces, in his class, another disabling obstacle (while he believes he has a second in his wife and child). The young Michael Henchard, like Eustacia Vye, is deeply ambitious, but Hardy chooses not to show the process by which, having shed one supposed impediment at Weydon, he manages to transcend the other in Casterbridge and reach his limited but real as well as symbolic power as Mayor. The narrator tells us that it is his great energy that has subdued others, made him rich, and persuaded the ruling class of Casterbridge that they would do well to let him, rough as he is, run their Town Council. We may, on reflection, not feel that such an explanation is fully adequate, but the fact that we are habituated to calling the novel *The Mayor* substantially helps Hardy persuade the reader to credit his brief account. It is almost as if we are persuaded to believe that the office was Michael Henchard's birthright.

It is not only his crossing of social barriers and his rise to power which are handled cursorily, but also his wielding of power. We are presented with no real evidence about what difference it made to any aspect of Casterbridge that Henchard was mayor. In part we accept that it is Henchard's wealth that represents his real power, and that his mayoralty is a sign of his power rather than an addition to it; but it is also true that Hardy is much more interested in the personal than in the political or social uses of power. It is further true that if the desire for the power that wealth and office can bring were all that motivated Henchard, if to be Mayor of Casterbridge sufficed him, then however tragic his fall, Hardy would scarcely be interested in him.

When Henchard has finally told Elizabeth-Jane that she is his daughter the narrator comments:

He was the kind of man to whom some human object for pouring out his heart upon—were it emotive or were it choleric—was almost a necessity. The craving of his heart for the reestablishment of this tenderest human tie had been great during his wife's lifetime, and now he had submitted to its mastery without reluctance and without fear. (p. 125)

At this stage in the novel the desire to love is as strong in Henchard as the desire for power; and there is a further connection with *The Return of the Native*. In the same chapter as that already quoted from, 'Queen of Night', the narrator announces concerning Eustacia Vye: 'To be loved to madness—such was her great desire' (p. 66). We can adapt this announcement also to Henchard thus: 'To be permitted to love to madness—such was one of his two great desires.'

Vye's method of ruling others is through their passionate enslavement to her, it is her only available way to power; seen thus simply, she is what many contemporary readers of the novel would have called a bad woman. Henchard wants to subdue others through his passionate devotion to them. The fragment from p. 125 quoted above refers to Elizabeth-Jane, but it could apply equally to Farfrae earlier in the novel. Henchard's relationship with Farfrae is complicated, however, by his other desire. While Henchard still retains his office and his wealth, his desire for the power they bring remains strong, but (once an appropriate object appears in the person of Farfrae) his latent and perhaps not quite so strong desire to be allowed to love comes into conflict with his desire for power. It is not inevitable that it should do so: Farfrae might have been a woman (though Henchard's rather remote affair with Lucetta is all the evidence we have that he can be moved to love a woman as he loves Farfrae), in which case love need have been no obstacle to the maintenance of Henchard's power; he might have been a doctor who cured him of some obscure illness instead of curing his wheat, in which case, similarly, there need have been no opposition between Henchard's twin desires. But as circumstances (or the novelist) would have it, Farfrae's arable knowledge and his economical efficiency, his very qualifications for the position of manager, bring about a conflict in Henchard between his desire to maintain his status, and his desire to love Farfrae.

When the crisis comes, when it is apparent that Farfrae's authority in business carries more weight with the farming community than Henchard's, when Henchard perceives himself in danger of being 'honeycombed clean out of all the character and standing that he's built up these eighteen year' (p. 107), the narrator carefully points out that it would be possible for Henchard to compromise by getting Farfrae to marry Elizabeth-Jane, and (by implication) for him to retire gracefully from active business, providing the cash to finance his son-in-law's success. The firm would still be Henchard and Farfrae, and he might mellow into a Casterbridge landmark. But Henchard cannot voluntarily mingle and thus diminish his two desires; they will remain incompatible and in conflict so long as the obstacle to one is the object of the other.

From this crisis in the narrative the sequence of Henchard's attempts to love is rapid. Abandoning Farfrae as an object of love he turns to Elizabeth-Jane, only to find that she is not his daughter, and that the kiss of her cheek 'he had prefigured for weeks with a thrill of pleasure' tasted of dust and ashes. Abandoning Elizabeth-Jane he turns to Lucetta, only to find that she has turned to Farfrae. In his bid to retain the power of wealth and status he drives to economic and social ruin. The graphic emblem of his defeat is the replacement of his own name by Farfrae's on the sign above his old headquarters, but Farfrae has not only taken over Henchard's business, he has also married the woman Henchard intended to marry, and has pretty well bought all that Henchard possessed. When Farfrae becomes mayor the reversal is complete, though Henchard's desire for power is not yet fully quenched.

Abandoned by Lucetta he turns inward and to drink. His first act, though, under the renewed influence of alcohol is to force the church choir to sing the commination psalm at Farfrae; such hate is only the obverse of his love. Farfrae now treats him patronizingly as an object for charity, unable to recognize him as the same man who befriended him at the beginning of his time in Casterbridge; this patronage provokes Henchard to competition once again, first to test (at the royal visit) how far his once secure power still resides with him and then (after his social powerlessness is made evident even to him) to demonstrate that his physical strength will provide him with another kind of power over Farfrae. But beneath this hostility to Farfrae is the abiding love.

He wrestles Farfrae, and has him at his mercy. Farfrae says he should take his life: 'Ye've wished to long enough.' Henchard's reply, as their eyes meet, their bodies in a close violent embrace, is (bitterly) 'O Farfrae—that's not true. . . . God is my witness that no man ever loved another as I did thee at one time. . . . And now—though I came here to kill 'ee, I cannot hurt thee! Go and give me in charge—do what you will—I care nothing for what comes of me!' (p. 273). The sequel makes it clear that the desire to be allowed to love Farfrae is by no means yet dissipated: after Farfrae goes Henchard was so thoroughly subdued 'that he remained on the sacks in a crouching attitude, unusual for a man, and for such a man. Its womanliness sat tragically on the figure of so stern a piece of virility' (p. 274).

Why is the posture of submission womanly? Perhaps because it is conventionally the role of the woman to play the weaker part, to long for reconciliation, for reinstatement of regard, of affection, to want to sue for the return of love. Henchard murmurs to himself: 'He thought highly of me once. ... Now he'll hate me and despise me for ever', and the narrator continues: 'He became possessed by an overpowering wish to see Farfrae again that night, and by some desperate pleading to attempt the well-nigh impossible task of winning pardon for his late mad attack'. When Henchard does find him he says: 'Oh, Farfrae, don't mistrust me—I am a wretched man, but my heart is true to you still!' (p. 286) Henchard, the bull-like man, the man of strong appetites, powerful desires, apparently thoroughly masculine, overturns the conventional expectations of the novel's Victorian readership; his passion is in submission rather than domination; he wishes to give love, to adore, rather than to be adored. Like Eustacia Vye, he is in erotic terms a character subversive of the norms of the dominant culture.[3]

Farfrae, the representative of that culture in the novel, doesn't believe him, probably cannot comprehend him. He has insufficient imaginative sympathy to understand the complex of desires in Henchard, he cannot respond to the richness and power of a phrase like 'my heart is true to you still' in the mouth of a man.

The episode has finally buried Henchard's desire for power, and he finally ceases to be mayor. His desire to love is all that remains, and Elizabeth-Jane is now the only possible object for that desire. Under pressure from overpowering need, in a characteristically impulsive moment, he tells Newson that his daughter is dead. From that moment of radical deception he is loving on borrowed time.

He sees Elizabeth-Jane and Farfrae often together: he hates the possibility of their union, he cannot accept that such a marriage would be good for her and for him any more now than he could when he and Farfrae first began competing commercially. The narrator says that uncompromising powerful impulsive desire is 'the idiosyncrasy of Henchard's which had ruled his courses from the beginning, and had mainly made him what he was. Time had been when such instinctive opposition would have taken shape in action' (p. 304), but now the 'netted lion' schools himself in restraint as he tries to hang on to Elizabeth-Jane. Henchard is to the community of Casterbridge dangerous like a wild animal; thus the network of allusions connecting him with the bull that threatens Lucetta and Elizabeth-Jane, and the references to his 'tigerish affection' (p. 91), and (after his defeat) to himself as a 'netted' and 'fangless' lion (pp. 303, 309). So long as his energy and strength can be harnessed safely for the good of the community it is prepared to give him the right he craves to assume power as mayor and to use for its benefit that energy and strength. Casterbridge is, however, relieved when, through Henchard's misjudged application of those energies in his commercial competition with

Farfrae, it can deprive the barely controllable individual of power. And now he suppresses his instincts and desires in subjection to the perceived will of the beloved.

Later on the same page the narrator comments further on Henchard's subjection: 'The *solicitus timor* of his love—the dependence upon Elizabeth's regard into which he had declined (or, in another sense, to which he had advanced), denaturalized him.' It is a decline because though he needs desperately to be allowed to show human affection, he has up to now never submitted his own will or need or desire to any object of his affection, has never sought to alter his nature in order to retain affection; it is an advance because his life (and those of others) might have been less painful if he had tried earlier to alter his nature, and now at the last gasp he is beginning to see that there are communal needs and rights which in ordinary human intercourse, let alone loving relationships, require respect. In his bare need, perhaps for the first time in his life, the desire to be loved is equal in him with the desire to love.

Once we develop from the narrator's hint these alternative views of Henchard's dependence on Elizabeth-Jane, we are also forced to consider our response to the transformation that he has effected. Do we regret the Henchard who was proud, fiery, driven by imperious desires, uncaring of consequences, ruthlessly honest, but destructive of himself and others around him if they could not stand up to him, or escape? Or do we feel it is right, or a cause for gladness, that he is humbled, socialized, taught to respect and consider the lives and needs of the community if he would gain his own ends, that he becomes devious, indirect, but potentially a productive member of the social organism, a proper relation for the proper Elizabeth-Jane?

It is not an easy opposition to resolve, and it is clearly possible to hold both views at the same time, as perhaps Hardy did. In the event the question is not sustained for long, for the final object of Henchard's desire to love is removed from him by the return of Newson, and all possibility of his socialization ends; all that remains is death.

His last words are in his will, which ends:

> & that no man remember me.
> To this I put my name.
>   Michael Henchard.

For most of his life Michael Henchard's ambitious and passionate nature has sought the power of wealth and status—to make a name in the world. The name he ultimately achieves is Mayor of the town of Casterbridge. This name, to be known thus throughout the region, provides him at last with a space for his ambition to fill; but as he enjoys it, he finds it is not enough. It is deeply ironic, if not tragic, that his pursuit of the well-beloved reduces him at last to his bare name and an attendant, though futile, injunction that the name itself be allowed to subside into oblivion. Despite Henchard's will it is certain that Casterbridge will remember him; to have been Mayor is to have left several indelible marks in the records of the town.

So far I have only explored the first element of Hardy's early title, but it is also important that Henchard and Farfrae are mayors of *Casterbridge*. There is, though, already an extensive critical discussion of Casterbridge, to which I do not wish to add very much.[4]

Though the narrator spends a substantial number of words evoking the town and its inhabitants for us, the impression we derive from his account is by no means homogeneous. The narrator of any Hardy novel is a complex organism, and in this instance he speaks with (at least) three separate accents. The physical detail of the town derives from the Dorchester experienced by the schoolboy Thomas Hardy, walking in every day from Bockhampton in the 1840s and 50s, very much in the same way as Egdon Heath in *The Return of the Native* is the recreation of the vision of the same boy who played on Puddletown Heath in the days before he went to school—the distortions of observable reality are of the same kind in either case.

Analysis of Casterbridge is sometimes in the voice of that boy grown up and living in the town, intimately re-experiencing it, and sometimes in the voice of the cosmopolitan author from the metropole, revisiting the home town from which he has risen, patronizing it by building a *pied-à-terre* on its outskirts.

Casterbridge is sometimes seen as an extension of the countryside. The functions of the town are thoroughly ruralized, and '[b]ees and butterflies in the cornfields at the top of the town who desired to get to the meads at the bottom ... flew straight down the High Street without any conscious-ness that they were traversing strange latitudes' (p. 58). It is the countryside concentrated, as if it were a group of rural parishes compressed into a nar-rower space, 'shepherds in an intramural squeeze' as the narrator describes the inhabitants of the suburb of Durnover (p. 92); the professional class that makes up the Town Council are the equivalent of the landed gentry, the vil-lage craftsmen represented by the shopkeepers (who sell agriculturally useful goods) and tradesmen (who deal in agricultural produce and perform agri-cultural services), the peasantry by the patrons of Peter's Finger. But there are distinctions as well as similarities.

Architecturally and historically the antiquity of Casterbridge as an urban community is carefully established, its close clutter of shops and dwellings and public buildings physically opposes the scattered countryside, sharply divided from the surrounding fields by the dark square of avenues that encloses it. Though all activity in the town is designed to serve the ends of the farmer and the surrounding rural parishes—markets, fairs, bulls and butterflies—yet still the gathering below the bow window of the Kings Arms hotel, carrying unsatisfactory loaves of bread, shouting through the window at the mayor, has a distinctly urban feel to it. For all its agricultural interdependence, Casterbridge is the home of essentially urban people. The professionals—doctors, lawyers, teachers—need the base of population to flourish. The bustle of life observed by the idle rich (Lucetta) is very different from the prospect from a manor-house window; at the other end of the social spectrum the dwellers of Mixen Lane—a fragment of the town notably outside the neat enclosing framework of hedges—are recognizably slum-dwellers.[5]

It is also true, however, that Casterbridge is contrasted with what we might think of as cities; it is not enough simply to consider town and country oppositions in Hardy. Casterbridge is urban without doubt, but it has a kind of intermediate existence which contrasts radically with metropoles; the context of comparison is partly size, partly economic function, and partly human behaviour:

> The yeomen, farmers, dairymen, and townsfolk, who came to transact business in these ancient streets, spoke in other ways than by articulation. Not to hear the words of your interlocutor in metropolitan centres is to know nothing of his meaning. Here the face, the arms, the hat, the stick, the body throughout spoke equally with the tongue. (pp. 61–2)

The responses and interactions that Hardy describes are essentially rural, having nothing of characteristic metropolitan inwardness. It is a matter of expressiveness, of energy, vitality, of living your meaning, which in cities has become overlaid with the middle-class restraints of polite custom and behaviour, or the working class restraints of secrecy and indirection. Henchard attempts a similar process when he tries to enforce standard speech on Elizabeth-Jane—the upper-middle class of the rural town aping the middle-class of the metropole. The narrator makes the direct functional comparison of rural with manufacturing towns. The latter 'are as foreign bodies set down, like boulders on a plain, in a green world with which they have nothing in common' (p. 62), a description that parallels the earlier description of Casterbridge: 'it stood as an indistinct mass behind a dense stockade of limes and chestnuts, set in the midst of miles of rotund down and concave field.' The essential urban similarity is in the 'mathematical line' (p. 29) separating town and country; the essential difference is the harmony in which the town of Casterbridge lives with its surrounding fields and downs, the symbiosis between the two.

It is a further complicating element in the reader's experience of Casterbridge that the narrator, or at least one of the narrative voices, that of the metropolitan sophisticate, is predictably patronizing about the place, talking of 'the venerable contrivances and confusions which delighted the eye by their quaintness, and in a measure reasonableness, in this rare old market town . . .' (p. 62)

It is thus hard to pin down in a single definition Hardy's imaginative recreation of Dorchester, and perhaps its ambiguity is essential: both urban and rural, more urban than rural, yet so far from what most readers in 1886 as well as the present would immediately represent to themselves as urban, that it seems at once rural again. Henchard is the least urbane of men, and only in such a shiftingly envisioned place could he plausibly be mayor.

Casterbridge, however, and its inhabitants are quite sufficiently urban to provide in concentrated form material for a sharp insight into economic oppression, a community at war with itself, the first that Hardy consciously offers in his novels. While Henchard presides over a banquet at the best hotel, at which guests were 'sniffing and grunting over their plates like sows nuzzling for acorns' (p. 35), the poor in the streets finger inedible bread. The same night Christopher Coney says to Farfrae 'we be bruckle folk here—the best o' us hardly honest sometimes what with hard winters, and so many mouths to fill, and Goda'mighty sending his little taties so terrible small to fill 'em with' (p. 53), and in the morning Henchard urges the Scotsman to 'a solid staunch tuck-in' on pigeon-pie and home-brewed ale, at which his plate is heaped 'to a prodigal fulness'. With characteristic irony Hardy notes that in Peter's Finger ex-poachers and ex-gamekeepers, equally victims of arbitrary rural class-power, swap stories of their bloody fights conducted over the rights of a few men to keep food away from those who need it. The condition of life, seen from the perspective of Mixen Lane, is one of perpetual economic struggle or collapse, and from this essentially urban point of view the novel alight further be read as a tale of class revenge.

'I do like to see the trimming pulled off such Christmas candles' (p. 267). Thus Nance Mockridge on Lucetta at the high-point of her life— wealthy, married to the Mayor of Casterbridge, in the public eye at a civic ceremony as the first lady of the town and all tho surrounding country-side. The skimmity-ride, anticipation of which stimulates Nance's remark, is Jopp's personal revenge on Lucetta for not helping him to a place, but for Nance Mockridge and others like her it represents the levelling of Lucetta to Mixen Lane, the vivid demonstration to the Casterbridge world and to Lucetta herself that she is no different from the white-aproned women in the doorways of the Lane. It is an unintentional product of the event that it reduces Lucetta further, to the ultimate condition of all humanity; and the revelation the ride embodies ensures that (unlike Henchard, the man with whom she is coupled in the ride) she is rapidly forgotten by all after her death, and particularly by her husband.

The revenge of Mrs Goodenough the furmity-seller is equally powerful and, directed against the function and the man at the centre of the novel, has wider ramifications. The immediate situation—Henchard the ex-mayor, the magistrate, sitting in the court's 'big chair', still retaining position, authority, the appearance of wealth, Mrs Goodenough standing before him, seedy, vulgar, penniless—offers so strong a contrast, that when she reveals Henchard's wife-selling and proclaims that he is morally unfit to judge her, the reader, who has always known of the wife-sale, still feels a sense of shock at the revelation. This is perhaps the central moment of the novel, the moment when the tragic hero is confronted with the consequences of his own moral flaw, the moment when the mayor understands that his power and his name will disappear. It is appropriate that it comes for the furmity-seller as a triumphant moment of class-revenge, but it is also appropriate in that Mrs Goodenough, more sharply than other characters, perceives the equality of all human beings in their weaknesses. As she talks to Susan of past days, she says:

> nobody could go, without having a dish of Mrs Goodenough's furmity. I knew the clergy's taste, the dandy-gent's taste; I knew the town's taste, the country's taste, I even knew the taste of the coarse shameless females. (p. 24)

Her litany of customers spans in a concentrated form the range of society; none was exempt from her own illicit trade, all are rendered alike in her account, the vicar with the prostitute.[6]

This reconnection of Mrs Goodenough and Michael Henchard contains, on reflection, more than the revenge of the underclass on the ruling class. The furmity-seller is Henchard's nemesis, but she is also his replicator in several ways.

Neither is a native of the area. The grain-based food she sells is not altogether what it seems, it has a hidden agenda, which Henchard's 'perverseness' finds out swiftly; the grain we hear Mayor Henchard has sold was similarly not what it seemed—the bread from his growed wheat is held to be 'unprincipled', as one might say the laced furmity is 'unprincipled'. When Susan returns to Weydon eighteen years after her sale to Newson, she finds Mrs Goodenough 'an old woman haggard, wrinkled, and almost in rags ... once thriving, cleanly, white-aproned and chinking with money—now tentless, dirty, owning no tables and benches' (p. 23). The reader is offered no account of her decline, but her 'steeped' aspect in court at Casterbridge a year later, and the drunk and disorderly charge brought against her there, suggest that a partial cause at least might have been the too ready consumption of her profits. On the other hand the secret of her illicit dealing was bound to be found out at some time by someone in authority, by undercover excise officers, for example. The deleterious influence of alcohol and secrets on Henchard's career is evident.

Mrs Goodenough has a different, though hardly reliable, explanation of why she has come down in the world: 'Lord's my life—the world's no memory; straightforward dealings don't bring profit—'tis the sly and the underhand that get on in these times' (pp. 23–4). The irony of this account is matched by the irony of Henchard and Jopp's manifestly improbable suggestion that Farfrae uses witchcraft to succeed in business, a suggestion followed swiftly by Henchard's visit to Conjuror Fall (pp. 184–6).

The furmity-seller, when interrogated by Susan at Weydon, faithfully recovers from her memory Henchard's instruction of seventeen years before to tell any woman who asked for him that he had gone to Casterbridge, when there was no inducement for her to do so, save common humanity.[7] It is similarly one of the deeply saving graces of Henchard that, amidst the multitude of wrong things he does, there is the startling and instinctive doing of the morally right thing.

Thus, when Mrs Goodenough and Henchard are brought face to face again in the court at Dorchester, Hardy has carefully prepared the reader to accept, almost before she announces it, equality between mayor and prisoner (in more than their common humanity), and further prepared the reader for Henchard's rapid disintegration. In part perhaps Hardy's motive for reintroducing her is the basic strategy which suggests that two similar careers establish a higher degree of mimetic verisimilitude than one, that the replication indicates a truth about the human condition; but in fact such replication can be taken much further in analysis of the novel.

None of the major characters in the novel is a native of Casterbridge or even of South Wessex. Save for a vague unstressed interlude while Dr Chalkfield is mayor, the chief citizens of the town are foreigners, and their wives are foreigners. All enter the novel with barely enough money to survive upon, and all at some time achieve or marry wealth and power. From the current point of view in the novel we may say that Lucetta was brought down by class-warfare, as was Henchard, and (possibly) the furmity-woman. All of which leads to the question: Is there any reason to think that Farfrae will not be similarly reduced? Does the fiercely repetitive nature of the plot more or less force us to the conclusion that Farfrae too will be driven to a fall by the underclass of

Casterbridge, and Elizabeth-Jane with him? Well, I would like to postpone considering this question until later, since there are other issues raised by the extended title of the novel that have first to be taken into account.

For the first edition of the novel, it will be remembered, Hardy augmented the title to read: *The Mayor of Casterbridge: the Life and Death of a Man of Character*, adding two further elements that provoke discussion. There is a fairly straightforward though superficial reason available for the introduction of 'Life and Death'. The stress in the earlier simpler title on the office rather than the individual left the way open for perverse readings of the novel that would give as much consideration to Farfrae as to Henchard, or even more perverse, that might argue that Farfrae, the surviving mayor at the end of the novel, is the true centre of the narrative. I have no wish to explore these possibilities, though it is easy enough to imagine how an argument might be framed, setting aside in the process only the whole tonal structure of the novel. It was perhaps in part to dissociate himself from any such possible reading that Hardy developed the more elaborate title, pinning the name Mayor firmly to the name Michael Henchard.

The effect of introducing the phrase 'Life and Death' goes, however, beyond that proposed in such an explanation. It raises two questions: first, if Hardy wishes thus to stress Henchard's life in the novel, why are twenty years of his brief maturity passed over; and second, what in the novel suggests that Henchard's death should be held thus in balance with his life?

An answer to the first question can be reached by reconsidering Henchard as mayor from a slightly different point of view. When Susan and Elizabeth-Jane see him through the window of the King's Arms, Henchard has reached a crucial moment in the development of his life. Aged forty, he has fulfilled the prediction he made of himself to the company in Mrs Goodenough's tent at Weydon: 'I'd challenge England to beat me in the fodder business; and if I were a free man again I'd be worth a thousand pound before I'd done o't" (p. 10).[8] He is wealthy; and more, he is the first citizen of his chosen town. The progress of his life for the last nineteen years is summarized by his success, and Solomon Longways provides the essentials for the reader (and Elizabeth-Jane); first that he is lonely, and then that he is

> the powerfullest member of the town-council, and quite a principal man in the country round besides. Never a big dealing in wheat, barley, oats, hay, roots, and such-like but Henchard's got a hand in it. Ay, and he'll go into other things, too; and that's where he makes his mistake. He worked his way up from nothing when 'a came here; and now he's a pillar of the town. Not but what he's been shaken a little to-year about this bad corn he has supplied in his contracts'. (p. 37)

Farfrae, passing the hotel, hears Henchard defy anyone to make the bad corn good again, and cannot resist entering Henchard's life.

Henchard has achieved all the material goals his imagination can suggest to him, and he knows they are not enough; he is alone, 'stately and vertical, silently thinking' (p. 40), while his fellow diners melt into drunken bonho-mie. The whole of his life since rejecting Susan, even including his misty affair with Lucetta in Jersey, has been merely a preparation for the moment in which he meets Farfrae and conceives a passionate love at first sight for him. The personal has re-entered his life, and his crisis begins, the conflict between his twin desires the course of which has already been sketched. Hardy implies, perhaps, in his expanded title, that Henchard's significant life, which was sus-pended when he failed to find Susan and Elizabeth-Jane, resumed only when he drew Farfrae into it.

The result is the inexorable and distinctly rapid process towards death, more than one death. He dies as a man of wealth and power, as mayor, long before he dies bodily. Once he is bankrupted and all that he possessed is auc-tioned, 'there was quite a sympathetic reaction in the town, which till then for some time past had done nothing but condemn him' (p. 220). Henchard's life as a public man is ended, framed for the townsfolk to examine. 'Now that Henchard's whole career was pictured distinctly to his neighbours, and they could see how admirably he had used his one talent of energy to create a position of affluence out of absolutely nothing—which was really all he could show when he came to the town as a journeyman hay-trusser with his wimble and knife in his basket—they wondered, and regretted his fall' (like the chorus in a classical tragedy). He seeks bodily death through suicide, but is metaphorically and painfully reborn for a brief life as a man for whom love is all-in-all; but the object of his love is withdrawn, and finally naked of desires, even of the desire for nourishment, taking all responsibility for all his actions into himself, he wastes away, and dies indeed.

This death is as strong evidence as one could wish to show how Hardy strained at the boundaries of realist fiction. The closest parallel is with Heath-cliff, though the agent of Henchard's death is no spirit once human, but, perhaps, 'the coming universal wish not to live' (*Jude the Obscure*, p. 355). The death at an early age, through self-neglect and mental self-torture, of Louis Trevelyan (in Trollope's *He Knew He Was Right* [1869]) is a good example of how a fully realist novelist handles a similar situation. Henchard dies when he does because that is when he must die, because the imaginative logic of the narrative demands it; we only do not question his death, because we know it is right.

And then, finally, there is in the title the phrase that has remained cru-cial for very many interpreters of the novel: 'a man of character'. My attempt to understand what such a description of Henchard implies turns on a passage from John Stuart Mill's *On Liberty*. There is a certain amount of external evidence that Hardy knew the piece well, for he wrote on 20 May 1906 to *The Times* (the occasion was the centenary of Mill's birth) of his hearing Mill speak in 1865, identifying him as 'the author of the treatise *On Liberty* (which we students of that date knew almost by heart)' (*Life and Works* p. 355). In these days we are not so familiar with On *Liberty*, and in order to establish the connection between Hardy's creation and Mill's analysis, substantial quotation from the third chapter, *Of Individuality*, is not redundant, if read with Henchard's character in mind.

Mill is concerned to show that contemporary society is mistakenly distrustful of extraordinary individuals who have unique talents in various directions; in these lines he discusses the significance of the person who possesses powerful desires and impulses:

> To a certain extent it is admitted, that our understanding should be our own: but there is not the same willingness to admit that our desires and impulses should be our own likewise; or that to possess impulses of our own, and of any strength, is anything but a peril and a snare. Yet desires and impulses are as much a part of a perfect human being, as beliefs and restraints: and strong impulses are only perilous when not properly balanced; when one set of aims and inclinations is developed into strength, while others, which ought to coexist with them, remain weak and inactive. It is not because men's desires are strong that they act ill; it is because their consciences are weak. There is no natural connexion between strong impulses and a weak conscience. The natural connexion is the other way. To say that one person's desires and feelings are stronger and more various than those of another, is merely to say that he has more of the raw material of human nature, and is therefore capable, perhaps of more evil, but certainly of more good.

The man of strong desires and impulses, Mill says, is potentially a greatly good man, so long as there is a balance in him between his desires and impulses and his conscience. This is a way of formulating the essence of much tragedy, for we may suppose that it is rare for any individual to hold within them this essential balance. More often, like most of Shakespeare's tragic figures, the intensity of desire and the power of its impulsive expression is at crucial moments uncontrolled by the conscience acting through the will. And so it is with Henchard. Amongst them the narrator and the other characters draw frequent attention to Henchard's deeply impulsive nature, put in service of his powerful ambition and his underlying desire to love. At the same time events demonstrate that at crucial moments in his life his conscience proves inadequate to the task of controlling his impulses. At first it seems like some diminishment of this condemnation that when he sells his wife, when he directs the commination psalm at Farfrae, when he interrupts the royal visit to Casterbridge, when he all but kills Farfrae in the hay-loft, he does so under the influence of alcohol, the effect of which is to put his conscience to sleep. But this is only the postponement of responsibility, for he deliberately drinks in order to dull his conscience, in order to allow his impulses to have free rein. And to make clear what Henchard is capable of, his final destructive impulsive act, when he tells Newson that his daughter is dead, is performed when he is perfectly sober.

Nevertheless readers have always recognized that Henchard has a greater potential, a fuller humanity than anyone else in the novel. It is in part his tragedy that his potential is not fulfilled. The identification of Mill's account with Henchard is reinforced in the continuation of the paragraph from *On Liberty*:

> Strong impulses are but another name for energy. Energy may be turned to bad uses; but more good may always be made of an energetic nature, than of an indolent and impassive one. Those who have most natural feeling, are always those whose cultivated feelings may be made the strongest. The same strong susceptibilities which make the personal impulses vivid and powerful, are also the source from whence are generated the most passionate love of virtue, and the sternest self-control. It is through the cultivation of these, that society both does its duty and protects its interests: not by rejecting the stuff of which heroes are made, because it knows not how to make them.

It is Henchard's extraordinary energy which allows him to surmount the prejudices of the ruling society of Casterbridge and compels them to elect him mayor, and, as Mill reiterates the supremacy of the energetic nature when combined with 'the most passionate love of virtue, and the sternest self-control', we recognize again the potential within Henchard that is essentially unfulfilled.[9]

Immediately Mill defines what he means by 'character', and here is the source for the final element in Hardy's title:

> A person whose desires and impulses are his own—are the expression of his own nature, as it has been developed and modified

by his own culture—is said to have a character. One whose desires and impulses are not his own, has no character, no more than a steam-engine has a character. If, in addition to being his own, his impulses are strong, and are under the government of a strong will, he has an energetic character.

The remainder of the passage from *On Liberty* that I wish to quote turns from the definition of the potential Carlylean hero to a brief account of why contemporary society finds it hard to accept such individuals:

> Whoever thinks that individuality of desires and impulses should not be encouraged to unfold itself, must maintain that society has no need of strong natures—is not the better for containing many persons who have much character—and that a high general average of energy is not desirable.
>
> In some early states of society, these forces might be, and were, too much ahead of the power which society then possessed of disciplining and controlling them. There has been a time when the element of spontaneity and individuality was in excess, and the social principle had a hard struggle with it. The difficulty then was, to induce men of strong bodies or minds to pay obedience to any rules which required them to control their impulses. To overcome this difficulty, law and discipline, like the Popes struggling against the Emperors, asserted a power over the whole man, claiming to control his life in order to control his character—which society had not found any other sufficient means of binding. But society, has now fairly got the better of individuality; and the danger which threatens human nature is not the excess, but the deficiency, of personal impulses and preferences.

Thus, if we follow Mill, we can say that Henchard is a man of energetic character, but one dangerous to society because the strength of his impulse to power and of his desire to love is at crucial moments in his life not matched by the strength of his conscience operating through his will to prevent such impulses and desires infringing on the rights of others. Mill recognizes that society is wrong (and ultimately deprives itself of potential for growth) to outlaw people of individual energy (and in fact the town council of Casterbridge does not initially do so with Henchard, but rather harnesses his energy—without however caring particularly for the individual who possesses it).

At the same time, however, Mill accepts that society has a right to protect itself when the operation of such energy limits the potential of others for growth. 'The means of development which the individual loses by being prevented from gratifying his inclinations to the injury of others, are chiefly obtained at the expense of the development of other people.' This point raises serious questions for the reader of *The Mayor of Casterbridge*; Farfrae and his wife Elizabeth-Jane are the most prominent and the most punctiliously proper representatives of society in the novel, and they reject Henchard, abandon him, outlaw and ultimately condemn him to death.[10] Following Mill, they are right to do so, for even if he has expiated the crime of selling his wife, he has sinned again in telling Newson his daughter is dead. However it seems clear from the hostility the narrator displays towards Farfrae at the end of the novel, and the coolness that seems the keynote of Elizabeth-Jane's nature, that Hardy and his narrator do not intend the reader to take Mill's position. There is no equivocation about Henchard's act of denial—it is wrong; but the narrator ensures that the reader understands why the impulse to lie is so powerful for Henchard in a way neither of his judges does. Farfrae is incapable of distinguishing the man from the function, seeing him only as a day-labourer—he judges largely by the surface, and when he sees something deeper, he says: 'with a man of passions such as his there is no safeguard for conduct' (p. 242), forcing us to judge between passions and conduct, warmth and cold, anarchy and disruptiveness and moral conformity to conventions of behaviour—the range or the limits of human potential. Elizabeth-Jane is sympathetic, kind, loving even, but she has so little passionateness herself that it is impossible for her to comprehend her step-father. Even Newson, who is not bothered by the 'trick' once he has become reunited with his daughter, and treats the matter as a practical joke, is wrong in this instance.[11] It is no joke, but rather the desperate instinctive grasping of a passionate man for his last chance of happiness in a society that has little sympathy or understanding for the passionate and the energetic.

If we are inclined to forgive or even to approve Henchard's lie to Newson, then we are parting company with Mill, and becoming ourselves revolutionaries against Victorian society. This is Hardy's ultimate critique—or maybe his amplification—of Mill's ideas on a man of character. A social theorist cannot deal in individual cases, and Hardy's application of Mill's ideas reveals Hardy's fundamental discontent with a society that can abandon a man such as Henchard to death. But we cannot rest content with such a conclusion, for at the same time Hardy shows that the strength and energy that drives Henchard to success drives him equally rapidly to defeat, and the working out of this sequence suggests that Victorian society is not unique in penalizing powerful energies and desires, that the nature of human existence anywhere in the world and at any time ensures that the controlled and the equable alone prosper.

This is a familiar proposition in Hardy criticism. Though the success of the mediocre is seldom found in so naked a form as it is in *The Mayor of Casterbridge*—perhaps Gabriel Oak's triumph in *Far From the Madding Crowd* is the only comparably powerful statement of the idea—from Sergeant Troy to Jude Fawley and Sue Bridehead Hardy's novels offer a series of individuals who try in some way to fight social convention and the nature of human existence, and are destroyed in the conflict.

The Life and Death of the Mayor of Casterbridge: A Story of a Man of Character is permeated with confusing and conflicting accounts of why things happen in the world the way they do. If Henchard is 'a man of character', then the place to begin an investigation of these accounts would seem to be with the notion that character is fate, even though the context in which the issue is raised in its definitive form concerns Farfrae rather than Henchard:

> Whether it was that his northern energy was an overmastering force among the easy-going Wessex worthies, or whether it was sheer luck, the fact remained that whatever he touched he prospered in. . . . But most probably luck had little to do with it. Character is Fate, said Novalis, and Farfrae's character was just the reverse of Henchard's. (p. 115)

There is little doubt that this is one of the theses the novel tends to validate. When (to refer to an example that also relates to Farfrae) Lucetta says 'Donald's genius would have enabled him to get a footing anywhere, without anybody's help!' (p. 266) we accept that she is right, despite the narrator's subsequent doubts; we have no trouble in imagining him (had he turned Henchard's original offer down) the mayor of some Canadian grain-belt town. His character would ensure a similar fate.

There are, however, certain unsettling features within this apparently authoritative passage. For instance, it is not unreasonable for the narrator to stress Farfrae's 'northern energy' as the character trait responsible for his success, but he then confuses file issue by saying that Farfrae was in character precisely Henchard's opposite. This is confusing since the reader cannot help but recall the narrator's previous assertion that it was Henchard's exceptional energy which had brought *him* success. How acute, we are led to ask, is the narrator as a judge of character? Another troubling detail is that most commentators suggest (intertextually) that Hardy's allusion to Novalis's idea cannot be read without reference to George Eliot's prior use of it in *The Mill on the Floss*, where Eliot's narrator calls the notion that character is destiny one of Novalis's 'questionable aphorisms' (Book VI, Chapter 6), and proceeds to suggest that circumstance is equally powerful in shaping our ends.

Up to a point, however, it is demonstrable that the natures of the major figures in the novel shape their own lives and those of others. But the greatest problem at the heart of the proposition that character is fate is its apparent exclusivity; it tends to limit to one the range of meanings of the name 'fate', a limitation which is strongly at odds with other formulations in the novel, and with the form of the narrative itself. On the one hand there is the notion of a personal fate—what happens to a person; on the other, there is abstract fate—a force that causes things to happen to all people. Novalis seems to have had the personal sense in mind: our future is what it is because we are the people we are. Ultimately his neat aphorism has insufficient potential for the analysis conducted by the narrative voices (or by the characters themselves), and there is a plethora of references in the novel to concepts like Providence, fortune and destiny, which exclude human agency altogether.

It is inevitable in any approximately realistic interpretation of Victorian society that some characters should attribute events to divine intervention. When Farfrae finally gives in to Henchard's impulsive, compulsive desire for him to stay in Casterbridge and become his manager it is because he is convinced that their encounter is 'Providence! Should anyone go against it?' (pp. 64–5). There is a conventional Christian overtone to the word 'Providence'; and his religious (if not Christian) understanding of causation is made clear in a parallel phrasing at a similar moment of decision (his acceptance of the mayoralty of Casterbridge). Farfrae says to Lucetta (who had hoped they would leave Casterbridge): 'See now how it's ourselves that are ruled by the powers above us! We plan this, but we do that . . .' (p. 243). The question is, how far do we accept Farfrae's approach to life, here or elsewhere?

That Hardy was attempting in the novel to draw a distinction between a religious understanding of a causative force and a secular one is suggested by two further passages from the novel: on p. 179 the narrator, considering the consequences for Lucetta and Elizabeth-Jane of the newly-fledged attraction between the former and Farfrae, says of Lucetta that she 'with native lightness of heart took kindly to what fate offered', and of Elizabeth-Jane that she 'wondered what unwished for thing Heaven might send her in place of [Farfrae]'. The tenuously religious Lucetta receives contentedly the chances that neutral 'fate' presents her with, but the deeply religious Elizabeth-Jane ponders on the agency of the explicitly Christian 'Heaven'.

A similar distinction is perceptible in a paragraph on p. 88 when the narrator says of Elizabeth-Jane that she retained a 'fear of the coulter of destiny despite fair promise', while reporting in the same paragraph that she says to herself (in interior monologue) that she will not be gay because it 'would be tempting Providence to hurl mother and me down, and afflict us again as he used to do'. Though 'he' is not capitalized, Elizabeth-Jane's identification of Providence with God seems to be implied, while the narrator uses the neutral 'destiny'.

Farfrae and his wife Elizabeth-Jane are the only characters to attribute agency to 'Providence' or 'Heaven', and though they do not invoke God directly this may well only be because they consider it unlucky or ungenteel or vaguely blasphemous so to do. By the end of the novel they have become representatives for the reader of all dominant social norms, and one of these, one indeed of the most important, is an observance of religious conventions. There seems to be some doubt, then, about a divine version of the causality of events.

Henchard himself is contradictory in this area as in many: he is the only major character to invoke God by name; he is a churchwarden; and yet there is no sense at all of him as a man who sets any store by Christianity or Christian observance.[12] For a brief time after he is saved from killing himself by the appearance of his effigy at the place he had chosen for his suicide, he wonders if his preservation is miraculous. The narrator comments: 'The sense of the supernatural was strong in this unhappy man, and he turned away as one might have done in the actual presence of an appalling miracle' (p. 297). Even when he sees that there is a natural explanation for the appearance of his image in the pool, he says 'Who is such a reprobate as I! And yet it seems that even I be in Somebody's hand!' (p. 299). It is just possible to imagine at this moment that Henchard has at last seen the light, will become born again, and thus finally integrated into society. On the next page, however, the narrator comments: 'the emotional conviction that he was in Somebody's hand began to die out of Henchard as time slowly removed into distance the event which had given that feeling birth', and at once we recognize how characteristic it is (character being [personal] fate) that his belief in a beneficent divine providence should be purely transitory.

When Henchard decides to forswear strong drink, he does it before God, in a church, head on a Bible; but he does so not out of religious conviction, but because the imagery and associations of the place and objects and ritual are appropriately solemn and portentous, and suit his current frame of mind. The narrator of Larkin's 'Church-Going' shares some of these apprehensions.

Henchard is impulsive, and his capacity for feeling is very great; for the most part he is unconcerned with supernatural agency, but at moments when emotions of some description are intensely roused in him, he turns outside himself. When, for instance, he discovers that Elizabeth-Jane is not his child the narrator analyses his response:

> His lip twitched, and he seemed to compress his frame, as if to bear better. His usual habit was not to consider whether destiny

were hard upon him or not—the shape of his ideas in cases of
affliction being simply a moody 'I am to suffer I perceive,'—'This
much scourging, then, is for me.' But now through his passionate
head there stormed this thought—that the blasting disclosure was
what he deserved. . . . Henchard, like all his kind, was superstitious,
and he could not help thinking that the concatenation of events
this evening had produced was the scheme of some sinister
intelligence bent upon punishing him. Yet they had developed
naturally. (pp. 126–7)

In this passage, as in the 'character is fate' passage, there is evidence of radical ambiguity. The narrator's account is that because the pain Henchard feels is
sharper than usual, sharper than he can easily contain, he turns outside himself,
speculating that the force ordering events in the world, neutral destiny in this
instance, (the existence of which he has apparently always implicitly accepted)
has for once judged him, and personally intervened with a punishment to match
the crime of wife-selling. The narrator, however, dismisses Henchard's 'sinister
intelligence' as the overwrought emotionalism of an unintellectual and superstitious man, and points out the traceable sequence of cause and effect that
had brought him to this moment. George Eliot would have been proud of her
disciple, and the reader is encouraged to feel thoroughly superior to Henchard.
But there are (at least) two narrative voices speaking to us in the novel on this
issue, voices that might be characterized as 'rationalist/realist'—the voice just
attended to, that finds a logical antecedent cause in the past of human action
for every present event—and 'determinist/immanent will'—the voice that uses
in many places 'destiny', 'fate' and other such words to indicate a force that
makes things happen quite independent of human agency.

Consider, for example the following: 'Ever since the evening of his wife's
arrival with her daughter there had been something in the air which had
changed his luck. That dinner at the King's Arms with his friends had been
Henchard's Austerlitz: he had had his successes since, but his course had not
been upward' (p. 135). Only twenty pages earlier the (a) narrator had denied
that luck had anything to do with Farfrae's success.[13]

Or again this, where the (a) narrator says that access to music might have
rendered Henchard less comfortless in his despair, 'for with Henchard music
was of regal power. . . . But hard fate had ordained that he should be unable to
call up this Divine spirit in his need' (p. 296). It isn't altogether clear why music
should be unavailable to him; even if he can't play himself, there is music in
Mixen Lane or he can go to hear church-music. But the point is that this narrator specifically invokes 'hard fate' whose ordinance has prevented the man from
gaining relief. How is this different from Henchard's 'sinister intelligence'?

Or lastly, this: 'Poor Elizabeth-Jane, little thinking what her malignant star had done to blast the budding attentions she had won from Donald Farfrae, was glad to hear . . .' (p. 166). There is a perfectly adequate sequence of cause and effect in the previous chapters to account for the growth of attraction between Lucetta and Farfrae, and yet we are told here that such a rational explanation is illusory, and that Elizabeth-Jane's personal 'malignant star' had in fact caused it all.

Since the narrative voice is fundamentally contradictory, not anyway a homogeneous thing, the reader is left free to choose one or all of these methods of accounting for the way things turn out. When Elizabeth-Jane watches by her mother's death-bed we are shown 'the subtle-souled girl asking herself why she was born, why sitting in a room, and blinking at the candle; why things around her had taken the shape they wore in preference to every other possible shape; why they stared at her so helplessly, as if waiting for the touch of some wand that should release them from terrestrial constraint; what that chaos called consciousness, which spun in her at this moment like a top, tended to, and began in' (p. 119).

There is no answer, and the narrator's silence in face of these direct questions is perhaps the most eloquent commentary of all on the issue. But there is the temptation for the critic of the novel to draw back one step further towards the creative fount, and consider the role of the Thomas Hardy who is the inscriber of the chaotic consciousness/es that 'guide' the reader through the fiction. In this novel the veil of realism over the fiction is stretched very thin in some places, particularly those that have to do with the way things happen. It might be said with some justice that it is T Hardy novelist who is fate. It is he who ensures that for Henchard and for others at the moment of intensest hope there comes crashing destruction of hope. This instrumentality of the author is closely tied up with another aspect of causality, a view that might be expressed by 'secrets are fate'.

It is possible to argue that the really disabling element in life is to have secrets; that much of the evil that occurs in this novel, and in others by Hardy—*Tess of the d'Urbervilles*, or *The Return of the Native* for instance— occurs because secrets have not been told (thus leading one to take a dim view of the ending of *Under the Greenwood Tree*).

> Had the incident [Henchard's selling his wife] been well-known of old and always, it might by this time have grown to be lightly regarded, as the rather tall wild oat, but well-nigh the single one, of a young man with whom the steady and mature (if somewhat headstrong) burgher of to-day had scarcely a point in common. But the act having lain as dead and buried ever since, the interspace of

years was unperceived; and the black spot of his youth wore the
aspect of a recent crime. (p. 218)

At any moment in Henchard's career in Casterbridge the revelation of this
secret would have been a setback, but coming as it does at the time of his
greatest financial difficulty, it prevents the possible extension of his credit
through the influence of his good name, and rapidly accelerates proceedings
against him for bankruptcy.

If Lucetta's secret liaison with Henchard had always been known,
then there would have been no skimmity-ride, and she would not have died
(though also she might not have married Farfrae). Henchard warns Lucetta
that Farfrae 'is sure to find out something of the matter, sooner or later', offering advice that he cannot follow himself.

The discovery of Susan's secret would have hurt Henchard at any time;
but it is so grotesquely painful as to be deliberate, not just as a fictional device
for effect, but as a direct statement from the novelist about the nature of
existence, that immediately after opening of himself 'without reluctance and
without fear' to Elizabeth-Jane as his daughter, Henchard opens a letter
which reduces all the anticipation, love, hope to a ruin of ashes. He finds she
is not his daughter.

Henchard keeps to himself his knowledge of Newson's return. The narrator notes of Henchard that 'a great change had come over him with regard to
[Elizabeth-Jane], and he was developing the dream of a future lit by her filial
presence, as though that way alone could happiness lie' (p. 290). In the next sentence Newson returns to destroy the dream—as the narrator memorably says,
'Henchard's face and eyes seemed to die.' Secrets, Hardy says throughout his
fiction, are destructive; but here as elsewhere it is not the fact of the secret's revelation that is so striking—if Newson is alive, then there is every reason why he
should exert himself to find Susan and his daughter; it is the timing of the revelation at the moment calculated to cause the deepest anguish that reveals nakedly
the malice of the author. Here, one might say, is Henchard's 'sinister intelligence'.
Hardy simply destroys the illusion of mimesis, removes his novel from the conventions of Victorian realism, and announces than the novelist is fate.

Study of his work, particularly of the last novels, *The Dynasts* and the
poetry, suggests though that there is for Hardy a deeper realism involved
in his manipulation, in that he is thus only reflecting the ill-managed plan
of causation in the world. What does it ultimately matter who or what is
responsible for what happens; Elizabeth-Jane's questions need no answer; it
is the pain or the pleasure that results which is important.

As the man of character leaves Casterbridge as fully bereft of all things
as when he had arrived there, the narrator summarizes for us his thoughts:

He experienced not only the bitterness of a man who finds, in looking back on an ambitious course, that what he has sacrificed in sentiment was worth as much as what he has gained in substance; but the superadded bitterness of seeing his very recantation nullified. He had been sorry for all this long ago; but his attempts to replace ambition by love had been as fully foiled as his ambition itself. His wronged wife had foiled them by a fraud so grandly simple as to be almost a virtue.

It was an odd sequence that out of this tampering with the social law [presumably the same social law that the narrator of *Tess* says Tess has been made to break] came that flower of nature Elizabeth. Part of his wish to wash his hands of life arose from his perception of its contrarious inconsistencies—of nature's jaunty readiness to support unorthodox social principles. (p. 319)

The first paragraph neatly catches the essence of Henchard's life; but the second is rather strange. It suggests that Henchard wants to die in part because the social law is not always supported by nature. But when has Henchard ever felt that conformity with society's orthodoxy was the only virtue in life? Perhaps what the narrator intends here is to say that Henchard shares the basic human wish to have life predictable, to have appropriate effect follow the cause; when it doesn't, when we seem sport for the gods (or nature), then life isn't worth living?

On the next page there is a further portentous narratorial commentary:

Externally there was nothing to hinder his making another start on the upward slope, and by his new lights achieving higher things than his soul in its half-formed state had been able to accomplish. But the ingenious machinery contrived by the gods for reducing human possibilities of amelioration to a minimum—which arranges that wisdom to do shall come *pari passu* with the departure of zest for doing—stood in the way of all that. He had no wish to make an arena, a second time, of a world that had become a mere painted scene to him. (320)

This passage bears a family resemblance to that at the end of *Tess of the d'Urbervilles* in which the narrator talks of the President of the Immortals at play with Tess, and it is relatively easy to set aside the mechanical machinery of the gods as proceeding from the frustrations of a cynical narrative voice. If the gods really rule the world, then any claim that character is fate is nonsense, and life and free-will an illusion. But by this time we know, despite the tone, that the voice making this statement represents only one aspect of authority in the novel, which is so fragmented as to be no authority at all.

There are other questions raised by the passage. What, for instance, are Henchard's new lights? Self-restraint; humility; socialization? And what 'higher' things might he be able to accomplish? Presumably higher in a moral sense, more directly beneficial to his fellow humans? And are we to believe that the series of events recounted in the novel has proved the world a vale of soul-making for Henchard? Apparently so, but this account seems to describe quite another man from the one we see trussing hay and wishing for death. The image of Henchard's past life conducted in an arena, full of conflicts with wild beasts and gladiators, taking up the whole Roman background to the narrative, is more appropriate.

The Mayor died a long while ago in the Casterbridge arena; Michael Henchard dies in a hut in the heart of Egdon Heath, the natural environment above all untamable by man. Like Eustacia Vye he dies because there is no longer any reason he can see to live, or because Hardy can see no reason for him to live; because ambition has dissipated and love comes to ashes and there is nothing else. Unaccommodated man is destroyed by vacancy within and by the elements without.

The last word in the novel is with Elizabeth-Jane:

> Her experience had been of the kind to teach her, rightly or wrongly, that the doubtful honour of a brief transit through a sorry world hardly called for effusiveness . . . her strong sense that neither she nor any human being deserved less than was given, did not blind her to the fact that there were others receiving less who had deserved much more. (p. 334)

The question raised by this summary is who or what gives to humans less or more? If character is fate, then Elizabeth-Jane's understanding is sharply awry. It is most likely that she would credit the Anglican Providence with agency, but the narrator who is interpreting her thoughts would more probably have some neutral concept like the Immanent Will in mind. The reader is at liberty to feel that Hardy has so manipulated the lives of his characters that to go beyond the idea that the writer is destiny serves no purpose.

Notes

1. In *Thomas Hardy: The Forms of Tragedy* (Detroit, 1975), Chapter 4.
2. Two of the three novels that Hardy wrote after *The Return of Ox Native*—*A Laodicean* and *Two on a Tower*—also contain studies of women whose lives are also conditioned by their lack of access to power in a male-dominated environment, despite the fact that one is rich and the other aristocratic. Paula Power's name is thus

fundamentally ironic, and though Lady Viviette Constantine loves and is loved in return, male authority determines her subsequent unhappiness and death.

3. Elaine Showalter's fine essay 'The Unmanning of the Mayor of Caster-bridge' reaches a similar conclusion by a different route. The essay is in *Critical Approaches to the Fiction of Thomas Hardy*, edited by Dale Kramer (London and Basingstoke: Macmillan, 1978) pp. 99–115.

4. See, for instance, the first chapter of David Enstice's *Thomas Hardy: Land-scapes of the Mind* (London and Basingstoke, 1979) with its reliance on A. Lindsay Clegg's *A History of Dorchester, Dorset* (London, 1972), and almost every substantial commentator on the novel.

5. Another aspect of the urban nature of Casterbridge is the rapidity with which gossip spreads through the community: 'By this time the marriage that had taken place was known throughout Casterbridge; had been discussed noisily on kerb-stones, confidentially behind counters, and jovially at the Three Mariners' (p. 217). The actions of prominent people in the town are speedily and intimately discussed by the workfolk and out-of-workfolk of the town. Similarly, at the beginning of the next chapter: 'The retort of the furmity-woman before the magistrates had spread; and in twenty-four hours there was not a person in Casterbridge who remained unacquainted with the story of Henchard's mad freak at Weydon Priors Fair, long years before' (p. 218). Gossip is one of the many potential agencies of events that the novel empowers, as for instance when inaccurate gossip about Farfrae's intentions with regard to purchasing a seed shop for the bankrupt Henchard creates enmity in the ex-mayor where none was intended (p. 241).

6. The incident is a triumph of a different sort for Henchard too, in that he does not use his authority to attempt to crush the woman, but at once accepts the inherent validity of her claim.

7. It is then a reasonably harsh criticism of Susan and of conventional morality when the narrator adds: 'Mrs Newson would have rewarded the old woman as far as her small means afforded, had she not discreetly borne it in mind that it was by this unscrupulous person's liquor her husband had been degraded' (p. 25). Elizabeth-Jane's concern for respectability, the anxiety of saving herself and her mother from categorization by observers as 'the lowest' must share in this criticism.

8. This speech echoes Thomas Leaf's unintentionally comic story at the end of *Under the Greenwood Tree*, in which a man is supposed to make a thousand pounds through a kind of natural multiplication. Henchard actually does it, though we have no details about how he does it. His achievement might also lead a reader to imagine that the tendency of this novel is to attack the institution of marriage.

9. There is a strong flavour of Blake underpinning the idea of energy in both Mill and Hardy: 'Energy is the only life, and is from the Body; and Reason is the bound or outward circumference of Energy. Energy is Eternal Delight. Those who restrain desire, do so because theirs is weak enough to be restrained; and the restrainer or reason usurps its place & governs the unwilling. And being restrain'd, it by degrees becomes passive, till it is only the shadow of desire' (from *The Marriage of Heaven and Hell*). Energy, defined in the *OED* as 'vigour of action, utterance, etc. Hence as a personal quality: The capacity and habit of strenuous exertion', has its earliest record in Coleridge 1809–10; but the word was in the air at the end of the eighteenth century as descriptive of painting and so on.

10. The narrator comments that 'Any suspicion of impropriety was to Eliza-beth-Jane like a red rag to a bull. Her craving for correctness of procedure was,

indeed, almost vicious' (p. 216). With regard to Farfrae a good example of his adherence to social conventions is on p. 307, where Henchard thinks how he could alienate 'the correct' Farfrae from Elizabeth-Jane by revealing her bastardy to him.

11. This novel defines 'practical jokes' as something rather more sinister and dangerous than I am used to considering them; there is also a considerable number of them. As well as telling a man his daughter is dead when she is alive, threatening to sell your wife is a joke (though actually doing it is not) (p. 14); making a man ride to work half-naked is a joke (p. 100); getting a potential husband's daughter to live with you is a joke (p. 150); a bull charging two women intends a practical joke rather than murder (p. 207), and the same is true of Henchard wrestling Farfrae (pp. 235, 239); Henchard's reading aloud of Lucetta's love-letters is a joke (p. 251, and Lucetta herself calls it 'horse-play' p. 249); some people think the skimmity ride 'too rough a joke', and for Jopp 'it was not a joke, but a retaliation' (p. 268). This extensive list might provide the basis for a study of playfulness in Hardy.

12. There are thirteen places in the novel where God is named, and Henchard is responsible for ten of them (the others are Christopher Coney, Joyce and the landlady of Peter's Finger). From the oath he swears before God in the church near Weydon Henchard uses the name freely, telling Farfrae to 'pray to God' that he may never suffer fits of desperate gloom (p. 78), saying to himself that God knows whether Lucetta will be contented to be put off with a cheque now Susan has returned (p. 81), using the exclamation 'Good God' twice to introduce chastisements of Elizabeth-Jane's Dorset speech and humble actions. As he looks forward to the day when his oath will be fulfilled, he says 'then I mean to enjoy myself, please God.' When he has Farfrae's life in his hands, and the Scotsman tells him to take it as he has long wished to, he replies 'that's not true! . . . God is my witness that no man ever loved another as I did thee.'

Apart from his oath-swearing, we never see Henchard in church (though as a churchwarden presumably he must go), and it is hard to imagine him there. The narrator repeatedly stresses Henchard's superstitious nature, and it would be possible to say that his frequent reference to God is an instinctive superstitious attempt to ward off evil consequences rather than a deeply held belief in the Christian God's power in the world. A different reading might suggest that Henchard is more open to the supernatural, more naturally religious, than any other character in the novel. As usual the ambiguity leaves us free to choose, to construct our own meaning.

13. The Napoleonic allusion also directs one's thoughts immediately to *The Dynasts* and the Immanent Will.

PETER WIDDOWSON

"Moments of Vision": Postmodernising Tess of the d'Urbervilles: or, Tess of the d'Urbervilles Faithfully Presented by Peter Widdowson

Anyone who has read *Tess of the d'Urbervilles* (and certainly any modern criticism about it) will be in no doubt that the novel is emphatically visual in many of its effects. There are those famous set-piece 'descriptions' of rural Wessex (not quite Dorset, let us remember); the inescapably scenic moments, such as the May-dance at Marlott as the novel opens or sunrise at Stonehenge towards the end, which render talk about Hardy's proto-cinematic techniques more than merely chic; and the narrative's obsessive voyeuristic gazing at Tess herself (especially that famous 'mobile peony mouth'[1]) which has made so many readers *wonder* a little about Thomas Hardy. But there is also a great deal of visual imagery in the novel of a rather more self-reflexive sort—a kind of metadiscourse about looking, seeing, perception, representation, imaging.

This is not new or unique to *Tess of the d'Urbervilles*, of course: it is everywhere apparent in Hardy's fiction—from the subtitling of *Under the Greenwood Tree* as 'A Rural Painting of the Dutch School' to the presence (betimes) of a photographer in *A Laodicean*; from the staged artificiality of the tableaux vivants in *The Hand of Ethelberta* to the blindness of Clym in *The Return of the Native*; from the astronomer's telescope in *Two on a Tower* to striking 'moments of vision' (a phrase I shall return to) such as that in *Desperate Remedies* (Hardy's first published novel) where Cytherea Graye, watching

From *New Perspectives on Thomas Hardy*, edited by Charles P.C. Pettit, pp. 80–100. © 1994 by Peter Widdowson.

her father and some masons at the top of a church spire—'it was an *illuminated miniature, framed in* by the dark *margin* of the window' (my italics)—suddenly sees him fall to his death: 'he reeled off into the air, immediately disappearing downwards'.[2] And there are the typographical signs and devices scattered throughout the text of *Jude the Obscure*—a novel significantly characterised by its author in his preface to the first edition (1895) as 'a series of seemings, or personal impressions'.[3]

But self-conscious techniques of visualisation are particularly insistent in *Tess*, a novel also prefatorily described by Hardy as 'an impression'[4]—a significant word, perhaps, given his fascination with the late 'impressionist' paintings of J. M. W. Turner.[5] Chapter 2, for example, opens with a reference to a 'landscape-painter', and from there on—as J. B. Bullen has pointed out—the novel abounds with overt or covert references to pictures.[6] There is also the complex ambiguity of the narrator's point of view or stance—towards Tess in particular. For instance:

> As she walked along to-day, for all her *bouncing handsome womanliness, you* could sometimes *see* her twelfth year in her cheeks, or her ninth *sparkling from her eyes*; and even her fifth would flit over the *curves of her mouth* now and then.
>
> Yet *few* knew, and *still fewer* considered this. *A small minority*, mainly strangers, would *look long at her* in casually passing by, and grow momentarily fascinated by her freshness, and wonder if *they* would ever *see* her again: but *to almost everybody* she was a *fine and picturesque* country girl, and no more. (Ch. 2, p. 52)

My italics draw attention to the voyeurism of the passage, but the uncertainty of focus ('you ... few ... still fewer ... a small minority ... almost everybody') and the peculiar logic of the syntax in the second paragraph ('Yet ... but ... and no more') make it very difficult to say who sees her like this and whether the narrative is attempting to distance itself from the erotic imaging the passage in fact delivers or is fully complicit in it. Furthermore, there is the continual presentation of Tess in terms of the way she is 'seen' by others—most especially, of course, Alec and Angel—until her 'character' seems to be composed entirely of other people's images of her (a point I will return to later). And there are the many other instances where the narrative deploys strikingly visual devices and motifs, from the filmic long-shots (the farm-girls picking Swedes at Flintcomb-Ash) and close-ups (Tess's mouth), to the final scene where Angel and Liza Lu, 'their eyes rivetted' to the gaol's flag-pole, watch the 'black flag' unfurl which denotes that Tess has been hanged (notice how, at this point, a novel which has fetishised Tess's visual presence throughout now signals its absence by her displacement into a black flag).

It is quite possible to think, therefore, that *Tess of the d'Urbervilles* is actually in some way *about* seeing and representation. After all, Hardy himself describes it in the preface to the first edition—although we can never really trust that wary old ironist and least self-revealing of writers—as 'an *attempt to give artistic form* to a true sequence of things' (my italics). And he also claims, by way of the novel's hugely contentious subtitle ('appended', he would have us believe in a prefatory postscript of 1912, 'at the last moment' and with no premeditation), that his 'Pure Woman' is '*faithfully presented* by Thomas Hardy' (my italics). Does the phrasing here suggest just how ironically conscious he was of representation as a potent source, precisely, of *mis*representation? Had the image, as we all now know in these post-modern times, already substantively replaced 'the thing itself' for Hardy? Was he already discrediting the notion that there is an ultimate reality, or true essence, outside of history and discourse—such as 'human nature', for example, or even perhaps: *pure woman*? But a discussion of this key term in Hardy's disingenuous subtitle—and a central theme of critical commentary on *Tess*—must wait for a moment, although, as we shall see the 'pure woman' and her attendant debate in fact focuses the issues of seeing and representation which I have suggested the novel so insistently raises. Certainly a good deal of recent criticism emphasises these issues as crucial terms in discussing *Tess of the d'Urbervilles*—an emphasis which derives principally from two very contemporary critical sources: feminism and post-structuralism. In order to explain what I mean here, I need to reflect briefly on the general state of the last two decades of Hardy criticism, before returning to the problems of 'seeing', (mis)representation and pure women.

While selecting work from the past twenty years for the Macmillan *New Casebook* on *Tess*, I found that with a few honourable exceptions, all the really interesting material came after 1980. It appeared that work from the 1970s, even that of high quality and sophisticated in its own terms, somehow 'belonged' to an earlier critical phase[7]—rather like those automobiles which are still being made new and still function adequately, but which, when you lift the bonnet, clearly betray a prior generation of technology. I do not mean to be gratuitously dismissive, nor to foster a 'whig' view of literary-critical history as continually 'progressive', nor do I wish to be wilfully partial and partisan, but so much critical writing on *Tess* in the 1970s, with its emphases on plot, 'poetic structure', character, 'ideas' and imagery (sometimes symbolism), *does now* seem passé, beside the point, going nowhere—except over well-trodden (some might say exhausted) ground.

What gradually becomes apparent, despite an obsessive innovativeness and self-presentation of *difference*, is that by far the greatest proportion of criticism on Hardy's fiction in the 1970s was held within the (by then) traditional parameters of critical intelligibility.[8] These were fundamentally humanist-realist in origin, promoting notions of a unified human subject ('the individual', 'character') at the centre of the general scheme of things—metaphysical, natural and social ('environment')—and of the artist's prime responsibility and achievement as being to represent this relationship with veracity (or with 'realism'). This, in turn, implies, on the one hand, the existence of an external reality to be copied—a given 'real world' and 'characters' both knowable and describable—and, on the other, the possibility of deploying a language which could accurately *describe*—not mediate—that reality, one which had a precise referentiality and would 'tell things as they really are'. What lies at the heart of such an essentialist worldview is a belief that everything has an ultimate ontological reality, an irreducible essence, quite outside its material, historical or discursive circumstances (things as they *really* are). The commonest (and most ideologically potent) expression of this is the notion of 'Human Nature'—the proposition that whatever the circumstances, and with the best will in the world, human beings cannot change their basic nature, or have it changed for them: that they are, as it were, trapped by their own very humanness. But it is, of course, this 'essential' human nature which artists are most praised for depicting, and their 'realism' is, paradoxically, at once their ability to represent the contingent reality of everyday life, *and*, by way of this, the essential unchanging reality of 'human nature' itself. In its attempt to render this essence visible by describing it in referential language, realism too is essentialist.

Hardy, against the grain of much of his writing, has, from the earliest reviews, been hauled into consonance with such a worldview and such an aesthetic. Borrowing his own phrase, 'Novels of Character and Environment',[9] to praise what are generally regarded as his 'major' novels, critics have characteristically seen Hardy, 'at his best', as the tragic humanist-realist of Wessex, finding essential human nature in the lives of his rural protagonists (and in his 'rustic chorus') pitted in conflict with 'Fate' or 'Nature' (much less often with 'Society'). This, together with his descriptions of nature and his evocation of a 'passing' rural community, has been regarded as his major achievement, and accounts for the elevation into canonic texts of about eight out of his fourteen novels (the six 'minor novels' fail in various ways to fit this mould[10]). Even so, Hardy presents problems, and it is noteworthy how much damage-limitation criticism has had to go in for in order to wrench this 'flawed genius' into the canon and tradition. Hardy's 'faults' are said to be: his tendency to 'melodrama'; the excessive use of chance and coincidence in his plots; his 'pessimism'; his parading of 'ill-digested' ideas; his at times pedantic, awkward, mannered style; and, over and above all these—indeed subsuming them—his tendency to 'improbability' and 'implausibility'; in other words, his failure to be 'realistic', or, to put it yet another way, to represent 'essential reality' accurately. These 'faults' and 'flaws' bedevil even his major works, where they have to be ignored or explained away, but they are the principal cause of his 'failure' in the 'minor novels'.

All too often, and however sophisticated the particular inflexions of critical inquiry in the 1970s, many of these governing coordinates remained unchallenged. Certainly there were innovative approaches, with a kind of high-powered humanistic formalism (emphasising imagery, symbolism, 'poetic structure' and so forth) replacing the older 'character'/'Fate'/Tragedy/ rural–elegy nexus, but fundamentally similar underlying assumptions (about Hardy's humanism, about his 'flaws', and especially about his 'uneasy' relation to realism) continued to determine the critical positions taken up. There was little attempt, for example, to rethink the tendency to reject large chunks of Hardy's texts simply as bad writing; little sense that viewing them through a realist lens might result in them appearing 'improbable', and that perhaps the lens was wrong; little inquiry into the nature and function of Hardy's language (except perhaps its 'poetics'); little inquiry into his 'inadequate' characterisation (because 'character' itself remains an unproblematic concept) or his contingent plotting; little thought that perhaps Hardy was an anti-realist, challenging and demystifying the limits and conventions of realism and humanist essentialism. But the fundamental inadequacy of most of the 1970s criticism which I have been generalising about is not so much its residual subscription to the conventional critical stereotypes of Hardy's fiction, but rather its failure to admit, disguised by grandiloquent evaluations and judgements, that it was inadequate to the task of dealing with the *entire textuality* of the literary works it had in hand. All novels, but Hardy's especially so, are riddled with contradictory discourses, are inscribed throughout with faultlines thrown up by the clash of competing discursive 'plates' just below the text's surface, and it is surely the job of criticism, not to reject them as 'failures of taste', but to explore and explain the significance of the work *as a whole*. It is instructive to compare criticism from the seventies with the many eighties essays[11] which focus on the dynamically unstable textuality of Hardy's fictional writing: its plural discourses and competing styles, its irony, mannerism and self-deconstructing artificiality, its self-conscious vocabulary and modes of address, its language of tension. But the perception of these features is the reflex, I have suggested particularly, of feminist and post-structuralist initiatives and it is to these that we will return in a moment.

However, there is one impressive piece of scholarship from the 1970s which should first be acknowledged as fundamentally influential in the

contemporary redirecting of attention to Hardy's textuality in relation to *Tess*:
J. T. Laird's *The Shaping of Tess of the d'Urbervilles* (1975), a book which traces
the evolution of the novel from its earliest stages of manuscript composition, through various editions and revisions, to the 'quasi-definitive' version
of the Wessex Edition of 1912. Despite a rather unnerving self-contradiction
when Laird seems to suggest, *contra* his own exhaustive proof of the insta-
bility of the text, that 'studying the author's creative processes ... eventually
leads to a surer and deeper understanding of the meaning of *the definitive
text*' (my italics),[12] his work nevertheless reveals the extent and significance
of Hardy's revisions and emendations, how conscious their effects were, and
how a detailed examination of the textuality of *Tess* reinforces the sense that
'representation' and notions of a 'pure woman' are bedrock issues in the novel.
Much criticism since 1975 has been deeply beholden to Laird in its pursuit
of textual *cruces* to explain the signifying effects of *Tess*, and his work has been
taken further since—most particularly in the monumental Oxford edition of
the novel edited by Juliet Grindle and Simon Gatrell[13]—and in the latter's
Hardy the Creator, whose critical method its author calls 'textual biography'
and which establishes how extensively and radically Hardy revised his texts
in a subversive, experimental practice of writing, a practice which, as Terry
Eagleton has put it, shows a 'novelist whose work ... is always on the point of
breaking through its own containing forms'.[14]

   But it is with the intervention of feminism and post-structuralism that
Hardy criticism significantly begins to retool. From the start of his novel-
writing career, of course, critics noticed and focused upon 'Hardy's Heroines',
and there are many essays entitled thus (or alternatively 'Hardy's Women'),
most of which reproduce, not surprisingly, the sexual stereotyping of dominant gender ideology.[15] *Feminist* criticism, conversely, aims to decode the
sexual/textual politics of literary texts, and has therefore been especially concerned with the *representation* of women; with the whole construction of gender in discourse; and with the notion of the 'male gaze', its consumption of
women and its tendency to reproduce its own images and fantasies as female
sexuality. In this respect, Hardy's novels are an ideal site on which to explore
such issues—and not by any means necessarily from a position of hostility to
his representation of women, but rather from a recognition of the complexity
and innovativeness of what he seems to be doing.

   Alternatively, post-structuralist criticism, most obviously in Deconstruction, has re-emphasised textuality as the primary concern of criticism—though
not as evidence of the integrated wholeness of the text as great work of art so
beloved of New Criticism, but on the contrary, as a fissured, riven, deranged,
unstable linguistic terrain. In this case, too, Hardy's texts—and in particular
their evident artificiality, self-reflexiveness about modes of perception and

reproduction, and their contradictory constituent discourses—offer themselves as fertile ground for analysis.

A seminal early essay,[16] in the contexts of both textuality and gender, is one by John Goode called 'Woman and the Literary Text' (1976), in which he suggests that we can only see the 'political implications' of a work by attending to its 'formal identity', and that in relation to Tess what we witness (and are implicated in) is 'the objectification of Tess by the narrator', especially by way of making her 'the object of consumption' of Alec and Angel (and then of us as voyeuristic readers consuming with our eyes both the text and, hence, Tess herself). The effect is to make us 'the subject of her, and thus guilty of the object images whose contradictions she is subject to'. In other words, Tess is composed of all the 'object images' the novel defines her as, primarily deriving from male lookers and including the narrator/Hardy and us as readers in our collusion with those images: nubile country-girl, plump arms, erotic mouth, etc. Goode comments that this is why, 'whatever Hardy's own ideological commitment, no frame will hold his novel in place', or, to put it another way, why the text's discourses *have to be* accepted as contradictory. These themes are extended in Goode's later (1979) essay, 'Sue Bridehead and the New Woman', where he suggests that Sue is an 'exposing image' in the 'taking of reality apart' which *Jude the Obscure* effects—most particularly of the mystifications inherent in conventional notions of love and marriage.[17] More recently, Goode's pioneering and radical recognition of the textual/sexual politics and subversive anti-realism of Hardy's fiction have received sustained expression in his *Thomas Hardy: the Offensive Truth*, a book described by Terry Eagleton as 'alert to Hardy's fiction ... as transformative practice, disruption, intervention, texts which ... often enough meditate on the act of writing as a metaphor of their preoccupations, [and which show] astonishing ... radicalism of gender as well as class'.[18]

What is happening to Hardy, as a reflex of his new critical reproduction in the 1980s and 1990s is that he is in the process of being post-modernised. The foregrounding of sexual politics in *Tess*, and of the tensions incident on a late-nineteenth-century male novelist writing so ambiguously about his 'pure woman' heroine, about the destructive maleness of his two heroes' relations with her (especially the—apparent—ambiguity of seduction and rape), and about marriage, separation, bigamy, extramarital sex and childbirth, all imply a writer whose 'consciousness' is in some sense being recast in the mould of feminist thinking about sexuality and patriarchy.

More obviously post-structuralist in its variously stylistic, semiotic and deconstructive analyses of the complex, riven, heteroglossic textuality of *Tess*, equal amounts of contemporary criticism all point to the unstable play of the signifier as the nodal experience of the novel. In other words, we have a text which has indeed become a disruptive 'series of seemings', one which, in its destabilising formal dynamics 'disproportions' (Hardy's own word—see below, p. 92) reality by revealing how slippery language is, how 'meaning' (and hence ideology) is constructed within discourse, and, precisely therefore, how representation becomes misrepresentation. By disturbing and displacing 'reality' (together with its servant, Realism) in the defamiliarising discourse of his own texts, Hardy exposes (or, more exactly, as a creature of post-modernism *is made to* expose) the mystifications, naturalisations and (mis)representations by which the dominant ideology and culture sentence us all to lives of false being.

However, before I alchemise Hardy once and for all as a post-modernist (and throw away the stone), let me more properly register—so that I can bring it into sharper focus in the following section—that in his own historical period, and certainly when he was publishing his poetry, Hardy was indeed a contemporary of the Modernists. It may be that the critical industry, already in his lifetime busily at work on him as both poet and novelist (combined, let us admit, with not a little self-fashioning[19]), had so constructed him as the great proto-Georgian poet, as the humanist-realist rural-tragedian, as Grand Old Man of English Letters, that the *modernist* in Hardy could not then or later easily be perceived. Of course, it is a critical truism to say that he is a 'transitional' writer, but I wonder now just *how* transitional, or whether Hardy was not in fact already *there*, already a Modernist. D. H. Lawrence recognised it in the *Study of Thomas Hardy* (1914), written as he launched into the work which was to become *The Rainbow* and *Women in Love*, and Ezra Pound hailed him as a contemporary poet; but still, it is only with hindsight and the clearing of the critical trees that the innovative anti-realism and self-conscious modernity of much of Hardy's fictional *oeuvre* comes into view. Which is why, I suggest, it has been so simple for recent criticism to find the ingredients in him for a transmogrification into post-modernist.

Well, you might say, who would have thought it: 'good little Thomas Hardy', the poet of Wessex and the English countryside, the great humanist tragedian of the 'Novels of Character and Environment', the elegist of a passing rural tradition, etc., suddenly becoming subversively post-modern. But then, literary criticism never could quite handle Hardy: didn't make it to F. R. Leavis's Great Tradition; always 'flawed' by contingency, melodrama and improbability; neither securely 'Victorian' nor 'modern'; uncertain whether he is primarily novelist or poet. But in neither genre has Hardy ever really been made to *fit* (except by a lot of critical manhandling and dismissal of recalcitrant elements), which makes one think, doesn't it, that our disruptive post-modern Hardy may, after all, be nearer the mark. It is with this in mind that I now return to my two focal themes: 'seeing'/representation and the notion of Tess as '(a) pure woman'.

* * *

With characteristic ambiguity of utterance, Hardy entitled one of his later volumes of poetry *Moments of Vision* (1917). The ambiguity of the word 'vision' is readily apparent: at once the literal 'seeing/sight' (as in '20/20 vision'), the metaphysical notion of imaginative revelation ('she had a vision'), and the proleptic ability to see through or beyond the immediately determinate ('he has vision', 'her vision of the future'). The ambiguity of the cluster of inflections around 'moments', however, is rather less obvious. Of course, 'moments' are brief fractions of time, usually implying stopped fragments in the temporal process (as in 'wait a moment', 'magic moments' or 'moment of truth'), and this is certainly the upper meaning in Hardy's title: particular instances of 'vision'. But there are two other senses which also haunt the fringes of the word: first, that of serious consequence ('momentous', 'matters of pith and moment'); second, and for my purposes here more significant, that within physics which means the measure of a turning effect (as in 'the moment of a force'). So Hardy's title may imply that the instants of 'vision' are important ('moments' of great 'moment'), but also that the vision is somehow itself in motion, turning, swinging round a point, pivoting.

If we think for a (dare I say) moment of the effect of a turning vision—in the most literal sense—then we must conceive of a 'seeing' which moves round its object (consider astronauts observing Earth from their circulating spacecraft), and which can theoretically move round it through 360 degrees in any direction, i.e., in three-dimensional mode. Move round your chair, *looking* at it, and you will, at various stages, see it from all sides and all angles (downwards, upwards, sideways, etc.). In other words you will be able to apprehend it as a totality, a three-dimensional object. But two things may strike you: one, if you 'stopped' the moment when you were theoretically looking straight up at it from below (chair suspended absolutely vertically above you), the 'image' from that 'moment of vision' would look remarkably unlike one's standard received image of a chair (think of the kind of trick-photography which takes familiar objects from unfamiliar angles: where a bucket, for example, taken from directly above, becomes no more than a set of concentric circles). Two, how on earth (and I use this phrase, here, not *merely* as a manner of speaking) would you represent, *in visual terms*, your total apprehension of the total, three-dimensional chair—the chair in all its chairness? How, indeed, would you 'see' it all, all in one moment? Two senses of 'moment'—turning and stopped instant of time—clash here in fundamental contradiction: one is, precisely, in *motion*, in time; the other, equally precisely, is still, 'stopped', out of time. Is there any way of resolving this physical impossibility? Well, yes—if we return to the other term in Hardy's title: 'vision'.

For vision, in what I have called its metaphysical senses, allows us (but especially the creative artist) to break out of the space/time trap of the third dimension, and enter that zone of relativity beyond the determinate factors of time and space. Put simply and crudely, 'vision' allows us to 'see' the future, or 'envisage' another world; it would also enable us to see, in one totalising 'moment' (in this case, *both* stopped instant *and* full circular movement) all of our chair at the same time. It is not without point, here, when approaching so visual an artist as Hardy (and indeed one who draws heavily on painting for both his terms of reference and his imagery[20]), to note that this liberation from space/time, this envisioned *simultaneity* of experience, was the principle on which the modernist painters, only a dozen years after *Jude the Obscure* (why don't we think of Hardy and Picasso as contemporaries?—Picasso was well into his 'Metamorphic' phase when Hardy died in 1928), based their dis-locations of conventional (realist/mimetic) form. That is why one can see both profiles of a face simultaneously in Cubist portraits, or a violin dismantled with all its planes simultaneously displayed on the two-dimensional picture-surface of a modernist still life.

'Vision', then, both as momentary revelation (what James Joyce, only ten years after *Tess*, was to call an 'epiphany') and as 'turning' or destabilis-ing perception, is a way of breaking out of the conventional, the normative, the familiar, the naturalised fictions of 'common sense'. Indeed it ruptures a (bourgeois) world constructed very largely by the cultural ideology of a Real-ism which 'tells things as they really are' and has a profound antipathy to the 'improbable' or 'implausible'—qualities which are themselves frequently the result of, precisely, 'vision' and 'the visionary'. For Hardy, vision in this binary sense ('double-vision'?) is a way of 'defamiliarising', of 'making strange'—and I strategically choose the formalists' terms to signal once again his consanguin-ity with modernism—the naturalised world of conventional perceptual real-ity, of 'seeing things as they really are'. It is subversive in many ways, and not least in its anti-realist stance—which may help to explain the troubled history of Hardy's place in the conventional canon of English fiction and the diffi-culty many critics have had in comprehending the apparently schizophrenic textuality of his novels. It is worth adding here that Hardy himself was not just 'doing defamiliarisation' by chance—as an automatic and unwilled reflex of his (unconscious) proto-modernist mind. On the contrary, he was thinking about it throughout his writing life, but especially from the 1880s onwards; and his last, highly self-reflexive and self-conscious work of fiction, 'Florence Emily Hardy's *The Life of Thomas Hardy*' (he composed it himself, before his death, in the 1920s[21]), is full of concepts and phrases which at once define 'vision' as what we would now call 'complex seeing' and which would, had they been written by a twentieth-century cultural theorist, have equal currency with terms like 'defamiliarisation' and 'baring the device' or the Brechtian notion of 'alienation'.

Prior to the 1880s, Hardy's views show a more purely Romantic conception of the visionary function of art: 'irradiating . . . with "the light that never was" . . . a hitherto unperceived beauty . . . seen to be latent . . . by the spiritual eye'.[22] But by 1886 Hardy is reflecting: 'novel-writing as an art cannot go backward. Having reached the analytic stage it must transcend it by going still further in the same direction. Why not by rendering as visible essences, spectres, etc., the abstract thoughts of the analytic school?' And later in the same passage he proposes the use of 'abstract realisms', significantly stating that this project was actually carried out, not in a novel, but in 'the more appropriate medium' of his immense epic poetic-drama, *The Dynasts* (p. 177). What is clear, if nothing else, is that Hardy was being pressed against the limits of conventional realism. The following year, in expressing his admiration for the paintings of 'the much-decried, mad, late-Turner', he rejects 'the original realities—as optical effects, that is' in favour of the 'expression of . . . abstract imaginings' (p. 185). Taken in conjunction with his remarks about 'impressions' and 'seemings' in the prefaces to the novels of the 1890s referred to earlier, it is clear that notions of 'vision', and how to realise it formally, were much on Hardy's mind. But it is in a couple of memoranda from 1890 (while he was completing *Tess*) that his most prophetically modernist utterances are made:

> 'Reflections on Art. Art is a changing of the actual proportions and order of things, so as to bring out more forcibly than might otherwise be done that feature in them which appeals most strongly to the idiosyncrasy of the artist.'
>
> 'Art is a disproportioning—(*i.e.* distorting, throwing out of proportion)—of realities, to show more clearly the features that matter in those realities, which, if merely copied or reported inventorially, might possibly be observed, but would more probably be overlooked. Hence "realism" is not Art.' (pp. 228–9)

It is here, I think, that the core of Hardy's fictional aesthetic is to be found, and the informing frame of reference for a reading of *Tess*: art is a 'disproportioning' of reality—realism is not art. In other words, 'vision' (abstract imaginings), swinging round its 'moment', makes visible 'essences' (the notion of a 'pure woman', for example). But at the same time, vision 'distorts', 'disproportions', those representations of reality ('copied or reported inventorially') which are the naturalised (mis)representations of Realism, in order to expose essentialist misrepresentation for what it is (how can there, in fact, be 'a pure woman' or 'pure woman'?), and to illuminate another truth which those misrepresentations obscure: that 'reality' is only ever *discourse*—'seemings', 'imaginings', 'impressions'.

'My art', Hardy wrote in 1886, 'is to intensify the expression of things ... so that the heart and inner meaning is made vividly visible' (p. 177). Tess, that most 'vividly visible' of novels, may be an example of Hardy 'intensifying the expression' in order to bring into view precisely that 'expression'—the discourses of representation themselves—for scrutiny and demystification in order to exemplify the fact that 'expression' is its own very 'heart and inner meaning', that the 'reality' of an image is the image itself, that its only reality is what it constructs through representation. 'Expression' does not copy 'things as they really are', it forges images in its artifice. Tess may indeed be 'a pure woman', but *only as she is imaged*, only as the 'artificial' construct of representation—and who knows whether this is true or false: except, unless we miss the irony (for Hardy knows full well the claim is nonsense), when she is *'faithfully* presented by Thomas Hardy'.

Let us now turn, at last, to that subtitle itself, and consider it as the pivot of a 'moment' around which *Tess of the d'Urbervilles* swings in exemplification of Hardy's disproportioning art discussed above. The two main senses of the phrase 'a pure woman' are readily evident: the ethical/sexual (the use of which in relation to Tess as fornicator-murderess so incensed Hardy's Victorian critics), and the ontological/archetypal (in which she would be, were Bob Dylan her bard, 'just like a woman' in every respect). There is also the further related sense of the generic as 'ideal'—again, perhaps, in two inflexions: both prototypical and perfect. I am not primarily concerned here with the ethical sense, although for Hardy at the time it was clearly a strategic assault on the moral attitudes of his readers and *their perception* of purity. It is that other essentialist meaning that is of interest to me, and especially in relation to Hardy's concern with making 'visible essences' noted above. The novel is full of phrases which indicate that he was thoroughly conscious of this second sense and probably more interested in it than the contemporary moral issue. Let me start with the two most obvious examples: at Talbothays, in the early morning idyll with Angel, Tess is described as 'a visionary essence of woman—a whole sex condensed into one typical form' (Ch. 20, p. 187); and later, as she approaches Flintcomb-Ash, the narrative, in an odd shift of tense and focus, presents her in this way: 'Thus Tess walks on; a figure which is part of the landscape; a field-woman pure and simple, in winter guise' (Ch. 42, p. 355)—where the phrase 'pure and simple' could mean a pure, simple field-woman, but clearly actually implies the essential stereotype. (Much earlier, during the harvesting at Marlott, the narrative has already given us this generalisation: 'A field-man is a personality afield; a field-woman is a portion of the field; she has somehow *lost her own margin*, imbibed the *essence* of her surrounding, and assimilated herself with it' [Ch. 14, pp. 137–8, my italics]— so that Tess, too, the 'field-woman pure and simple', must also be subsumed within this characterisation—or rather, *de*-characterisation.) Further, as we have seen, when Tess is first introduced in Chapter 2 she is described as 'a fine and picturesque country girl, and no more' (p. 52, note that word 'picturesque' and the phrase 'and no more'), and later again, just after the generalisation about field-women above, she is called, in an oddly contradictive phrase, 'an almost standard woman' (Ch. 14, p. 141). Elsewhere, the narrative regularly generalises about women—for example, on Tess's 'rally' after the death of her child, it muses: 'Let the truth be told—women do as a rule live through such humiliations, and regain their spirits, and again look about them with an interested eye' (Ch. 16, p. 158)—a sentence remarkable both for its patriarchal patronising (do men—by implication of finer sensibility—not 'regain their spirits' then?) and for that revealing phrase 'an interested eye'. Again, in relation to the dairymaids' passion for Angel at Talbothays, we are told they are involuntarily overwhelmed by 'an emotion thrust on them by cruel Nature's law'; and, in an even more insulting instance of chauvinistic essentialism, 'the differences which distinguished them as individuals were abstracted by this passion, and each was but portion of one organism called sex' (Ch. 23, p. 204)—'pure women' indeed, and just like the field-women who have lost their 'own margin'. For Angel, of course (and for the narrator too?), Tess is archetypally this 'organism' in the famously erotic passage when she has just awoken on a summer afternoon:

> She had not heard him enter, and hardly realized his presence there. She was yawning, and *he saw the red interior of her mouth* as if it had been a snake's. She had stretched one arm so high above her coiled-up cable of hair that he could see its satin delicacy above the sunburn; her face was flushed with sleep, and her eyelids hung heavy over their pupils. The brim-fulness of her nature breathed from her. It was a moment when *a woman's soul* is more incarnate than at any other time; when the most spiritual beauty bespeaks itself flesh; and sex takes the outside place in *the presentation*. (Ch. 27, p. 231, my italics)

Is this what Hardy means by 'a pure woman' in his subtitle? But notice again, as in all these quotations, how he seems to be doing the very opposite of establishing Tess's 'character'; that, conversely, in rendering her as essence—'a woman's soul'—he is making her an enigma, unknowable, subject only to speculation (rather as Hardy's later disciple, John Fowles, was to do with Sarah Woodruff in *The French Lieutenant's Woman*), and inimical, therefore, to the *raison d'etre* of a fictional realism which finds its very heart in well-rounded 'character'.

But, of course, it is the continuous textual 'presentation' (notice Hardy's use of the word at the end of the last quotation above) of Tess that makes the obsessive (and usually erotic) imaging of her as something to look *at*, as something *seen*, as a visual *object*, so inescapable. Space prevents a full account of the number of occasions her mouth (again, see the above quotation) is fetishistically focused upon—for example, 'To a young man with the least fire in him that little upward lift in the middle of her red top lip was distracting, infatuating, maddening' (Ch. 24, p. 209). But her smile and her eyes also receive continual attention ('her rosy lips curved towards a smile' [Ch. 5, p. 79], 'a roguish curl coming upon her mouth' [Ch. 29, p. 247], 'her eyes enlarged, and she involuntarily smiled in his face' [Ch. 9, p. 103]), as do her neck, her arms, her hair and general deportment ('Tess stood there in her prettily tucked-up milking gown, her hair carelessly heaped upon her head' [Ch. 29, p. 2471]). Equally heavily emphasised is the 'bouncing handsome womanliness' of her figure (see the quotation at the beginning of this paper); even Angel at his most idealising—in the passage where he sees her as the 'visionary essence of woman' (see above, p. 93)—is still aware that there weren't many women 'so well endowed in person as she was' (Ch. 20, p. 186); and for Alec she is of course the true *femme fatale* (not, by the by, necessarily a scheming woman or 'siren', merely 'irresistibly attractive'): 'She had an attribute which amounted to a disadvantage just now; and it was this that caused Alec d'Urberville's *eyes to rivet themselves upon her*. It was a luxuriance of aspect, a fulness of growth, which made her appear *more of a woman* than she *really* was' (Ch. 5, p. 82, my emphases; note both the male gaze and the physical essentialism implied by the phrases 'more of a woman' and 'really'.) And later it is this voluptuousness which starts the process of de-converting Alec as preacher: 'his eyes, falling casually upon the familiar countenance and form, remained contemplating her. . . ."Don't look at me like that!" he said abruptly' (Ch. 45, p. 388)—an inversion which must surely be the most brilliant evocation in fiction of male perfidy and the double standard, for who, after all, is doing the looking? It is further worth noticing in passing that it is not just Tess who is made into a sex-object by the text: Car Darch, just before Alec has sex with Tess, is described thus: 'she had bared her plump neck, shoulders, and arms to the moonshine, under which they looked as luminous and beautiful as some Praxitelean[23] creation, in their possession of the faultless rotundities of a lusty country girl' (Ch. 10, pp. 111–12).

In late twentieth-century terms, the above descriptions would surely amount to 'soft' pornography, or at least to accurate representations of the titillatory visual devices employed therein. And the text further emphasises this voyeuristic stance in its recurrent verbal and narrative objectification ('the presentation') of women in the novel. The 'club-walking' girls in Chapter 2, for instance, are taking part in 'their first *exhibition* of themselves' (p. 49, my italics here and below); the Clare brothers are 'on-lookers' at 'the *spectacle* of a bevy of girls dancing' (pp. 52–3); Tess, after her first visit to Trantridge, 'became aware of the *spectacle* she presented to [her fellow-travellers'] surprised vision: roses at her breast; roses in her hat; roses and strawberries in her basket to the brim' (Ch. 6, p. 84); Mrs Durbeyfield, 'bedecking' Tess for the sacrifice to Alec, is so proud of 'the girl's *appearance*' that she is led to 'step back, like *a painter from his easel*, and survey her work as a whole'; and in order to let Tess 'zee' herself, she hangs a large 'black cloak [surely the 'black flag' of Tess's hanging] outside the casement, and so made a large reflector of the panes' (Ch. 7, pp. 89–90). On other occasions the text pans back from Tess and reduces her (once again de-characterising her in the process) to an insignificant dot on the landscape: 'Tess stood still upon the hemmed expanse of verdant flatness, like a fly on a billiard-table of indefinite length, and of no more consequence to the surroundings than that fly' (Ch. 16, p. 159); 'the two girls crawl[ed] over the surface of [the 'desolate drab' field] like flies' (Ch. 43, p. 360).

Throughout the novel, then, Tess in particular is highly visualised as an object of 'vision' in the swinging 'moment' of the text's gaze. Only on two significant occasions does she disappear from view: once, when she is hanged, with Angel and Liza-Lu's eyes 'rivetted' (like Alec's on her body) to the gaol flag-pole, and she becomes merely 'a black flag' (Ch. 59, p. 489); the other when, in the old phrase precisely, Alec commits 'the act of darkness' with her: 'The obscurity was now so great that he could see absolutely nothing but a pale nebulousness at his feet, which represented the white muslin figure he had left upon the dead leaves. Everything else was blackness alike' (Ch. 11, pp. 118–19). It is as if, paradoxically and pointedly, the novel implies that the essence, the 'pure woman', can only be 'presented' as visualisations, only as she *appears*, but that the basic 'realities' of her existence (sex, death) are unknowable, unrepresentable—like those innermost secrets of 'character' that no one quite comprehends or can describe in other people, however well one knows them.

And let us be clear: we know almost nothing substantive about Tess's 'character', for the novel never attempts to penetrate her secret being. It may tell us things *about* her (she 'spoke two languages' [Ch. 3, p. 58]); give us her views (about the 'blighted star', for example); and show her spirited moments of mettle (to Alec's male cliché, '"that's what every woman says"', she retorts in implicit rejection of 'pure woman' essentialism: '"Did it never strike your mind that what every woman says some women may feel?"' [Ch. 12, p. 125], just as she tells Angel to 'call me Tess' when he insists, in the 'visionary essence' scene, on idealising her with names like Artemis and Demeter [Ch. 20, p. 187]). The novel may further appear to try and characterise her state of mind—'she looked upon herself as a figure of Guilt intruding into the haunts of Innocence ... she fancied herself such an anomaly' (Ch. 13, p. 135)—but only, we note, at a detached psychologistic distance; it may try and explain her love for Angel ('its single-mindedness, its meekness; what long-suffering it guaranteed, what honesty, what endurance, what good faith' [Ch. 33, p. 279]), but the more the text produces phrase after defining phrase, the more a palpable sense of her love recedes—just as earlier, despite all its words, the narrative signally fails to describe her eyes: 'neither black nor blue nor gray nor violet; rather all those shades together, and a hundred others ... around pupils that had no bottom' (Ch. 14, pp. 140–1). For all this 'characterisation', then, we really 'know' Tess very little indeed—which is presumably why so much critical argument has raged over whether she is 'passive' or not, whether she is 'pure' or not, indeed whether she is a 'fully-rounded character' at all.

Which is, I would suggest in conclusion, to beg the question. For *Tess of the d'Urbervilles* is precisely *not* a novel attempting to offer us a 'knowable' character, but rather one which exposes *characterisation* itself as a human-ist-realist mystification (producing 'visible essences'), and which parades the misrepresentation that 'characterisation' involves by subjecting to irony the falsifying essentialism of 'faithfully presenting a pure woman'. In her excel-lent essay of 1982, 'Pure Tess: Hardy on Knowing a Woman',[24] Kathleen Blake remarks that the novel 'really scrutinizes the sexual typing that plays havoc with a woman's life', while George Wotton in his book *Thomas Hardy: Towards a Materialist Criticism*, in suggesting that we recognise 'class and gender conflicts ... as conflicts of perception in the multifarious acts of seeing of the characters who inhabit Wessex', points out that Hardy's 'production (writing) determines consumption (reading) by casting the reader in the role of seer'.[25] In other words, we may say that Hardy's 'moments of vision' dis-proportion characterisation and character so that we can 'see' how they func-tion. Tess as a 'character' is no more than an amalgam—often destructively contradictory—of 'images' of her as perceived by individuals and by 'society': Angel idealises her, Alec sees her as sex-object, the narrative voice fetishises her, society regards her as prodigal, the novel 'faithfully presents' her as 'a pure woman' (with all the ironies that phrasing invokes). But Tess *has no character at all*: she is only what others (most especially the author) construct her as; and so she is herself merely a 'series of seemings' or 'impressions'. This, of course, gives the final ironic twist to the notion of her being '(a) pure woman', since there can be no such thing as 'essential character' when a woman is merely the construct of male socio-sexual images of her desired form (although my basic point here need not be limited to *gender*-stereotyping). Hardy's novel, then, well ahead of its time, seems to be dismantling the bourgeois-humanist (patriarchal and realist) notion of the unified and unitary human subject, and to be doing so by way of a discourse so self-reflexive and defamiliarising about representation, so unstable and dialogical, that it deconstructs itself even as it creates. Which is why, I believe, we can justly discover a contemporary post-modern text in *Tess of the d'Urbervilles*.

NOTES

An amended version of this essay appeared as the editor's introduction to the *New Casebook on Tess of the d'Urbervilles* (London: Macmillan, 1993).

1. Thomas Hardy, *Tess of the d'Urbervilles* (1891), ed. David Skilton, with an Introduction by A. Alvarez, Penguin Classics Edition (Harmondsworth, [1978] 1987) Ch. 2, p. 51. All further references to the novel are to this edition, and appear in brackets in the text.

2. Thomas Hardy, *Desperate Remedies* (1871), ed. with Introduction by C. J. P. Beatty, New Wessex Edition (London, 1975) pp. 46–7 (pbk).

3. Thomas Hardy, *Jude the Obscure* (1896), ed. with Introduction by Terry Eagleton (and notes by P. N. Furbank), New Wessex Edition (London, 1974) p. 23 (pbk).

4. 'Author's Preface to the Fifth and Later Editions' (1892), *Tess*, p. 38. Hardy, in the same sentence here, also quotes Schiller on 'representation' and 'poetical representations'.

5. See Florence Emily Hardy, *The Life of Thomas Hardy 1840–1928* (London, [1962] 1975) p. 185, for a typical memorandum (Jan. 1887) on this subject during the period of the composition of *Tess*.

6. For extensive treatment of this subject, and of Turner in particular, see Chapter 8 especially, 'Patterns of Light and Dark in *Tess of the d'Urbervilles*', in J. B. Bullen, *The Expressive Eye: Fiction and Perception in the Work of Thomas Hardy* (Oxford, 1986).

7. This 'phase' is perhaps exemplified at its best by R. P. Draper's earlier casebook, *Hardy: The Tragic Novels* (London, 1975), and by Albert J. LaValley's, *Twentieth-Century Interpretations of Tess of the d'Urbervilles* (Englewood Cliffs, N. J., 1969).

8. For an extended analysis of these by the present author, see Peter Widdowson, *Hardy in History: A Study in Literary Sociology* (London, 1989), especially Chapter 1, 'The Critical Constitution of "Thomas Hardy"'.

9. This singularly preemptive and subsequently ubiquitous phrase in Hardy criticism appears in Hardy's 'General Preface' to the Wessex Edition of his works in 1912 (which is reproduced in each volume of the Penguin and New Wessex editions of his novels). It occurs when he is 'classifying', and, in effect, hierarchically evaluating, his fictional *oeuvre*—with the ones so described clearly privileged.

10. Widdowson, *Hardy in History*, pp. 44–55 especially, for a discussion of critical treatment of the 'minor novels'.

11. With those, for example, collected in my Macmillan *New Casebook on 'Tess'*, and in recent volumes, such as Harold Bloom (ed.), *Modern Critical Interpretations of Thomas Hardy* (New York, 1987), and Lance St John Butler (ed.), *Alternative Hardy* (London, 1989).

12. J. T. Laird, *The Shaping of 'Tess of the d'Urbervilles'* (Oxford, 1975) p. 4. For a slightly fuller critique of Laird's stance, see my *Hardy in History*, pp. 30–1. There is a further essay by Laird on the textual development of *Tess*, 'New Light on the Evolution of *Tess of the d'Urbervilles*', in *Review of English Studies*, 31: 124 (Winter 1980) pp. 414–35.

13. Thomas Hardy, *Tess of the d'Urbervilles*, ed. Juliet Grindle and Simon Gatrell, the Clarendon Edition (Oxford, 1983).

14. In the Editor's Preface to John Goode, *Thomas Hardy: The Offensive Truth* (Oxford, 1988) p. vii.

15. For a fuller account and analysis of this, see in particular Chapter 13, 'The Production of Meaning: "Hardy's Women" and the Eternal Feminine', in George Wotton, *Thomas Hardy: Towards a Materialist Criticism* (Goldenbridge, 1985).

16. In Juliet Mitchell and Ann Oakley (eds), *The Rights and Wrongs of Women* (Harmondsworth, 1976). The following quotations, *passim*, are from pp. 255, 253, 254. Two other influential essays on the textuality/sexuality nexus are: Mary Jacobus, 'Tess: The Making of a Pure Woman', in Susan Lipshitz (ed.), *Tearing the Veil: Essays on Femininity* (London, 1978) which first appeared in *Critical Quarterly*, 26 (October 1976); and J. Hillis Miller, 'Fiction and Repetition: *Tess of the d'Urbervilles*', in Alan Warren Friedman (ed.), *Forms of Modern British Fiction* (Austin, 1975). This was reprinted, in revised form, as the chapter, '*Tess of the d'Urbervilles*: Repetition as Immanent Design', in Hillis Miller's *Fiction and Repetition: Seven English Novels* (Cambridge, Mass., 1982), and again, with Jacobus above, in Bloom (ed.), *Modern Critical Interpretations*.

17. In Mary Jacobus (ed.), *Women's Writing and Writing about Women* (Beckenham, 1979). See especially, pp. 100, 107–8.

18. Editor's Preface to Goode, *Thomas Hardy*, p. vii.

19. I have already implied this in Note 9 above, in reference to Hardy's own categorisation of his novels in the General Preface of 1912. But we also have to remember that he himself, in fact, wrote Florence Emily Hardy's supposed biography of him, *The Life of Thomas Hardy 1840–1928*, in the years immediately preceding his death, and so effectively composed his own 'life' as he wished it to be perceived. An account of this characteristically self-protective subterfuge is to be found in the first chapter of Robert Gittings's *Young Thomas Hardy* (Harmondsworth, [1975] 1978).

20. See Bullen, *The Expressive Eye*, for full discussion of this.

21. See above, note 19.

22. *The Life of Thomas Hardy*, p. 114 (see note 5 above). All further references are given in the text.

23. Praxiteles was a fourth-century BC Greek sculptor whose work celebrated sensuality (for example, in depicting naked gods for the first time).

24. The essay appeared first in *Studies in English Literature*, 22: 4 (Autumn 1982) pp. 689–705, but has been reprinted in Bloom (ed.), Modern Critical Interpretations.

25. Wotton, *Thomas Hardy*, p. 4.

ROBERT SCHWEIK

The "Modernity" of Hardy's Jude the Obscure

The range and variety of Hardy's influence on modern novelists has by now been more than amply demonstrated,[1] and the connection of some aspects of his *Jude the Obscure* to subsequent developments in the novel has long been acknowledged: it has become a commonplace to say, for example, that Hardy strongly influenced the treatment of human sexuality in the modern novel from D.H. Lawrence onward. As Ian Gregor put it, 'where *Jude* ends *The Rainbow* begins'.[2]

But if the influence of Hardy's *Jude* on the history of the novel is unquestionable, its 'modernity' has been sharply disputed. One reason for the dispute lies, I think, in the way that claims for—and denials of—the 'modernity' of *Jude the Obscure* tend to be set forth. Irving Howe, for example, describes *Jude* in the following terms:

> *Jude the Obscure* is Hardy's most distinctly 'modern' work, for it rests upon a cluster of assumptions central to modernist literature: that in our time men wishing to be more than dumb clods must live in permanent doubt and intellectual crisis; that for such men, to whom traditional beliefs are no longer available, life has become inherently problematic ... and that courage, if it is to be found at all, consists in readiness to accept pain while refusing the comforts of certainty.[3]

From *A Spacious Vision: Essays on Hardy*, edited by Phillip V. Mallett and Ronald P. Draper, pp. 49–63. © 1994 by Robert Schweik.

Such sweeping claims for the 'modernity' of *Jude* have led to equally sharp denials, perhaps the most categorical of which is that by C.H. Salter:

> [Hardy] uses the word *modern* vaguely and applies it to much that is not really modern or only trivially so, and sometimes as a term of reproach. He expresses a pessimism not produced by modern causes, but timeless and congenital.... Hardy's idea of tragedy is simple and medieval.[4]

In disagreements of this kind, both sides tend to make sweeping assumptions that 'modernity' is reducible to some central ideological stance which a work of art might or might not reflect. But, particularly in the nineteenth and twentieth centuries, works of high art tend to exhibit exceptional diversity of form and matter—an array of more or less distinct, often obscurely related, widely varying, and frequently conflicting attitudes and techniques—and an equal diversity of relationships to their cultural context. Finding some centre in that diversity is an exercise in futile reductivity, and assuming there is such a centre is all but useless, I think, in attempting to define the 'modernity' of a work of art like *Jude*—especially given the conclusions of recent studies about its profound ambiguities.[5]

Rather, in art history—and particularly for the nineteenth and twentieth centuries—it is far wiser to proceed on the assumption that whatever may be said to constitute the 'modernity' of a given work of art must inevitably be the product of selective retrospection: the identification of some of its features, from out of many others, that may be said to be 'modern' in their day because, from the vantage point of a later time, they can be seen to have been at the leading edge of one or another notable change beginning to take place in the arts. Describing the way any given work of art combines such features can be a useful way of identifying its peculiar kind of 'modernity'. It is in this way that I want to consider the 'modernity' of *Jude the Obscure*. The claim I make here is that in *Jude*—apart from the ways in which Hardy rendered his characters' sexuality—it is possible to identify three techniques remarkably similar to those beginning to be adopted by other artists in different countries and in different media at almost exactly the same time, and that, in this respect, *Jude the Obscure* was at the forefront of three important developments in the history of Western art—and 'modern' in that way. The changes I am concerned with are these:

1. the growing practice of ending works of art in ways that deny the audience a sense of resolution and closure,
2. the emergence of the kinds of unusual distortion and simplification characteristic of certain forms of expressionist art, and

3. the beginnings of a practice of mixing sharply conflicting artistic modes in a single art work.

Subsequently these strategies would be exploited in extreme forms in many works of art associated with 'modernism'.

Some of the ways *Jude* embodies these features have been partly described;[6] others have not, however, nor has their striking conjunction in the novel and their relationship to the emergence of parallel strategies in other art forms in the years 1893–4 been pointed out.

Techniques for Denying Readers a Sense of Final Resolution and Closure

A greater willingness to find new kinds of endings was one notable consequence of the growing rage for innovation in late nineteenth- and early twentieth-century art, and those innovations were put to an enormously wide range of artistic purposes. Among these was the use of a complex of devices for creating a more open-ended art work—one which, in Robert Martin Adams' phrase, included 'a major unresolved conflict with the intent of displaying its unresolvedness'.[7] Devices to create that kind of 'openness' came to be employed with greater frequency and obviousness from the end of the century onward.

Some few signs of an increasing willingness of novelists to exploit such endings began to appear after the middle of the nineteenth century in England and on the Continent. For example, in both *Madame Bovary* (1857) and *The Sentimental Education* (1869), Flaubert gave the final words to a character who speaks simplistic banalities that leave the reader with no concluding authorial overview which might create a surer sense of resolution. Of the multiple endings Dickens wrote to *Great Expectations* (1861), the first would have denied readers the sense of resolution that comes from the conventional use of a marriage to suggest an achieved happiness. Hardy, too, claimed that in the composition of *The Return of the Native* he had intended to have a more 'open' ending—again without a marriage—but was discouraged from doing so by the conventions required by serial publication.[8]

From that time forward, however, the endings of Hardy's major fiction reveal a tentative movement toward the use of less resolved endings. A marked lack of resolution is notable in *The Woodlanders*, for example, though it is softened by Marty South's final apostrophe to Giles Winterborne.[9] Even at the conclusion of *Tess*, Hardy provided a very important suggestion of some possibility of a happier future for Angel Clare in the company of a 'spiritualized' Tess: her younger sister, Lisa Lu.[10] It was only with *Jude* that Hardy finally created a narrative ending which not only left major issues emphatically unresolved but also suggested pointedly that the suffering and deprivation endured by one of its major characters would continue.

What is striking about *Jude* is both the multiplicity of techniques Hardy exploited in it to create that unresolved open-endedness, and also the way one of those techniques was paralleled by a similar development in music at almost exactly the same time.

To emphasize the lack of resolution in *Jude*, Hardy adopted at least three major devices. First, as Alan Friedman has noted, the counterpointed treatment of marriage and funeral at the end of the novel deprives both marriages of the traditional effect of closure these familiar endings usually have. Second, as Daniel Schwartz and Peter Casagrande have pointed out, *Jude the Obscure* has an 'iterative structure' of remarriages and returns of scenes and characters and a 'cyclical' plot pattern which help create a sense of pointless getting nowhere. David Sonstroem's diagram of the monotonously repeated back-and-forth pattern of Jude's movements in the novel suggests in still another way just how very repetitive its structure really is.[11]

But certainly the most powerful of the formal devices Hardy used to create the sense of unresolved open-endedness notable in *Jude* is the prolonged pattern of Jude's gradually diminishing aspirations and repeated checks on them which come in increasingly quick succession, and at progressively lower levels, in ten stages:

1. Jude first aspires to become a Bishop. (I, 1–9)[12]
2. Frustrated by Arabella's trick, he less confidently tries again; but, rejected by the college masters, he recognizes the collapse of his university hopes. (II, 1–7),
3. He then aspires to enter the church as a licentiate; but, baffled by Sue's marriage to Phillotson, he spends the night with Arabella, and experiences a weakening of his faith and his ambition for ecclesiastical life. (III, 1–10)
4. Jude nevertheless persists in his studies; but, when Sue flees to him, he finds his feelings for her inconsistent with his ecclesiastical ambitions, burns his books, and abandons his hope to be a clergyman. (IV, 1–3)
5. Jude next seeks fulfillment with Sue; but he is frustrated by her sexual reticence and her unwillingness to marry which brings upon them such social disapproval that they are driven to wandering from town to town. (IV, 5; V, 4–7)
6. After years of wandering, Jude aspires only to live peacefully in Christminster; but, returning there, he feels his humiliation more keenly and is faced with the catastrophe of his children's deaths and Sue's distraught reaction to it. (V, 8; VI, 3–7)

7. Sue's return to Phillotson reduces Jude to a bare hope for her possible return; but even this small aspiration is destroyed by her intransigence and by Jude's entrapment in a loveless marriage with Arabella. (VI, 3–7)

8. In the end Jude is reduced to seeking nothing more than his own death by exposing himself to the rain and cold; but even his suicide attempt is thwarted by a recovery that enables him to return to work. (VI, 8–10)

9. When his health finally does break down, Jude's last wish for water goes unheard, his barely whispered quotation of Job is mocked by the repeated 'Hurrah' of the Remembrance Day crowd, and his death itself becomes only a vexing inconvenience to Arabella as she goes about the business of attracting a new lover. (VI, 11)

10. In the final image of the novel, even Jude's remaining books—the relics of his previous ambition—seem 'to pale to a sickly cast' at the Remembrance Week noise, while the novel's last words emphasize that Sue's suffering will continue. (VI, 11)

If we were to represent graphically this pattern of Jude's progressively declining aspirations and the repeated checks upon them, they would appear as a line with a succession of peaks representing his aspirations followed by a subsequent decline, the peaks and valleys becoming progressively lower and flatter, until reduced to scarcely more than a ripple—but never quite terminating because even the finality of Jude's death is compromised by the prediction that Sue's pitiful sufferings will go on.[13]

The increasing employment of 'open' endings in the history of the novel after the publication of *Jude* has been extensively studied—notably by Alan Friedman, Beverly Gross, Frank Kermode, David H. Richter, and, most searchingly, by Maria Torgovnick.[14] These studies make clear that when Hardy published *Jude* in 1895 he was at the leading edge of what would become a widespread use of unresolved endings in literature. Such endings began to be more commonly used in the decades immediately following the publication of *Jude*; they show up in such disparate novels as Lawrence's *Sons and Lovers* (1913), Ford's *The Good Soldier* (1915), and Forster's *A Passage to India* (1924). And, in later fiction such devices appear with greater frequency and in more extreme forms—often in major touchstones of 'modernist' literature. Faulkner's *Absalom, Absalom!* (1936) and some of Samuel Beckett's works—to cite just two very different examples—are notorious for the ways they deny audiences a sense of resolution.

So much did such endings become a staple of twentieth-century literature that they have achieved the status of having become themselves conventional;

as Maria Torgovnick wryly observed, 'by the nineteen-sixties and nineteen-seventies, the "open" ending had become too trite and expected to have great imaginative force'.[15] In short, the multiple formal features Hardy exploited to create a sense of lack of resolution in *Jude* put that novel squarely at the beginning of a movement toward unresolved endings which would quickly emerge as one characteristic feature of much modern literature.

There are parallels in music to such literary narrative strategies,[16] and it is not surprising to find the emergence of similar devices in music beginning almost precisely at the time *Jude* was published. Note, for example, the remarkable structural similarity between Hardy's *Jude* and the conclusion of the final movement of Tchaikovsky's *Sixth Symphony* which premiered just two years earlier on October 28, 1893, at St. Petersburg. Tchaikovsky not only ended it with a slow movement—something all but unheard of in the history of the symphony—but devised a series of sweeping musical lines in which the melody seems to heave itself up, then collapse back down, then repeat that pattern at a lower pitch; instead of resolving into a well-defined conclusion, they grow darker in color, and finally die very gradually away in an extraordinarily long diminuendo to the *pppp* of Tchaikovsky's final notation.

That unusual final movement unsettled the audience at its premiere; structurally it bears a striking resemblance to the pattern of successively diminished aspirations and defeats which is one of the central formal features of Hardy's novel. Moreover, Tchaikovsky's note on his *Sixth Symphony* emphasizes that he had in mind a program in which life is imaged as first impulsive passion and confidence leading to disappointments, collapse of hopes, and death[17]—a program that squares remarkably with Hardy's obvious intentions in *Jude*. It is not at all surprising that some ten years later, after Hardy had heard the *Sixth Symphony*, he would write that he detected the 'modern note of unrest' in Tchaikovsky's music.[18]

And, as in the history of literature since Hardy's *Jude*, so in the history of music, since the first performance of Tchaikovsky's *Sixth Symphony* in 1893, a wide range of strategies which create a sense of lack of resolution emerged, and, again, they were put to increasingly varied uses. Just three years after the first performance of the *Sixth Symphony*, Richard Strauss ended his *Thus Spoke Zarathustra* (1896) in a torturously indecisive way by allowing a B major/C major conflict of tonalities to go entirely unresolved. Gustav Mahler, to mention yet another example, ended his *Ninth Symphony* (1910) with scattered musical phrases that seemingly trail into nowhere; and, just one year later, Igor Stravinsky chose to end his 1911 version of *Petrushka* by having the orchestra fade to a whisper and end on an unresolved melodic dissonance—a C natural followed by an F sharp. In fact, within twenty years such endings became as much a commonplace in modern music as in modern literature;

today, discussion of circularity and a sense of getting nowhere common in the works of such composers as Philip Glass and David Del Tredici and in the writings of John Barth, Thomas Pyncheon, and Donald Barthelme has reached the level of the Sunday Supplement article.[19]

My first observation, then, is that in denying his readers a sense of resolution in *Jude the Obscure*, Hardy was at the forefront in adopting a technique which, in many variations, would figure prominently in subsequent developments not only in modern literature but in modern music.

Expressionist Elements in Jude

A second feature notable in *Jude* puts that novel at the beginning of a very different development in literature—and one that played an important role in the history of the visual arts as well. In some places in *Jude*, Hardy adopted a style in which he attempted to intensify the expression of feeling and attitude by exaggeration, simplification and distortion—in short, by the use of devices which are among the distinctive elements of certain kinds of 'expressionist' art. What is striking about *Jude* is the relatively narrow range in which Hardy employed those narrative strategies and the intensive use he made of them to create a single character. Well-known notes by Hardy from the period 1886–1890 testify to his interest in such devices:

> My art is to intensify the expression of things. . . .
> The 'simply natural' is interesting no longer. The much-decried, mad, late-Turner rendering is now necessary to create my interest. (192)

> Art is a disproportioning—(i.e., distorting, throwing out of proportion)—of realities, to show more clearly the features that matter in those realities. . . . (239)[20]

Hardy's emphasis on intensification and distortion to convey the artist's subjective sense of reality is consistent with the practices and theories of expressionist art whose precursors in literature and painting were emerging just at the time Hardy wrote *Jude*. Of course 'expressionism' took a wide variety of forms, but intense subjectivity, hyperbole, simplification and distortion to emphasize extreme, often pathological psychological states are some features often associated with it. In *Jude* such 'expressionist' features appear in places where characters exhibit exaggerated psychological states and the narrator's comments involve extreme distortions of reality—for example in Hardy's description of Jude's despair when he is confronted with the difficulties of learning Latin and Greek:

... he wished ... that he had never been born.

Somebody might have come along that way who would have asked him his trouble, and might have cheered him. ... But nobody did come, because nobody does; and under the crushing recognition of his gigantic error Jude continued to wish himself out of the world. (I-4)

Such extreme exaggerations of feeling and distortions of reality—'but nobody did come, because nobody does'—constitute one major stylistic feature of *Jude*. They appear in such hyperboles as Mrs. Edlin's comment, 'Weddings be funerals 'a b'lieve nowadays', but, most importantly, Hardy used this mode to render Little Father Time almost entirely out of anti-realistic exaggerations. Time is a walking hyperbole; the following quotations are entirely characteristic of the language in the novel—both description and dialogue—used to depict him:

He was Age masquerading as Juvenility. ... [H]is face took a back view over some great Atlantic of Time, and appeared not to care about what it saw. (V-3)

The boy seemed to have begun with the generals of life and never to have concerned himself with the particulars. (V-3)

'His face is like the tragic mask of Melpomene'. (V-4)

'The doctor says there are such boys springing up amongst us. ... He says it is the beginning of the universal wish not to live'. (VI-2)

'I should like the flowers very very much, if I didn't keep on thinking they'd be all withered in a few days!' (V-5)

'I ought not be born, ought I?' (VI-1)

The use of such techniques to convey an emotionally charged view of reality was emerging in literature, specifically in the plays of August Strindberg, just about the time Hardy produced *Jude*. As early as 1887, Strindberg's play *The Father* made a sharp departure from current realistic conventions; and by 1898, just three years after the publication of *Jude*, Strindberg had completed two parts of his *To Damascus* trilogy, the first fully expressionist literary work in which canons of realism are violated in favor of manipulating highly simplified characters expressive of extreme feeling. Typical features of Strindberg's expressionist mode are notable in such lines as these which he gave to his character 'Stranger' in *To Damascus*:

> ... If I even knew why I was born—why I should be standing here—where to go—what to do! Do you believe that we can be doomed already here on earth?
> ... when I thought I had found happiness, it was only a trap to lure me into a greater misery. . . . Whenever the golden apple fell into my hand, it was either poisoned or rotten at the core.
> ... my fate is being ruled by two different forces, one giving me all that I ask for, the other standing beside me tainting the gift, so that when I receive it, it is so worthless that I don't want to touch it.[21]

Father Time would be entirely at home in such a play; even his nickname would be consistent with Strindberg's device of using general rather than specifically personal names.

Expressionist techniques such as Strindberg exploited in his dramas just at the time *Jude* was published were also appearing in Germany in the plays of Frank Wedekind, whose *Spring's Awakening* (1891) shocked audiences by its exploitation of grotesque caricature, its use of scenes with absurdist elements and, in the last act, its abandonment of realistic conventions by the introduction of that eerie character, The Man in the Mask, to express Wedekind's views. Subsequently the use of generalized characters and other devices pioneered by Strindberg and Wedekind appeared almost simultaneously in such disparate productions as Oskar Kokoschka's *Murder, Hope of Women* (1907), Wassily Kandinsky's *The Yellow Sound* (1909), Schoenberg and Poppenheim's *Expectation* (1909), and later in such literary works as Eugene O'Neill's *The Great God Brown* (1925) and Sean O'Casey's *The Silver Tassie* (1928). Characters that serve as metaphors for ideas and extremes of feeling, as Hardy's Father Time does, would subsequently appear prominently in 'modernist' literature: James Joyce, for example, used a variation on that technique to depict Bloom's innermost desires in the 'Circe' section of *Ulysses*, and, in extreme form it may be found in such works as Kafka's *The Transformation* where the metaphor becomes embodied as realistically treated fact.

Hardy's use of such techniques in *Jude* just at the time when expressionism was emerging in the literature of Europe was paralleled by a similar development in painting. In December, 1893, just two years before *Jude* was published, Edvard Munch exhibited his proto-expressionist collection titled *The Frieze of Life* in Berlin.[22] There are images among those works which vividly replicate expressionist elements in *Jude*: Munch's painting titled *The*

Girl and Death, for example, might serve as a visual rendering of Mrs. Edlin's observation 'Weddings be funerals 'a b'lieve nowadays', and his well-known *The Scream* could scarcely find a more fitting counterpart in the fiction of his day than in Hardy's Father Time.[23]

Furthermore, Munch's description of his paintings as 'nature transformed according to one's subjective disposition' and his expressed intention to paint not physical appearances but emotional reactions to them[24]—these all accord with Hardy's views quoted earlier. Munch's use of deformed, hallucinatory images and intensification of natural color had an enormous impact on many artists who have subsequently been identified with 'expressionism': clearly he influenced the *Die Brücke* painters, especially Emil Nolde, and served as an immediate model for the later twentieth-century expressionists who formed the Berlin *Sezession* and others who followed them.[25]

In short, by exploiting distinctly expressionist elements in *Jude*, Hardy was once again at the beginning of a powerful movement toward one manifestation of 'modernism' in art—one that cut across national boundaries and appeared in parallel ways in different mediums.

Employing Sharply Contrasting Artistic Modes

In 1887 Zola wrote to Strindberg criticising his play *The Father* for what today would be called its expressionist elements—the 'schematic nature' of its characters, their 'lack of reality', the use of types rather than individuals and Strindberg's 'lack of concern for naturalistic plausibility'.[26] It certainly would not have occurred to Zola to consider injecting a character from a Strindberg play into one of his novels. Yet, that, in effect, is what Hardy did in *Jude the Obscure*. The expressionist devices Hardy used to render Father Time in *Jude* were very much like those employed by Strindberg—and sharply at odds with the bulk of the novel.

As Michael Millgate has pointed out, Time is the sole arguable exception to the more firmly realized other characters in *Jude*,[27] and the styles Hardy adopted throughout the bulk of the novel were in the tradition of realistic fiction.[28] Such scenes as the fight that erupts at the meeting where Phillotson contests his dismissal (IV-6) had, as Hardy was aware, something of Fielding's comic realism,[29] but in *Jude* this Fieldingesque manner blends into styles and techniques more characteristic of Flaubert and Zola. In Jude's deathbed scene, for example, Hardy set Jude's dying words against the background of the cries of the Remembrance Week crowd—a strategy reminiscent of Flaubert's device of having Rodolphe's seduction of Emma Bovary take place against the backdrop of speeches at an agricultural fair. And equally memorable are those scenes which strike us, as they struck Hardy's contemporaries, as Zolaesque:[30] the scene where Jude and Arabella take tea in an 'inn of an inferior class' (I, 7) has elements reminiscent of *The Dram Shop*, for example, and the pig-killing (I, 10) of *The Earth*.[31] In short, Father Time's appearance in *Jude the Obscure* is as if a character from Strindberg's *To Damascus* had somehow wandered into a novel of Fielding, Flaubert, Zola—or Hardy.

At the time *Jude* was published, the beginnings of such mixing of sharply contrasting artistic modes were just appearing in Western art. One striking early example is Joris-Karl Huysmans' *En Rade* (1887) which so jarringly combined dream and reality that Zola wrote a letter to Huysmans complaining that the result was a 'confusion qui n'est pas de l'art'.[32] In the later work of Henrik Ibsen this mixing of sharply contrasting artistic modes took the form of conjoining the domestic realism of his earlier period with the symbolism notable in his plays from *The Wild Duck* (1884) onward, so that in *The Master Builder* (a play Hardy saw in 1893),[33] Ibsen's symbolism rubs shoulders with a realism as markedly different from it as Solness's references to a 'proper castle in the air' are to the 'real foundation' he proposes to build under it.[34]

This practice of mixing sharply contrasting artistic modes would subsequently become one of the most distinctive features of modernist art. One thinks of the quotations and allusions to literary and musical classics juxtaposed against gritty scenes of contemporary British life in *The Waste Land* (1922), and the similar collage-like mixing of sharply contrasting modes in Ezra Pound's *Cantos* (1917–1970). Virginia Woolf exploited another variation on the same strategy in *To the Lighthouse* (1927) by abruptly shifting from the minutely detailed and intensely personal interior monologues of the first and last sections of the novel to the impersonal, detached, and sweepingly general narrative style of the 'Time Passes' section. And, again, the device was pushed to its extreme limits in Joyce's *Ulysses* (1922), where shifts from one stylistic mode to another, sometimes within the space of a single chapter, occur with bewildering variety.

Conjoining sharply contrasting literary modes in one novel—as Hardy combined elements of literary realism with those of literary expressionism in *Jude*—also has a parallel in music: it is as if a composer were to have different parts of an orchestra playing in two dissonant musical keys in the same composition. And, in fact, at just the time Hardy was working on *Jude*, precisely that kind of development was taking place in music. Some time between 1892 and 1895—just about the time Hardy published *Jude*—Charles Ives added an 'Interlude' to his *Variations on 'America'* in which he combined F major with A-flat major.[35] In the following years other composers began to exploit that same technique: Richard Strauss's modulation from G-minor to D-minor over a G flat major pedal chord in the love music of *A Hero's Life* (1898), Ravel's *Water Games* (1901) which juxtaposed C-major and F-major; Prokofiev's piano composition *Sarcasms* (1912–14) with B-flat minor in the left hand playing against F-sharp minor in the right. And, in the works of one modern composer, Darius Milhaud, the technique was pushed to the extreme of using three and four keys simultaneously. By 1920 the practice had already become so widespread that in the following decade it prompted a series of published analyses.[36]

Conclusion

If here we seem to be at a far remove from Hardy, my point is that, in his mixing of expressionistic and realistic modes in *Jude* in 1895, he was again at the forefront of a development which cut across artistic forms and national boundaries and led to major formal innovations characteristic of some of the touchstones of later twentieth-century art.

In her *Hardy and the Sister Arts*, Joan Grundy speculated about whether there were features in *Jude* which anticipated such later artistic developments as Cubism or Futurism and noted that 'the experience of modern life imaged at the start of the novel ... certainly suggests a context similar to that out of which such art movements have sprung'.[37] I have attempted here to point out some of the ways *Jude* was indeed part of a context out of which a number of distinctive features of modernist art have emerged. Hardy's use of multiple formal devices which convey a sense of unresolved and problematic open-endedness; his adoption of an expressionist style in portions of the novel; and, even more, his mixing of sharply contrasting literary modes—all these are striking instances of his early use of distinctive formal strategies which would show up with growing frequency in modern literature and other artistic mediums. The increasingly pervasive use of those strategies in the arts from the publication of *Jude* onward makes clear that Hardy was working at the leading edge of some of the major artistic movements of his day, and by identifying these particular features it is possible to specify in a relatively precise way just how Hardy's *Jude the Obscure* may be said to have been in its time a 'modern' novel.

Notes

1. See Peter J. Casagrande, *Hardy's Influence on the Modern Novel* (Totowa, NJ: Barnes & Noble Books, 1987).

2. Ian Gregor, *The Great Web: The Form of Hardy's Major Fiction* (Totowa, NJ: Rowman and Littlefield, 1987), p. 233.

3. Irving Howe, *Thomas Hardy* (New York: The Macmillan Company, 1967), p. 134.

4. C. H. Salter, *Good Little Thomas Hardy* (Totowa, New Jersey: Barnes and Noble Books, 1981), p. 26.

5. See, for example, Ramon Saldivar's '*Jude the Obscure*: Reading and the Spirit of the Law', in Harold Bloom's *Thomas Hardy's Jude the Obscure* (New York: Chelsea House Publishers, 1987), pp. 103–118, and the summary points made by

Gary Adelman, *Jude the Obscure: A Paradise of Despair* (New York: Twayne Publishers, 1992), pp. 29–30, 98, and 107.

6. In *Hardy and the Sister Arts* (London: Macmillan, 1979), p. 26, Joan Grundy briefly suggests a possible formal connection of *Jude* to Cubism, Futurism, and Vorticism, but does not pursue the matter further; also, in 'Some Surrealist Elements in Hardy's Prose and Verse', *Thomas Hardy Annual*, No. 3 (London: Macmillan, 1985), Rosemary Sumner has pointed to relationships of some aspects of Hardy's art—though not of *Jude*—to certain features of works of DeChirico, Ernst, Picasso, Magritte, and Duchamp.

7. Robert Martin Adams, *Strains of Discord: Studies in Literary Openness* (Ithaca, NY: Cornell University Press, 1958), p. 13.

8. See Carl J. Weber, 'Hardy's Grim Note in *The Return of the Native*', *Papers of the Bibliographical Society of America*, 36 (1942), 37–45. About how the present conclusion of *The Return of the Native* reinforces the doubts raised by the novel rather than resolves them, see Robert Schweik, 'Theme, Character, and Perspective in Hardy's *The Return of the Native*', *Philological Quarterly*, 41 (1962) 757–767.

9. Robert Schweik, 'The Ethical Structure of Hardy's *The Woodlanders*', *Archiv für das Studium der Neuren Sprachen und Literaturen*, 211 (1974) 31–44.

10. On the way the relationship of Angel Clare and Liza-Lu forms a kind of 'new marriage', see Jan B. Gordon, 'Origins, History, and the Reconstitution of Family: Tess's Journey', *Thomas Hardy*, ed. Harold Bloom (New York: Chelsea House Publishers, 1987), pp. 115–135.

11. See Alan Friedman, *The Turn of the Novel* (New York: Oxford University Press, 1966), pp. 71–74; Daniel R. Schwarz, 'Beginnings and Endings in Hardy's Major Fiction' in *Critical Approaches to the Fiction of Thomas Hardy*, ed. by Dale Kramer (London: Macmillan, 1979), pp. 33–34; Peter Casagrande, *Unity in Hardy's Novels: 'Repetitive Symmetries'* (London: Macmillan, 1982), p. 203; and David Sonstroem, 'Order and Disorder in *Jude the Obscure*,' *English Literature in Transition*, 24 (1981), p. 9.

12. All references to the text of *Jude the Obscure* are to the Wessex Edition (London: Macmillan, 1912) and are indicated parenthetically by part numbers in Roman numerals followed by chapter numbers in Arabic numerals.

13. Fernand Lagarde's 'A propos de la construction de *Jude the Obscure*', *Caliban*, 3 (January, 1966), 185–214, argues—mistakenly, I think—for a pattern of rising hopes in the first four parts of the novel and only then declining, rather than the pattern of persistent and inexorable decline I point to in my analysis.

14. See Alan Friedman, *The Turn of the Novel* (New York: Oxford University Press, 1966); Beverley Gross, 'Narrative Time and the Open-ended Novel', *Criticism*, 8 (1966), 362–76; Frank Kermode, *The Sense of an Ending* (New York: Oxford University Press, 1967); David H. Richter *Fables' End: Completeness and Closure in Rhetorical Fiction* (Chicago and London: University of Chicago Press, 1974); and Maria Torgovnick, *Closure in the Novel* (Princeton: Princeton University Press, 1981), pp. 202–204.

15. Torgovnick, p. 206; see also Richter, pp. 2–7.

16. See, for example, Anthony Newcomb's analysis in 'Schumann and Late Eighteenth-Century Narrative Strategies', *Nineteenth–Century Music*, 11 (Fall, 1987), 164–174.

17. John Warrack, *Tchaikovsky* (London: Hamish Hamilton, 1973), p. 266.

18. Michael Millgate, *Thomas Hardy: A Biography* (New York: Random House, 1982), p. 448.

19. See, for example, Donal [*sic*] Henahan, 'The Going-Nowhere Music—And Where it Came From', *New York Times*, Section 2, Arts and Leisure, Sunday, December 6, 1981, pp. 1, 25.

20. Thomas Hardy, *The Life and Work of Thomas Hardy*, ed. by Michael Millgate (London: Macmillan, 1984), p. 183. Subsequent page numbers are provided parenthetically.

21. August Strindberg, *To Damascus I*, in *Eight Expressionist Plays by August Strindberg*, translated by Arvid Paulson (New York: New York University Press, 1972), pp. 140–141.

22. The confusing use of the term *impressionism* in early twentieth-century painting is partly sorted out in Victor H. Miesel's 'The Term Expressionism in the Visual Arts (1911–1920)', ed. by Hayden V. White, *The Uses of History: Essays in Intellectual and Social History Presented to William J. Bossenbrook* (Detroit MI: Wayne State University Press, 1968), pp. 135–152.

23. Exemplars of the Munch works referred to are all in the Munch Museum, Oslo, and are reproduced in Arne Eggum's *Edvard Munch: Paintings, Sketches, and Studies*, trans. by Ragnar Christophersen (New York: Clarckson N. Potter, Inc., 1984), illus. nos. 7, 12, and 238.

24. Reinhold Heller, *Edvard Munch: The Scream* (New York: Viking Press, 1973), p. 23.

25. Edward Lockspeiser, *Music and Painting: A Study in Comparative Ideas from Turner to Schoenberg* (New York: Harper and Row, 1973), p. 133.

26. Quoted in R.S. Furness, *Expressionism* (London: Methuen and Company, 1973), p. 4.

27. Michael Millgate, *Thomas Hardy: His Career as a Novelist* (New York: Random House, 1971), p. 323.

28. For a differing view, particularly with respect to the realism of Hardy's treatment of Sue Bridehead, see Phillip Mallett, 'Sexual Ideology and Narrative Form in *Jude the Obscure*', *English*, 38 (Autumn, 1989), 211–224.

29. Hardy to Edmund Gosse, November 20, 1895, in Richard Little Purdy and Michael Millgate, eds., *The Collected Letters of Thomas Hardy: Volume II 1893–1901* (Oxford: Clarendon Press, 1980), p. 99.

30. See, for example, the review by Jeannette L. Gilder titled 'Hardy the Degenerate', *World*, 13 (November, 1895), 15 and, also, the comments by Edmund Gosse and R.Y. Tyrrell recorded in R.G. Cox's *Thomas Hardy: The Critical Heritage* (London: Routledge, 1970), pp. 266 and 293.

31. Hardy recorded passages from English translations of Zola's *Abbé Mouret's Transgressions* and from *Germinal* in his '1876' notebook; see *The Literary Notes of Thomas Hardy*, ed. by Lennart Björk (Göteborg: Acta Universitatis Gothoburgensis, 1974), I, 403–405 and II, 189–191.

32. Emile Zola, *Correspondance* (Paris: F. Bernouard, 1928–29), letter of the 1st of June, 1887, p. 679. On the way *En rade* represents a movement from naturalism to a more 'expressionist' kind of art, see Ruth B. Antosh, 'J.-K. Huysmans' *En rade*: L'Enigme Résolué', *Bulletin de la Société J.-K. Huysmans*, 23 (1987), 33–43.

33. Hardy, *The Life and Work of Thomas Hardy*, p. 272.

34. Henrik Ibsen, *The Oxford Ibsen*, Vol. VII, ed by James Walter McFarlane, with translations by Jens Arp and James Walter McFarlane (London: Oxford University Press, 1966), p. 432.

35. Charles Ives, *Variations on 'America' (1891) for Organ / 'Adeste Fidelis' in an Organ Prelude* (1897) (New York: Music Press, 1949); this very early use of bitonality is notable particularly in the 'interlude' of measures 75–90. However, on p. [ii] an unsigned 'Note' to this edition suggests that the 'interlude' was not composed by 1891 but added some years later, and the subsequent questions raised by Maynard Solomon in 'Charles Ives: Some Questions of Veracity', *Journal of the American Musicological Society*, 40 (Fall, 1987), 443–470, do not increase confidence in the earlier date.

36. See, for example, J. Deroux, 'La Musique polytonale', *La Revue musicale*, 1921 (no. 11) and 1923 (no. 4), and A. Machabey, 'Disonance, polytonalité, and atonalité', *La Revue musicale*, 1931 (no. 116).

37. Joan Grundy, *Hardy and the Sister Arts* (London: The Macmillan Press, 1979), p. 66.

SAMUEL HYNES

How to Be an Old Poet:
The Examples of Hardy and Yeats

Ten or twelve years ago I wrote an introduction to a volume of Hardy's poems in which I considered the consequences for the poetry of the fact that most of it was written in the last decades of a long life.[1] I want to return to that subject here, but in a different way, expanding it to include another great modern poet, and shifting it upward to the level of theory: The Theory of Old Poets. That's how our thinking about art works, isn't it? We have an idea, time passes, the idea grows, spreads, changes, until particulars begin to look like principles, and we have a *theory*. I'm a decade and more older than I was when I first wrote about Hardy and old age. And so, I might add, are you. A decade nearer our own old age: high time we thought about it.

When in my theorizing I use the term Old Poets—with those capital letters—I mean, obviously, poets who lived a long time. But not all poets who live past middle age become Old Poets. Some fall silent at the end, as Eliot and Larkin did. Some go on in their poems being their younger selves: Robert Graves, for example. Graves was ninety when he died, and was still writing poems in his eighties, but his bargain with the White Goddess seems to have been that she would continue to inspire him on the condition that he continued to write the kind of poems he had always written. Some poets abandon poetry altogether for another medium: like Kingsley Amis,

From *Reading Thomas Hardy*, edited by Charles P.C. Pettit, pp. 172–87. © 1998 by Samuel Hynes.

103

who turned to fiction—I suppose because it was a better form in which to be bilious about the world.

But most poets go on being poets, and in time become old poets (note the lower case here), just as old painters, old gardeners, old carpenters, old literary critics go on practising their crafts long past the age at which you might think they should retire. The reason is obvious: it's what they *do*, what they have always done; it fills their days, and more than that, it defines them to themselves. To the question: Who am I? our work provides us with an immediate and irrefutable answer.

But longevity isn't the sole defining condition of being an Old Poet: as I conceive the category, Old Poets are those who in their old age make poetry out of that state—make age not simply their subject, but the condition of consciousness in their poems, and so make the perceived world of age real to other minds.

Let me describe that world, as I find it in the work of Old Poets. It is a world of *less, fewer,* and *last*: there is less activity there than in our world, and less possibility of action; in the grammar of that world words like *act* and *love* are past-tense verbs. Things happen there for the last time, and that affects the poetic tone; for as Dr Johnson said, 'No man does anything consciously for the last time, without a feeling of sadness.' (The titles of eleven poems in Hardy's *Complete Poems* begin with the word *last*.)

So old age is a *tone*. It also has a spatial dimension. Age is a reduced space, the horizons closed in, the interiors confining and disfurnished, like an old, unoccupied house. Age is a place in which the present is less present than it is in the world of ordinary being; there are fewer people there, fewer friends. But if it is unpopulated by the living, it is crowded with the dead: age is ghost-haunted.

If space is different in the world of old age, so is time. Time there stretches backward like a long road taken, into the distant past; forward it has almost no length at all, only a little span, like a short corridor, with a closed door at the end.

This world of age is difficult to talk about. We mustn't be too easily sad or sentimental about what is, after all, only ordinary human reality; and we mustn't let ourselves become mortality-bores. The best of the Old Poets avoid those traps: they are neither sentimental nor boring; they simply confront the world time has given them, and compel it to be poetry.

It's an exclusive world, this poetic world of old age. Younger poets may visit it, in the poems of their elders, but they can't practise there. There is no place in Old Poet Theory for poems by younger poets in which they *imagine* age: 'Here I am, an old man in a dry month' won't do; nor 'Grow old along with me! / The best is yet to be'; nor 'Do not go gentle into that good night.'[2]

Those poems have permanent places in our English-language canon, but they don't tell us what age is *like*. They can't. For age clearly is one of those human experiences—like love, sex, war, and religion—that aren't anything like what you imagine they will be, before you've had them. (Auden said fame is like that, too.)

When I think about old age as a separate and distinct human condition I think of the Seven Ages of Man speech in *As You Like It*. Jaques's Seventh Age is pretty grim:

> Last scene of all,
> That ends this strange eventful history,
> Is second childishness and mere oblivion,
> Sans teeth, sans eyes, sans taste, sans everything.[3]

You must recognize, as I do, that those lines do not accurately describe old Hardy, or old Yeats, or any other Old Poet. And yet . . . I am caught by Shakespeare's sense of age as diminishment and loss—*sans, sans, sans*, what Hardy called time's 'takings away'—and of oblivion. And so, even though it isn't quite fair, I think of this poetry as Seventh Age poetry: poetry that is about the reality of loss-in-time, and how to live with it, and make poetry out of it.

Hardy and Yeats are Seventh Age poets, in this sense. But not in the same way. Indeed, I think they can be seen as two distinct subtypes, which we might identify with Shakespeare's two greatest old men: Prospero and Lear. Pause for a moment to think of those two figures of Age. Prospero, in the last act of *The Tempest*: calm, accepting, beyond action, having resigned his place in the public world of power to return to Milan and think about death. An old man who has accepted diminishment and has given it dignity: Hardy at Max Gate, voluntarily withdrawn from the literary marketplace of London, retired from the novel-writing that had made him famous, living the diminished life of age, and writing the poetry of that condition; the old poet as sage, the truth-teller, no longer an agent in his life, but an observer.

Then think of Lear: Lear on the heath, passionate and raging, without court or courtiers, without comforts, exposing himself to suffering—an old man who would rather be a mad diminished king than no king at all, tragic, and consciously so, playing the role of Old Man as Tragic Hero. Yeats in his late years, not withdrawn, still *in* the world but raging against it, a passionate public man, the old poetic self re-made once more as Seventh Age Hero, the old man who remains an agent in his life by an act of will.

So: two Old Poets, both role-playing, but in different roles, which, yet have this in common, that they make Old Poetry possible.

Just when the Seventh Age begins in a poet's life is unpredictable. No door slams on the earlier life, not at three-score-and-ten or any other age. But in individual cases one can usually locate the point of change quite precisely in the poetry, and if one knows the life one can conjecture reasons. It happened in Hardy's poetic career between the publication of *Time's Laughingstocks* in 1909 and *Satires of Circumstance* in 1914—between his seventieth and seventy-fifth year. The cause is perfectly clear: it was of course the death of Emma Hardy in 1912. It was Hardy's greatest loss, his greatest personal diminishment; Emma's death emptied his life of his strongest link with his own past, with youth, hope and happiness, and shifted her presence and all that she meant to him into the ghost-world of memory.

There is another thing to be said about the effect of Emma's death. She was Hardy's exact contemporary, and when someone our own age dies, we feel a tremor in our life: our own death takes on a felt certainty then that is quite different from the untroubling proposition that all men are mortal. That's why old people read obituary pages, starting with the death-dates; they hope they'll find that the dead are all older than *they* are, and that death can therefore be postponed into the uncertain future, and thought about another day. The death of a contemporary has a different message: it says death is *here*, in the present.

You can see this change to Seventh Age poetry in the 'Poems of 1912–13' that Hardy wrote immediately after his wife's death, most explicitly in the first poem, 'The Going':

> Well, well! All's past amend,
> Unchangeable. It must go.
> I seem but a dead man held on end
> To sink down soon. . . . O you could not know
> That such swift fleeing
> No soul foreseeing—
> Not even I—would undo me so!

But it is everywhere in his later poems, in poems about his coffin, his grave, his ghost—a curious line of posthumous poems by a living Old Poet.

For Yeats the point of change occurred somewhere in the 1920s, between *Michael Robartes and the Dancer* (1921) and *The Tower* (1928)—earlier in his life than in Hardy's (Yeats was only fifty-six in 1921). The cause seems of a different kind: the Troubles, the Irish Civil War, and the settlement that was a defeat for his dreams of a romantic Ireland made him an Old (and a bitter) Poet before his time. The great poems that came out of those last years, the final two decades of his life, are full of age and loss.

Two great poets become Old Poets, then, for different reasons that reflect their different relationships to the world. Hardy, the private man, suffers a private loss that leaves him memory-haunted; Yeats, the public man, suffers a public loss that leaves him haunted by his country's history, and by the impotence of poetry in the public world. In both cases the book that follows the loss is the poet's greatest single volume. What shall we make of that? That loss is gain, for a poet? That great art may come out of the diminishments of the Seventh Age of Man? The history of Western culture offers us considerable evidence that this may be true: old Michelangelo, deaf Beethoven, ageing Degas (who only became Degas, Renoir said, as his health and sight began to fail), Renoir himself, old and crippled, a brush strapped to his arthritic hand, still painting Renoirs.

When Seventh Age poets speak in their own voices they often do so in images of their diminishment. Here is a stanza from Hardy's most poignant poem of age, 'An Ancient to Ancients':

Where once we danced, where once we sang,
      Gentlemen,
The floors are sunken, cobwebs hang,
And cracks creep; worms have fed upon
The doors. Yea, sprightlier times were then
Than now, with harps and tabrets gone,
      Gentlemen!

And here are some lines from Yeats's poem of age, 'An Acre of Grass':

Picture and book remain,
An acre of green grass
For air and exercise,
Now strength of body goes;
Midnight, an old house
Where nothing stirs but a mouse.

You see the similarities: two passages of confinement, decay and loss, two imaged spaces emptied of human company—and of human energy, too, for Old Age's reality also has its kinetic aspect, life runs down at the end.

And yet, in these poems there are presences, not living but imagined, a company of the Old to be invoked against age. Hardy calls up classical authors who wrote into their old age: Sophocles, Plato, Socrates, Pythagoras, Thucydides, Herodotus, Homer, Clement, Augustin, Origen. And Yeats names old artists and their old creations, as images of how the mind's energy can defy age: Shakespeare's Timon and Lear, William Blake, Michael Angelo. By naming these aged heroes, Old Hardy and Old Yeats claim places in their company.

But not in the same way, not in the same tone. I suggested that Hardy and Yeats are two distinct types of Old Poet, one Prospero, the other Lear. Hardy, Prospero-like, ends his poem in a calm diminuendo, addressed to the young generation that will succeed him:

> And ye, red-lipped and smooth-browed; list,
> > Gentlemen;
> Much is there waits you we have missed;
> Much lore we leave you worth the knowing,
> Much, much has lain outside our ken:
> Nay, rush not: time serves: we are going,
> > Gentlemen.

A curious, energyless ending, like the soft speech of an old man short of breath, uttering one line at a time, and finally one phrase at a time:

> Much is there waits you we have missed; (breath)
> Much lore we leave you worth the knowing, (breath)
> Much, much has lain outside our ken: (breath)
> Nay, (breath) rush not: (breath) time serves: (breath)
> > we are going, (breath)
> > > Gentlemen. (long breath)

Yeats is very different; he roars into his last stanza on a crescendo that only settles into calm at the end—one clause, without a single mark of punctuation to locate a pause in it, one continuous burst of energy, one breath. And then the final stanza, ending in a two-line closing diminuendo, its own vision of diminishment:

> Forgotten else by mankind;
> An old man's eagle mind.

Forgotten: as a poet, that is: a condition to fear and resist, if you're Yeats, because *poet* was for him an essential, self-defining term. Do you remember his little poem 'To Be Carved on a Stone at Thoor Ballylee'? In it Yeats refers to himself as 'the poet William Yeats', and prays that the characters of the inscription he has had carved on a stone at his tower-home in the West of Ireland will survive, when all is ruin again. These characters do remain on the tower, and a visitor can see them there. But *characters* means more in the poem than the carved words on that stone: it means the characters of the poem we are reading, and of all Yeats's other poems. Yeats isn't saying that they will certainly remain: what is certain is that ruin will return, in the cycle of changing things. Those last lines are more a prayer than an affirmation of the permanence of poetry: *may* they remain; *may* the words of a poet defeat forgetfulness.

Hardy is different, in many ways. First, in the absence from his poems of himself as a poet. You can't imagine him writing: 'I, the poet Thomas Hardy', because that isn't the role he plays in his poems. He isn't the artist, or the self-created hero; he doesn't re-make himself to play the poet's role on the world's stage. He is simply what he is, an old man who used to notice things, a country walker, a rememberer. It is extraordinary how completely Hardy controls the scale of himself in his world, keeping it all small; human-scaled, *un*-poetic.

Another difference concerns forgottenness. Yeats feared it; Hardy didn't. To be forgotten is a natural and inevitable fate in Hardy's world: the past fades, memory grows dim, the dead survive for a time in the minds of the living, and then cease to exist even there. We all know many poems on that general theme: 'His Immortality', 'The To-Be-Forgotten', 'The Ghost of the Past', 'Ah, Are You Digging on My Grave?' Annihilation is a principle that Hardy accepted calmly and without resistance: everything changes, dies, falls; nothing that exists is exempt from Time—not a man, not a star. Hardyans will catch my reference there: it is to 'Waiting Both', a poem from *Human Shows*, published when Hardy was eighty-five:

A star looks down at me,
And says: 'Here I and you
Stand, each in his degree:
What do you mean to do,—
        Mean to do?'

I say: 'For all I know,
Wait, and let Time go by,
Till my change come'—'Just so,'
The star says: 'So mean I:—
        So mean I.'

It is a poem of complete, motionless passivity: man stands on the earth, Star stands in the sky. Both wait. There is nothing else to do.

Yeats was no less aware of the power of Time and Change than Hardy was, but he played the theme differently. In his old poems the will to create confronts the inevitable destruction of Time in a tragic opposition. Yeats celebrates that confrontation: don't stand, he says; don't wait: act; resist Time. You'll lose, but it is mankind's glory to oppose destruction with creation. The late poems are full of statements of that theme: 'Lapis Lazuli', for example, and the last stanza of 'Two Songs from a Play':

> Everything that man esteems
> Endures a moment or a day.
> Love's pleasure drives his love away,
> The painter's brush consumes his dreams;
> The herald's cry, the soldier's tread
> Exhaust his glory and his might:
> Whatever flames upon the night
> Man's own resinous heart has fed.

Such energetic images of defeat, such strenuous verbs: *drives, consumes, flames*. The end is the same as in Hardy: everything passes, nothing escapes the force of Time. But the energy makes a difference. That energy animates all those Yeatsian heroes in 'An Acre of Grass'—Timon and Lear and William Blake and Michael Angelo. I find no such energy in Hardy's Ancients. They are quiet, past-tense heroes; they 'Burnt brightlier towards their setting-day', Hardy says; but that day came. There is no resistance there, no energy extravagantly spent in the war against Time: they are simply dead old thinkers, fixed and motionless, like portraits on a wall.

Old age is a time of necessary loss. It's also an embarrassment: anyone past middle age knows that; Hardy knew it, and so did Yeats. 'I look into my glass, / And view my wasting skin'—that's Hardy; 'What shall I do with this absurdity—/ O heart, O troubled heart—this caricature, / Decrepit age that has been tied to me / As to a dog's tail?'[4]—that's Yeats. If we look further into these two poems we will see that they express more than the decay of the flesh; they also reveal the separation between the outer and the inner self that all old people feel. Listen again to Hardy:

> I look into my glass,
> And view my wasting skin,
> And say, 'Would God it came to pass
> My heart had shrunk as thin!'
>
> For then, I, undistrest
> By hearts grown cold to me,
> Could lonely wait my endless rest
> With equanimity.

But Time, to make me grieve,
Part steals, lets part abide;
And shakes this fragile frame at eve
With throbbings of noontide.

This is the last poem in *Wessex Poems*: Hardy at about sixty. Wasting skin, fragile frame: the *exterior* is old. But inside is a heart that has not shrunk, but throbs as it did in the noontide of youth. That's the problem.

Now Yeats, at about the same age:

What shall I do with this absurdity—
O heart, O troubled heart—this caricature,
Decrepit age that has been tied to me
As to a dog's tail?
        Never had I more
Excited, passionate, fantastical
Imagination, nor an ear and eye
That more expected the impossible . . .

Again, on the outside there is the caricature Age, and inside, the passionate heart. In both poets the same self-contradictory old/young self.

How should an Old Poet deal with the dissonant reality of diminished flesh and undiminished heart? Hardy went one way—Prospero's way; Yeats went the other—the way of Lear.

Consider first Yeats/Lear. The Lear way with old age is to defy it, to deny diminishment, to proclaim the old heart's vigour. Be passionate, be furious, be insane if you have to; be physical, be sexual—frankly and grossly so. (Do I need to argue that these terms describe Lear? Surely not. Read the sixth scene of Act IV, one of Lear's mad scenes: 'Adultery? / Thou shalt not die: die for adultery! No: / The wren goes to't, and the small gilded fly / Does lecher in my sight. / Let copulation thrive . . .'. There's a full and passionate old heart here, undiminished, full-throttle.)

Old Yeats adopted Lear's way, not in his life (which was seemly enough—most of the time) but in his old poems. One way he did so was by inventing Learish characters as masks of himself, a gallery of old, half-crazy (or entirely crazy) surrogates: the Wild Old Wicked Man, Crazy Jane, Tom the Lunatic, an unnamed Old Man and Old Woman. Through these masks Yeats could speak passionately, directly, coarsely about age, sex and physical change; he could utter truths that would not have come properly from the mouth of an Irish senator and Nobel Prize winner—lines like 'Love has pitched his mansion in / The place of excrement'.[5]

Yeats's poems of age are often fiercely sexual, yet in most of them sex is not really the subject; it is, rather, the energy that drives the poems, a way of affirming the undiminished heart and the undiminished imagination, against the evidence of the diminished body. It is a strategy for an Old Poet. Yeats explained that strategy in a little poem called 'The Spur'. It's a poem about the themes of lust and rage in his later poems. But the poem isn't really about sexuality or anger; it's about how to be an Old Poet. Cherish the furious passions for their energy, it says; better to lust and rage in your poems than to be silent and forgotten.

And what about Hardy? What is Prospero's way with diminishment? It is the opposite of Lear's: acceptance; forgiveness; resignation; calm. By the end of *The Tempest* we know that for Prospero sex is a disturbance of youth—of people like Ferdinand and Miranda; that lust belongs to Caliban's world; and that rage is inappropriate to age. Prospero has reached the calm seas beyond those storms. Old Hardy was like that; or so it seems, from his poems. For there the passionate acts and issues of human existence have been transposed from the first-person lyric voice (such as Yeats used in his mask-poems) into sexual dramas from other, imagined lives: mismarriages, adulteries, betrayals, suicides and other satires of circumstance, sometimes witnessed by the speaker of the poem ('The Harbour Bridge'), sometimes told as local history ('The Mock Wife'), or folk-memory ('A Set of Country Songs'), but always distanced—passionate situations that happened to somebody else. And in the rare poems where the desire is first-person personal, it is in the past tense, remote in time, remembered as one might remember an accident or a sickness that one suffered long ago. I am thinking here specifically of poems like 'Louie' and 'Thoughts of Phena', but the distancing of the erotic is also true of the 'Poems of 1912–13'. Look at those poems again: love is present, and very movingly so; but desire is far back, in Cornwall, when Hardy and Emma were young. Sex is only history, in the now of those poems.

You can see the difference in present-tense sexuality between Hardy and Yeats in two small poems in which the poets regard young women. Do you remember Yeats's 'Politics'? It comes near the end of his posthumous book, *Last Poems*. In the poem, Yeats stands in the midst of a political conversation, but can't fix his attention on it, because there is a young girl present. The poem ends: 'But O that I were young again / And held her in my arms!' This is the Irish Senator being the decorous old Public Man in public, but privately feeling intense, present-tense desire.

And Hardy? The poem that comes to mind is 'The High-School Lawn'. Hardy (so often the old voyeur in his poems) peeps through a hedge at a whirl of pretty schoolgirls; but what he feels is not desire, but their common mortality:

A bell: they flee:
Silence then:—
So it will be
Some day again
With them,—with me.

How old must a man be, to see pretty girls and think of death?

Hardy, I conclude, was an old poet who was content to be entirely old, who was at ease with diminishment, and even with the prospect of approaching death, accepting silence, accepting forgottenness. A philosophical old man—like Prospero; the opposite of Yeats and Lear, and to me a more disturbing model.

I wonder if posterity, or the lack of posterity, had something to do with it. Yeats had a son and a daughter, and prayed for their future in poems; Hardy had none. Perhaps because Yeats had children, he thought also of other, non-genetic heirs, and named their inheritance in poems, most movingly in the third part of 'The Tower', which begins:

It is time that I wrote my will;
I choose upstanding men
That climb the streams until
The fountain leap, and at dawn
Drop their cast at the side
Of dripping stone; I declare
They shall inherit my pride,
The pride of people that were
Bound neither to Cause nor to State . . .

A will is an old man's utterance, a voice that is first heard from the grave. You have to believe in posterity to write one. Yeats's posterity here is what he called 'the indomitable Irishry', his own defiant and opposing people. In them he survives.

There is another sense of inheritance in Yeats. In 'Under Ben Bulben', his last lyric poem in the edition of *Collected Poems* that I prefer, he speaks to Irish poets who will come after him, as an aged parent might speak to his children:

Irish poets, learn your trade,
Sing whatever is well made,
Scorn the sort now growing up

All out of shape from toe to top,
Their unremembering hearts and heads
Base-born products of base beds.

You can hear the old man's anger building there against the ugly, artless, unremembering modern world—Yeats playing Lear to the end. But you can also hear the pride of continuance, Irish poet to Irish poet.

There is none of that in Hardy: no descendants, no choosing of heirs, no address to poets to come. The end, in his mind and in his work, was terminal and unconditional, and he accepted it with resignation. You hear none of Yeats's anger in Hardy's old poems, and no pride. He said to his wife Florence, just before his death, that he had done all that he meant to do, but did not know whether it had been worth doing.[6] Was that diminished pride the source of his calm at the end? The feeling, as he put it in a poem, that 'Nothing Matters Much'? Is that why, in the final poem of his *Collected Poems*, he resolved to say no more? Life and poetry ran down together, it seemed, and ended in silence—without continuance, and without regret.

Two old poets, at the close of life, regard their lives and their work, and think about worth. These are old thoughts, but they are not exclusively *poets'* thoughts: all old people must look back that way, in reflective self-assessment. Some readers must have noticed that that last point has hovered over this entire essay, that I haven't really been talking about Old Poets—or not only about Old Poets: I've been talking about Old Age. An unargued assumption all the way has been that poems chart life, or compose models of life lived, that poets can embody truth though they cannot know it (as Yeats said at the end). And that the poems of Old Poets (those capital letters again) may embody truths about old age, which we can learn. They say that age is a diminishment; that life empties then, as memory fills; that age is a time of loss (of friends, of powers, of hopes and expectations); and of self-judgement; and that death becomes a presence, like another person in the room. There is not much comfort in those truths; but then, we don't desire truth for its comfortableness, do we? We desire truth because that desire makes us human. We must know, and learn to live with what we know.

How to Be an Old Poet, then, is simply How to Be Old. Hardy and Yeats offer two possible ways, one modest, the other flamboyant, one accepting, the other opposing. Hardy put on old age like an old coat, and lived in it; it fitted him. Yeats made old age a set of gawdy theatrical costumes to *act* in. Two ways, nearly antithetical, of responding to and enduring what is both an unavoidable physiological fact and a state of mind. Is one way preferable to the other? I can see no objective way of answering that question: your own nature will answer it. But, the reader may say, surely I have leaned toward Yeats, and made him the hero of my essay; surely it is better to be a Wild Old Wicked Man than a Dead Man Held on End. If you think that, it may be because you have been seduced by Yeats's Old Man's Romanticism. For Yeats's old poems do have a high romantic style—'High Talk', he called it—and high romantic heroes, and grand settings and stage properties—the Sistine Chapel, the cathedral of Saint Sophia, the art of the Quattrocento. And great, defiant gestures: that, surely, is the way to be old.

Hardy's old poems have none of that: the talk is not high but plain, and there are no heroes and no works of art. Only life (and, occasionally, Life with a capital L), seen clearly through old eyes, as it is, as it has been. And spoken—not sung, not ranted—in a quiet, unclamorous voice. I want to end this essay with the sound of that old voice, as we hear it in an interesting sequence of Hardy's poems: 'For Life I Had Never Cared Greatly', from *Moments of Vision*; 'Epitaph', from *Late Lyrics*; and 'He Never Expected Much' and 'A Placid Man's Epitaph', both from the posthumous *Winter Words*. These are all poems of self-assessment that are also assessments of life itself: the old man not so much judging as defining his own existence in the world. Listen to them—both what they say, and the tone they say it in:

> For Life I had never cared greatly,
>   As worth a man's while;
>   Peradventures unsought,
>   Peradventures that finished in nought,
> Had kept me from youth and through manhood till lately
>   Unwon by its style.

> I never cared for Life: Life cared for me,
> And hence I owed it some fidelity.
> It now says, 'Cease; at length thou hast learnt to grind
> Sufficient toll for an unwilling mind,
> And I dismiss thee . . .
>   ('Epitaph')

And a stanza in which World addresses Hardy as a child:

> 'I do not promise overmuch,
>   Child; overmuch;
> Just neutral-tinted haps and such,'
>   You said to minds like mine.
> Wise warning for your credit's sake!
> Which I for one failed not to take,

> And hence could stem such strain and ache
>   As each year might assign.
>   ('He Never Expected Much')

And the last of his epitaphs:

> As for my life, I've led it
> With fair content and credit:
> It said: 'Take this.' I took it:
> Said: 'Leave.' And I forsook it.
> If I had done without it
> None would have cared about it,
> Or said: 'One has refused it
> Who might have meetly used it.'
>   ('A Placid Man's Epitaph')

These are all poems written in the last decade of a very old poet's life: if any poems are Seventh Age poems, these are. Consider what they express: the Old Poet themes of loss, diminishment and limitation. But not as an experience peculiar to the winding down of age; *all* existence is neutral-tinted, *any* action may come to nothing, any time. Yet there is no pain or bitterness in the poems; they share a calm serenity. They are solitary poems—one voice in emptiness, speaking to nobody; and yet three of them take the form of direct address—to Life, to World—as though in extreme old age, when loss has emptied his world, the Old Poet still has company, the company of All Existence, which speaks to him as honestly as he speaks to us. And speaks in imperatives, says: Take this. Leave that. Cease.

These poems are as consistent in their untroubled acceptance as Yeats's poems of crazy old people are in their wild defiance. Perhaps, like Yeats's, they are also mask-poems—a face to wear and a voice to speak with, in order that an old poet near his death might go on making poems, as Hardy did to the very end, to his death-bed. A way to face the Seventh Age of life as a poet, and as yourself.

How to be an Old Poet?—which, I have admitted, is really How to Be Old? Yeats and Hardy offer distinct responses to that question, but with some common factors. 'How to' suggests a set of instructions, like a recipe. It isn't, of course, that simple, but I think I can abstract a few general principles from their cases:

1.   Confront reality honestly: look into your glass.
2.   Don't turn away either from the past, which is long and full of failures, nor from the future, which will surely be brief.

3. Seek no consolations. To be honest, in old age, is to be unconsoled.

There is one more principle, and it is the most important.

4. Preserve the life of the imagination: feed it with memories and inventions; because imagination is life.

Which turns my proposition of a minute ago around: the answer to How to Be Old? is: Be an Old Poet.

NOTES

Quotations from Hardy's poems are taken from *The Complete Poetical Works of Thomas Hardy*, ed. Samuel Hynes (Oxford: Clarendon Press, 1982–95) 5 volumes. Quotations from Yeats's poems are taken from *The Collected Poems of W. B. Yeats* (London: Macmillan, 1950).

1. Introduction to *Thomas Hardy*, ed. Samuel Hynes (Oxford: Oxford University Press, 1984). The Oxford Authors series.

2. T. S. Eliot, 'Gerontion'; Robert Browning, 'Rabbi Ben Ezra'; Dylan Thomas, 'Do Not Go Gentle into that Good Night'.

3. Shakespeare, *As You Like It*, Act II, Sc. vii.

4. W. B. Yeats, 'The Tower'.

5. W. B. Yeats, 'Crazy Jane Talks with the Bishop'.

6. Thomas Hardy, *The Life and Work of Thomas Hardy*, ed. Michael Millgate (London: Macmillan, 1984) p. 478.

MICHAEL IRWIN

From Fascination to Listlessness: Hardy's Depiction of Love

I

The love which dominates Hardy's fiction is romantic or sexual. Other kinds of affection are featured, of course, but only in bit parts. The nature of his interest in this habitual theme is unusual—and perhaps unexpected in a writer famous for the creation of individualized characters. In relation to love, as to other aspects of human life, Hardy is concerned to generalize, to diagnose. He's constantly saying: 'This is what the thing called love is like. This is how it happens. Is it not strange? Why does it work like this? Why do these delights lead to these miseries?'

When Hardy is observing in this diagnostic spirit, his 'idiosyncrasy of regard', his tendency to see what other people don't, or to see familiar things from a different point of view, leads him to resort to a specialized personal vocabulary of key terms that come up again and again. Here is a selection of disparate examples: 'pulsation', 'organism', 'convergence', 'aspect', 'comer', 'flexuous', 'nerves', 'scan', 'indifference', 'morbid', 'vision', 'juxtaposition', 'irradiation'. A great deal can be learned about Hardy by an examination of his use of such terms, and by considering what it is in his view of life that makes him resort to them so *often*. 'Listlessness' and 'fascination' are words of this kind. In what follows I hope to use them as conceptual skeleton-keys to open up Hardy's ideas about love. I'll also be invoking, though less systematically, two or three of the other terms I've mentioned.

From *Reading Thomas Hardy*, edited by Charles P.C. Pettit, pp. 117–37. © 1998 by Michael Irwin.

Let me first, however, develop the point about Hardy's taste for asserting general positions. The habit is in evidence from the very start of his novelistic career:[1]

It has been said that men love with their eyes; women with their ears. (*Desperate Remedies*, Ch. 3.1)

It is an almost universal habit with people, when leaving a bank, to be carefully adjusting their pockets if they have been receiving money; if they have been paying it in, their hands swing laxly. (Ibid., Ch. 19.2)

... to have an unsexed judgment is as precious as to be an unsexed being is deplorable. (*The Hand of Ethelberta*, Ch. 8)

... in obedience to the usual law by which the emotion that takes the form of humour in country workmen becomes transmuted to irony among the same order in town. (Ibid., Ch. 26)

Not the lovers who part in passion, but the lovers who part in friendship, are those who most frequently part for ever. (Ibid., Ch. 37)

... darkness makes people truthful ... (*The Mayor of Casterbridge*, Ch. XVII)

Generalization being out of fashion I'd like to offer a paragraph or two in its defence. It is a mode that has suffered at the hands of the politically correct and has often been misrepresented in the process. Repeatedly it is pointed out that this or that general statement is a simplification. Well, yes, it would be: such is the nature of generalizations. They must be taken for what they are. In many workaday areas this doesn't seem to be too much of a problem. We may curse the BBC's meteorologists when it rains after they have said that it won't, but we don't stop listening to them. We accept the generalized status of the weather forecast. In this case, as in many others, the fallibility of the statement in question doesn't make it deceitful or pointless. Like all generalizations it should be judged in the light of context, scope and tone. Pope's warning that 'A little learning is a dangerous thing' is intended for potential critics: it isn't an argument against mass education. When Hardy says 'darkness makes people truthful' we know that he doesn't mean that it's impossible to lie at night. Typical responses to such statements should be: 'Is this broadly true?' or 'Is there something in it?' Often, as in this latter case, the claim is designed primarily to be suggestive. At a further stage the seeming generalization can be aphoristically provocative, as in Shaw's 'He who can, does. He who cannot, teaches.'

Hardy does on occasion deal specifically in this kind of aphorism, especially in passages of deliberately formalized comedy featured in *The Hand of Ethelberta*.[2] More basically he clearly assumes that there are observable common denominators in human psychology and conduct—as in the examples about darkness or one's deportment when leaving a bank. The assumption is intrinsic to his descriptive method, which regularly invites the reader to draw inferences: a man stands or moves in a particular way and is therefore (for example) unhappy or rebellious. Hardy likes to share with his readers his ability to observe, and the further ability to diagnose on the basis of the observation.

But he is aware of the limits of such diagnosis. A passage near the beginning of *Desperate Remedies* puts the case very fairly. Cytherea and Owen Graye have been left orphaned and destitute:

> There is in us an unquenchable expectation, which at the gloomiest time persists in inferring that because we are *ourselves*, there must be a special future in store for us, though our nature and antecedents to the remotest particular have been common to thousands. Thus to Cytherea and Owen Graye the question how their lives would end seemed the deepest of possible enigmas. To others who knew their position equally well with themselves the question was the easiest that could be asked—'Like those of other people similarly circumstanced!' (Ch. 1.5)

The tone is boldly confident, but in fact, in defiance of the prediction, the Grayes' future proves to be anything but typical. In no time at all they're involved in a maze of mystery, conspiracy and manslaughter. But equally Hardy knows, as he hints here and shows in comparable cases, that even the most orthodox life cannot seem merely 'typical' to the individual who leads it. We may inhabit generalizations, but we feel unique. Hardy's diagnosis of human behaviour typically acknowledges its own externality and allows for exceptions.

To return to my key-words: 'listlessness' and 'fascination' both figure in Hardy's first novel, *Desperate Remedies*, the former term frequently. A glance at some of the contexts in which it appears may suggest the coloration it has for Hardy:

... tracing listlessly with his eyes the red stripes upon her scarf ...
(Ch. 3.2)

Here she sat down by the open window ... and listlessly looked
down upon the brilliant pattern of colours formed by the flower-
beds on the lawn ... (Ch. 5.2)

... he listlessly observed the movements of a woman wearing a long
grey cloak ... (Ch. 9.3)

... his eyes listlessly tracing the pattern of the carpet. (Ch. 11.1)

... their eyes listlessly tracing some crack in the old walls, or
following the movement of a distant bough or bird ... (Ch. 12.8)

He listlessly regarded the illuminated blackness overhead ... (Ch.
15.2)

What this pattern of usage suggests is that, for Hardy, the word 'listless'
denotes an emptiness of mind, an absence of internal stimulus. The eyes
automatically seek an external one, but bring no inner resources to bear upon
it. In this frame of mind you 'idly trace', you see passively.

This mental inertia is a matter of common experience. But Hardy
also uses the word 'listless' in contexts in which feeling has been violently
numbed or confused. I'll give examples here, from *Far from the Madding Crowd*, which may serve to suggest how conscious, and consciously
expressed, is Hardy's interest in this extreme and peculiar state of mind. He
presents three parallel vignettes in which his main characters, Oak, Boldwood and Bathsheba, are shown in the heightened state of listlessness that
derives from shock. Each of the scenes takes place at dawn or daybreak,
and in the vicinity of a gate or broken fence, these factors hinting that the
life of the character concerned is about to enter a new phase—that this is a
turning point. In each case the scene which confronts him or her is in some
sense unnatural and forbidding, a metaphorical expression of the observer's
confused state of mind.

The first shows Gabriel Oak immediately after the discovery that his
whole flock of sheep has been destroyed:

Oak ... listlessly surveyed the scene. By the outer margin of the
pit was an oval pond, and over it hung the attenuated skeleton of
a chrome-yellow moon, which had only a few days to last—the

morning star dogging her on the left hand. The pool glittered like
a dead man's eye ... (Ch. V)

The second passage concerns Boldwood, in mental turmoil after receiving
Bathsheba's valentine. Having risen early he leans over a gate and looks
around:

> ... over the snowy down ... the only half of the sun yet visible
> burnt rayless, like a red and flameless fire shining over a white
> hearthstone. The whole effect resembled a sunset as childhood
> resembles age.
>   ... Over the west hung the wasting moon, now dull and
> greenish-yellow, like tarnished brass.
>   Boldwood was listlessly noting how the frost had hardened
> and glazed the surface of the snow till it shone in the red eastern
> light with the polish of marble ... (Ch. XIV)

After opening Fanny's coffin and being spurned by Troy, Bathsheba rushes
blindly out into the night. At random she goes through a gate into a spot
apparently reminiscent of the hollow in which Troy dazzled her with his
sword-play. At daybreak, when she comes to herself and looks about her, the
place seems very different:

> ... the general aspect of the swamp was malignant. From its moist
> and poisonous coat seemed to be exhaled the essences of evil things
> in the earth and in the waters under the earth. The fungi grew
> in all manner of positions from rotting leaves and tree stumps,
> some exhibiting to her listless gaze their clammy tops, others their
> oozing gills. (Ch. XLIV)

In each of these cases there might seem to be a contradiction between
the distortion and ugliness of what is seen and the reported listlessness,
or unresponsiveness, of the seer. But all three natural settings might have
looked quite different, even quite peaceful, to an untroubled observer. As I
implied earlier, the distortion is in effect a projection of appalled intensities
of feeling, and these intensities are so diverse as to cancel each other out
and produce the listless state. Hardy makes the point in describing Troy's
motionless stance over Fanny's coffin:

> So still he remained that he could be imagined to have left in him
> no motive power whatever. The clashes of feeling in all directions

confounded one another, produced a neutrality, and there was motion in none. (Ch. XLIII)

Thus for Hardy listlessness is likely to be found both before the beginning and after the end of a cycle of emotion. In the former phase it characteristically involves an appetite, a hunger, for the feeling which is absent. Eustacia and Mrs Charmond are chronically listless in consequence of an unfulfilled desire for passionate love. Another such character is Viviette in *Two on a Tower*, described by Tabitha Lark as 'eaten out with listlessness'. Hardy glosses the term a few pages later:

> The soft dark eyes ... were the natural indices of a warm and affectionate—perhaps slightly voluptuous—temperament, languishing for want of something to do, cherish, or suffer for. (Ch. III)

Each of the three women is roused from her languor by just the kind of romantic passion she has been craving. In each case the feeling experienced is described as 'fascination'.

Once again *Desperate Remedies* offers a convenient introduction to the term concerned. Its young heroine, Cytherea, has had a taste of the relevant emotion by the beginning of Chapter Three: 'A responsive love for Edward Springrove had made its appearance in Cytherea's bosom with all the fascinating attributes of a first experience ...' (Ch. 3.1). But she encounters it in more melodramatic fullness when meeting the daemonic Aeneas Manston for the first time. As she leaves him she thinks: 'O, how is it that man has so fascinated me?' (Ch. 8.4).

The episode that produces this reaction is suggestive of some of the factors that might be involved in 'fascination' as opposed to, say, 'interest' or 'attraction'. Not only is Manston physically handsome, he has a touch of diabolism about him, and has been playing the organ to her in an isolated and decaying Elizabethan manor house in the middle of a ferocious storm:

> The thunder, lightning, and rain had now increased to a terrific force. The clouds, from which darts, forks, zigzags, and balls of fire continually sprang, did not appear to be more than a hundred yards above their heads ...
>
> ... Cytherea, in spite of herself, was frightened, not only at the weather, but at the general unearthly weirdness which seemed to surround her there. (Ch. 8.4)

Perhaps it's hardly surprising that she sits 'spell-bound before him' and finds herself 'shrinking up beside him, and looking with parted lips at his face'. What seems to be involved is sexual attraction exaggerated by an element of shock to produce total imaginative absorption. The scene is typical of other episodes of 'fascination' in Hardy in that the effect produced is sudden, involuntary, and is achieved despite near-total ignorance of the individual found fascinating. It differs from many others in that elsewhere the dramatic external context, 'the general unearthly weirdness', can be absent, so that the fascination derives almost solely from the impassioned imaginings of the person who is fascinated.

That situation is at its diagrammatically clearest in the short story 'An Imaginative Woman', a case-study of fascination, in which the heroine, Ella Marchmill, never so much as meets the object of her adoration. She has to make do with his poems, his photograph and a few of his clothes—but her 'passionate curiosity' and 'subtle luxuriousness of fancy' do the rest. As nearly as may be she is made pregnant by the photograph. The feeling she unilaterally generates is strong enough to be the indirect cause of her eventual death.

Ella self-confessedly gets into 'a morbid state'. Her story is one of several in which Hardy suggests that passionate love, or something that seems very much akin to it, is a quasi-neurological phenomenon. In 'The Fiddler of the Reels' Car'line Aspent's 'fragile and responsive organization' makes her hypersensitive to the 'fascination' exercised by the music of Mop Ollamoor. At the climax of the story his playing reduces her to 'hysteric emotion' and convulsions. A similar vulnerability in Barbara, of the House of Grebe, is exploited by her sadistic second husband. Nightly, in bed, he invites her to stare at the statue of his predecessor, scrupulously mutilated to reproduce the terrible injuries he had suffered in a fire: ' . . . such was the strange fascination of the grisly exhibition that a morbid curiosity took possession of the Countess'. Against her will she does keep glancing at the hideous object until she is reduced to an epileptic fit. Each of the three stories is a caricature of the workings of love as displayed elsewhere in Hardy. Imaginative excitement preys upon a hypersensitive nervous system.

Various of the apparently more substantial relationships in Hardy's fiction start from reactions almost as hyperbolic. Dick Dewy has only to get a glimpse of Fancy Day's boot, and later of Fancy herself, with her hair down, illuminated in a window, to become a 'lost man'. De Stancy, in *A Laodicean*, is persuaded to spy on Paula Power taking exercise in her private gymnasium. The 'sportive fascination of her appearance' not only wins his heart forthwith, but causes him to abandon that same day his long-kept vow of teetotalism.

The paradigmatic case is probably that of Eustacia's infatuation with Clym in *The Return of the Native*. Though it is Book Third of the novel which is actually entitled 'The Fascination', the process has started well back in Book Second. Eustacia's attention is first attracted when she overhears a conversation about the newcomer by means of a chimney which functions as a sort of giant ear-trumpet:

> That five minutes of overhearing furnished Eustacia with visions enough to fill the whole blank afternoon. Such sudden alterations from mental vacuity do sometimes occur thus quietly. She could never have believed in the morning that her colourless inner world would before night become as animated as water under a microscope, and that without the arrival of a single visitor. (Book Second, Ch. I)

After spending 'the greater part of the afternoon . . . imagining the fascination which must attend a man come direct from beautiful Paris', she goes out at dusk to look at the house where he is to stay. She passes him in the darkness and, though she cannot see him, hears him say good-night. 'No event could have been more exciting':

> On such occasions as this a thousand ideas pass through a highly charged woman's head; and they indicate themselves on her face; but the changes, though actual, are minute. Eustacia's features went through a rhythmical succession of them. She glowed; remembering the mendacity of the imagination, she flagged; then she freshened; then she fired; then she cooled again. It was a cycle of aspects, produced by a cycle of visions. (Book Second, Ch. III)

That night she dreams of Clym, and the charm grows stronger. Hardy sums up her condition in a description to which I'll return—a description in which he again uses the word 'vision':

> The perfervid woman was by this time half in love with a vision. The fantastic nature of her passion, which lowered her as an intellect, raised her as a soul. (Book Second, Ch. III)

Truly a case of 'fascination': all these intensities are directed towards a man she has yet to set eyes on. When she does eventually come to see him, through pertinacious scheming, it is in unusual and heightened circumstances. As a newly slain Turkish soldier in the mummers' play, she has time and opportunity to study his face in detail through the ribbons that do duty for her visor. Later that night he does speak two casual sentences to her, but, as Hardy proceeds to explain, she scarcely needs this additional stimulus:

> She had undoubtedly begun to love him. She loved him partly because he was exceptional in this scene, partly because she had from the first instinctively determined to love him, chiefly because she was in desperate need of loving somebody. Believing that she must love him in spite of herself, she had been influenced after the fashion of the second Lord Lyttleton and other persons, who have dreamed that they were to die on a certain day, and by stress of a morbid imagination have actually brought about that event. Once let a maiden admit the possibility of her being stricken with love for some one at some hour or place, and the thing is as good as done. (Book Second, Ch. VI)

If *The Return of the Native* were the only Hardy novel you'd read you might linger on such a passage as this and think that, as in the short stories I've mentioned, he was exploring what he takes to be an aberrant emotional condition. The emphasis on Eustacia's lack of rational motive and the reference to 'morbid imagination' would certainly seem to convey such a suggestion. But comparison with other works shows that for Hardy this is what romantic love, in general, is *like*. This, he is claiming, is how 'fascination' works.

Regrettable as it might well appear, Hardy's views seem to be fairly summed up by the dubious Fitzpiers:

> Human love is a subjective thing ... it is joy accompanied by an idea which we project against any suitable object in the line of our vision ...
> ... I am in love with something in my own head, and no thing-in-itself outside it at all. (*The Woodlanders*, Ch. XVI)

Hardy displays this phenomenon again and again. 'Falling in love', the great antidote to listlessness, is shown to be a delusive process based on a subjective dream, a 'vision'. When the fascination gives way to reality, as eventually it must, listlessness sets in once more. Bathsheba is already talking 'listlessly' when she returns from Bath after her marriage. Angel Clare is listless on his wedding night.

The subjectivity of love is emphasized nowhere more strongly than in Hardy's later novels. Angel's emotional processes are sufficiently close to those of Fitzpiers for him to be able to say, truthfully, to Tess: 'the woman I have been loving is not you'. *The Well-Beloved* is exclusively a meditation on this very theme. Pierston, the main character, falls passionately in love with a series of women, over a period of forty years, including Avice Caro, her daughter and her grand-daughter. These fits of infatuation begin and end randomly. Nothing the unfortunate woman concerned says or does would seem to have any significant influence on the arousal, the prolongation or the termination of the feeling. The status of this parable is left uncertain, in the sense that it isn't clear how representative a figure Pierston is supposed to be. Although Hardy calls his novel 'a fanciful exhibition of the artistic nature' he also suggests in his Preface that the 'delicate dream' concerned 'is more or less common to all men'.

Two parenthetical comments may be made about *The Well-Beloved* by way of emphasizing the singularity of Hardy's views on love. Despite scattered references to Shelley, to Plato, to the Ideal or ethereal, Hardy never implies that the infatuated one might be content with worshipping from afar. Courtly love is never felt to be an option: the vision must be pursued in physical terms. If you are smitten you should go in and try to win. On the other hand there is no suggestion that the feeling concerned is appeased or extinguished by sexual conquest: Pierston is no Don Juan. The love Hardy writes about certainly involves sexual desire, but it is never simply a transcription of that desire. Fascination isn't lust in a fanciful package. The balance of needs is clearly displayed again in *Jude the Obscure*. For Jude, Sue is at first 'more or less an ideal character, about whose form he began to weave curious and fantastic daydreams'. In time, however, he also needs to make love with her in physical terms. Yet the fact that he eventually succeeds in this aim does nothing to diminish his devotion to her.

If I might risk a generalization of my own: I suppose most of us hope that the solipsistic aspect of 'falling in love' can be interfused with, and actually strengthened by, a growing sense of the 'objective' individuality of the loved one. What can seem unnerving in Hardy is the exclusivity of his concentration on the subjective element or phase. Noticeably absent from his work is that substantial aspect of real-life love-affairs which consists of *getting to know* the other person. Hardy's tendency is bluntly to disregard it. In *The Return of the Native* eleven chapters span the time between the conversation Eustacia hears down the chimney and what seems to be the possible beginning of Clym's courtship. The two are still on surname terms. The next chapter describes a lovers' rendezvous:

> 'My Eustacia.'
> 'Clym dearest.'
> Such a situation had less than three months brought forth.
> (Book Third, Ch. IV)

With one bound Clym has been trapped. The getting-to-know phase is similarly elided in *The Woodlanders* after Grace and Fitzpiers have become acquainted: 'There never was a particular moment at which it could be said they became friends; yet a delicate understanding now existed between two who in the winter had been strangers' (Ch. XIX). The social aspect of the relationship is left unimaginable. Perhaps Giles actually errs in trying to provide a social context for his courtship by holding a party for Grace. The project would probably have been doomed even with a less disastrous guest-list. Love, in Hardy's fiction, tends to stay hermetically sealed, a private and obsessive involvement between two individuals who scarcely know one another in the normal sense.

When I ask students to write about Hardy's view of love many of them notice the tendencies I've been sketching, and react uneasily. At twenty you don't want to believe that love might be no more than the passionate infatuations which Hardy describes. They look for an escape route, and almost always find the same one—an account of the eventual relationship between Oak and Bathsheba:

> Theirs was that substantial affection which arises . . . when the two who are thrown together begin first by knowing the rougher sides of each other's character, and not the best till further on, the romance growing up in the interstices of a mass of hard prosaic reality. This good-fellowship . . . is unfortunately seldom superadded to love between the sexes. . . . Where however happy circumstance permits its development the compounded feeling proves itself to be the only love which is strong as death—that love . . . beside which the passion usually called by the name is evanescent as steam. (*Far from the Madding Crowd*, Ch. LVI)

This, my students conclude, is the mature kind of love which Hardy 'really' espouses, the substantial love of a Gabriel Oak rather than the evanescent love of a Troy. It may be a consoling conclusion, but it overlooks some significant factors. One is an incidental comment in the penultimate paragraph of the novel: ' . . . Bathsheba smiled, for she never laughed readily now'. Another consideration is that *Far from the Madding Crowd* is an early work. It isn't easy to find comparable accounts of a seasoned relationship in Hardy's later novels. The love he is to portray again and again has much more to do with passion than with camaraderie.

But those seeking the escape route have good reason to do so. Here is a major author apparently arguing that romantic love is mere fantasy, self-defeating and short-lived. There would seem to be a depressing logic in

Hardy's position: intensity of feeling is an index of the furious imaginative energy that has gone into the creation of a 'vision'. The exposure of its unreality will bring an equivalent intensity of listless disappointment.

Hardy exaggerates the painful aspects of this process by isolating it from what, in real life, are usually considered mollifying consequences of fading passion. Child-rearing is typically the emotional or psychological parachute that permits a sufficiently gentle descent from the giddy heights of romantic love. Childless himself, Hardy denies his characters children. The birth-rate in his Wessex is generally pitiful. Some of his heroines perish too soon, some remain single, some die in childbirth. Little Time's Malthusian measures are almost predictable: he is rectifying an anomaly. The Fawley children are in danger of outnumbering those produced by the protagonists of all the other Wessex novels put together.

A prior point is that even weddings feature only irregularly and glumly. Several are aborted at the last minute, through misunderstandings or changes of heart. Those of Viviette, Cytherea and Ethelberta are desperate and loveless proceedings. Pierston eventually marries in his sixties, his rheumatic wife being brought to the church in a wheelchair. Hardy's habitual topic is the rising of the rocket of love: marriage is the stick hitting the ground.

II

At this point the argument forks. One of the alternative roads has been clearly sign-posted by a number of recent critics of Hardy. Progress along it would involve making points of approximately the following kind. Hardy's exclusive absorption in the excitements of romantic and sexual liaison is symptomatic of his essential immaturity—an immaturity he himself acknowledges in the Life.[3] He shows a morbid over-sensitivity to the symptoms of physical ageing, especially in the case of women. His novels are full of unhealthy sexual manifestations—voyeurism, fetishism, masochism masquerading as stoicism. This obsessiveness is all of a piece with the adolescent sexual susceptibility he retained to an embarrassingly late age and to his notorious estrangement from his first wife. He returns again and again to the shallow drama of flirtation and titillation, being incapable of portraying the kind of controlled, reciprocal love that he never experienced.

And so it would be possible to go on. This is a comfortable road, smooth-surfaced and much travelled—but I don't care to take it because I think it leads away from Hardy's actual writings and arrives nowhere very interesting. There is a further consideration: it would seem that many literary commentators are at home on that route for reasons of personal moral taste. They feel able to assume that a controlled, balanced view of romantic passion is available to all right-thinking and intelligent people. A comment such as 'she was in desperate need of loving somebody' would seem to mean little to them. It thus becomes a matter of easy confidence to award any author marks out of ten for maturity of sexual outlook, whether in art or life. I don't share this frame of mind. In fact one of the things I most value in Hardy is the way he grapples with the problems posed by the elusiveness, capriciousness and uncontrollability of love and desire. So I will take the other fork in the argument, which requires an attempt to empathize with Hardy's views.

Certainly his presentation of love poses difficult questions. If the account I've given is fair he would seem to allow virtually no middle ground between the listlessness or disengagement which leaves one less than fully alive, and the nervous excitability of deluded infatuation. Is he implying that it is actually impossible to 'fall in love' reasonably and justifiably? Intermittently he seems to suggest that there could be such a phenomenon as the right person, the right 'comer'. Could there? If Angel Clare had danced with Tess the first time he set eyes on her, if Bathsheba had accepted Gabriel Oak's initial proposal, if Farfrae had married Elizabeth-Jane before Lucetta appeared on the scene . . . Certainly things might still have gone wrong, but they would have gone wrong *differently*. Why does Hardy never tell that kind of story?

Then, for so convinced a Darwinian, he seems oddly oblivious to the evolutionary implications of his views on love. Repeatedly, and in the very grain of his descriptions, he shows that human beings are subject to the energies that dominate the animal and vegetable world. It might have been expected, then, that simple sexual appetite would loom large as a motive in his fiction. Fitzpiers does a little in this line, and Alec d'Urberville does more, but they are atypical. The love Hardy depicts is controlled by ideas, and even derives from them. Fascination, not lust, is the great driving force. What evolutionary hope can there be for a species spurred to breed by baseless fantasies and agitation of the nerves?

But I want to leave these queries suspended and attempt a defence, even a celebration, of Hardy's views on love. It entails looking at them from a vantage-point rather different from any adopted so far in this essay. My key terms, 'fascination' and 'listlessness', offer a possible starting point. Though Hardy uses them so often in relation to love they relate to a deeper dialectic in his work—a dialectic much analysed and discussed by critics. On the one hand he repeatedly refers to the unimaginable scale and antiquity of the universe we inhabit, in comparison with which the individual human being is an unnoticeable speck. On the other hand he regularly reminds us that each of these specks has an intelligence—perhaps the only intelligence—that apprehends the universe, and a passionate and unique inner life. When the emphasis is on the former consideration the human figure is reduced, as are Cytherea and Tess, to a depressed sense of being negligible—'one of a long row only'—a sense that conduces to listlessness. When the emphasis is on the latter there is a sudden surge of vitality, a revived feeling of uniqueness—very much the reactions associated with 'fascination'.

One of Hardy's recurring images offers both alternatives, both views of life, simultaneously. It is the image of a living creature suddenly illuminated in darkness:

> As Eustacia crossed the fire-beams she appeared for an instant as distinct as a figure in a phantasmagoria—a creature of light surrounded by an area of darkness: the moment passed, and she was absorbed in night again. (*The Return of the Native*, Book Fifth, Ch. VII)

> Gnats, knowing nothing of their brief glorification, wandered across the shimmer of this pathway, irradiated as if they bore fire within them; then passed out of its line, and were quite extinct. (*Tess of the d'Urbervilles*, Ch. XXXII)

In Hardyesque terms an unhappy man seeing these sights or reading these descriptions would feel the oppressive force of darkness, brevity, extinction. A happy man would respond to the irradiation, the glorification that serves as a metaphor for the vividness of the individual existence.

In these instances, as in countless others, the light is a literal one. But frequently it is figurative—the light of love. Pierston watches the second Avice, 'for the moment an irradiated being, . . . : by the beams of his own infatuation

> " . . . robed in such exceeding glory
> That he beheld her not"' (*The Well-Beloved*, Part Second, Ch. 9).

Tess feels despair when, after her confession, she realizes that Clare now sees her 'without irradiation . . . in all her bareness'.

Admittedly 'irradiation', or something very like it, can be achieved by more mundane means, such as conviviality and drink. Mrs Durbeyfield finds that, at Rolliver's, 'A sort of halo, an occidental glow' comes over life. Hardy says something rather similar, in the succeeding chapter, about Mr Durbeyfield and his fellow-drinkers:

> The stage of mental comfort to which they had arrived at this hour was one wherein their souls expanded beyond their skins, and spread their personalities warmly through the room. In

this process the chamber and its furniture grew more and more dignified and luxurious, the shawl hanging at the window took upon itself the richness of tapestry, the brass handles of the chest of drawers were as golden knockers, and the carved bedposts seemed to have some kinship with the magnificent pillars of Solomon's temple. (Ch. IV)

The irony in the passage modifies the transformations described, but doesn't annul them; ' . . . their souls expanded beyond their skins . . . ': the experience falls well short of the 'exaltation' that Tess achieves through love, or through gazing at a star, but it's a step in that direction. Hardy pursues the theme with greater intensity when describing the tipsy dancers walking home from Chaseborough:

> . . . however terrestrial and lumpy their appearance just now to the mean unglamoured eye, to themselves the case was different. They followed the road with a sensation that they were soaring along in a supporting medium, possessed of original and profound thoughts; themselves and surrounding nature forming an organism of which all the parts harmoniously and joyously interpenetrated each other. They were as sublime as the moon and stars above them; and the moon and stars were as ardent as they. (Ch. X)

'Terrestrial and lumpy' / 'sublime as the moon and stars': the polarities are those of listlessness and fascination. The ambivalence in the description of these revellers is structural; not incidental. Hardy is further developing a theme central to *Tess of the d'Urbervilles*: the process of falling in love will be shown to be similarly transformative. Angel Clare sees Tess as Artemis or Demeter; Tess is spiritually transformed by the sound of a second-hand harp only passably well played. Love resembles drunkenness in that it makes one see and hear things differently, feel more richly alive.

As a novelist Hardy can easily be misread because he modulates so effortlessly and unpredictably between realism and modernism. The critics least responsive to him are those unable to go beyond the literal reading. A little earlier I described Eustacia's early contacts with Clym in roughly such terms: an overheard conversation, a muttered good-night, a first sight of his face and she was already 'in love'. From a common-sense perspective, how absurdly precipitate. But Hardy isn't simply telling a particular story—he is showing what falling in love is *like*. We snatch glimpses, hear voices, make guesses, over-interpret, see things in dreams. The relevant section of *The Return of the Native* isn't simply a narrative that shows Eustacia succumbing to infatuation: it's an *expression* of that infatuation. To read it for the story alone is to extract a skeleton.

There's a comparison here with Shakespeare's comedies, which clearly had great influence on Hardy. In those plays the extravagances of plot become a means of suggesting the extravagances of romantic feeling. The suggestion is that love, at least among the young, produces behaviour so confused that it's *as though* they'd swallowed a magic potion, or come to question their own gender, or had fallen in love with identical twins. The same 'as though' is constantly operative in Hardy's fiction, making narrative simultaneously metaphor. The effect can be anywhere along the spectrum from comic to melodramatic. It's a commonplace that when one is infatuated one sees reminders of the beloved one everywhere. Hardy burlesques the idea in *Desperate Remedies* when Cytherea becomes aware that her lover's initials are branded on the buttocks of all the sheep in the vicinity of Knapwater House. An energetic lover may break through the reserve of a reluctant girl. *The Trumpet-Major* images such an irruption when Bob Loveday literally cuts through the partition-wall that separates him from Anne Garland. More grandiosely, in *A Pair of Blue Eyes* Hardy proposes an answer to the question 'What does it feel like to fall unexpectedly in love for the first time in your mid-thirties?' It feels something like hanging from the face of a high cliff in a powerful wind with a huge drop below your feet, with heavy rain falling upwards and a dark sea waiting to swallow you if you lose your grip.

In scenes which work something like that one—and Hardy's fiction is full of them—the effect could be described as operatic. The peculiar beauty of opera is that it can make two things happen at once. A story is told in words and actions but emotion can be projected into a fourth dimension of music. The story tells you who the heroine falls in love with, and why. Her aria tells you what that love feels like, and makes you share the feeling. The duplicity of effect is so easily understood by audiences for anything from *Evita* to *La Traviata* that it tends to be taken for granted, and its complexity overlooked. One justification of the mode could be stated in the following terms: 'If this lonely courtesan could project the love in her heart, it would be with this kind of beauty and passion.' Another might be expressed something like this: 'All of us would wish to capture, or to re-capture, the intensities of love. This aria, in its context, will enable you to do so.' Violetta sings for all of us.

With regard to opera I'm talking (in general) about the transcription of feeling into melody. In Hardy's work, of course, the transcription is into metaphor. I think most lovers of Hardy read him, and re-read him, whether they know it or not, primarily for the 'arias', those potent, memorable scenes—subjective correlatives—which in many cases may seem extraneous to the narrative proper, but are means of projecting the emotions which that narrative has unleashed.

To recapitulate: I am saying that Hardy's presentation of love is wonderfully adept at making us experience, or remember, the transforming power of passion; and I am arguing that he values this sensation as a type of the joy that can transform, 'irradiate', a dulled life of diurnal habituation and make us feel to the full the singularity of our separate existences. But in asserting this position I may seem to have drifted a fair way from my comments on Hardy's desire to anatomize, to diagnose. After all, he does again and again attribute the exalted sensations I'm talking about to self-delusion or 'morbid imagination', and in so doing he might well be said to be importing the literal view for which I've expressed a distaste. Is not the romantic love he brings to poetic life delusive or immature, however good it makes the lover feel? Isn't it—as he might be thought to imply in Tess—akin to mere drunkenness?

I conclude by offering two possible answers to these questions. The first is a summary 'yes'—but it's followed by (colon) 'but so what?' If you read the 'Digression on Madness' in Swift's *A Tale of a Tub*, you find that you are dialectically manoeuvred towards a conclusion that proffers alternative attitudes to life: you can be a Knave among Fools or a Fool among Knaves. The former is smarter than his fellows in being constantly aware, unlike the complacent Fools, of the essential animality of human existence. The price paid is cynicism and self-loathing. The Fool among Knaves, blind to this truth, is content with surfaces, happy because 'well-deceived'. Swift clearly presents these alternatives as a deliberate Hobson's Choice: heads you lose, tails you also lose.

At the risk of further simplifying what has already had to be a simplified summary I suggest that Hardy's position on love functions rather similarly. Fired with love you can be, at least for a short time, an optimist among pessimists, living in an irradiated world. Alternatively your head may point out that this transfiguration is merely the product of emotional need compounded with self-deception and over-heated imaginings. You can become a pessimist among optimists. But Hardy, I feel, differs from Swift in NOT making the alternatives a Hobson's Choice. His bleak honesty may repeatedly record his awareness that romantic love is largely, perhaps wholly, a matter of delusion. But always his heart, his imagination, his prose are saying 'Go for it, anyway: follow the instinct for joy.' He's in good company. Shakespeare continually describes love in terms of madness. Specifically he likens the lover to a lunatic in terms of capacity for delusion. But none of his comedies recommends that we take the cure.

My second answer is more complicated, and goes back to one of Hardy's comments on Eustacia, quoted earlier: 'her passion, which lowered her as an intellect, raised her as a soul'. What does he mean? How can something both lower you as an intellect and raise you as a soul? What 'lowers' is obvious: it's the fantastical, irrational nature of the feeling concerned. But how does the 'raising' come about?

I think, in the following way—which, incidentally, differentiates its 'irradiations' from those produced by drink. Love may be delusory for the reason given by Fitzpiers, in that it springs not from the character of the loved one, who is only uncertainly perceived, but from the character of the lover. But nevertheless there can be a richness in that love, derived not from its object but from its sources. What is quickened in the lover goes far beyond petty egotism: diverse perceptions and imaginings are fired and fused into transcendent feeling. This is the process which may be said to 'raise' the soul: your *being* is brought to life.

I haven't scope here to develop the point: I have space only for a single illustration of it, which happens to consist of one of my favourite passages in Hardy's fiction, the account of Avice Caro's funeral, as seen by Jocelyn Pierston:

> The level line of the sea horizon rose above the surface of the isle, a ruffled patch in mid-distance as usual marking the Race.... Against the stretch of water, where a school of mackerel twinkled in the afternoon light, was defined, in addition to the distant lighthouse, a church with its tower, standing about a quarter of a mile off, near the edge of the cliff. The churchyard gravestones could be seen in profile against the same vast spread of watery babble and unrest.
>
> Among the graves moved the form of a man clothed in a white sheet, which the wind blew and flapped coldly every now and then. Near him moved six men bearing a long box, and two or three persons in black followed. The coffin, with its twelve legs, crawled across the isle, while around and beneath it the flashing lights from the sea and the school of mackerel were reflected; a fishing-boat, far out in the Channel, being momentarily discernible under the coffin also. (*The Well-Beloved*, Part Second, Ch. 3)

It might seem reasonable to put questions such as: Why doesn't Hardy let Pierston arrive at the funeral on time and mourn properly? What has this overcrowded, hyperactive landscape-description to do with Pierston's love for Avice? The answer to the latter question, and the indirect answer to the former, is 'everything'. Pierston has never adequately recognized the individuality of Avice—he would be the first to admit to that charge—but his feeling for her has none the less been powerful: a concatenation of his responses to the rocks, the sea, the movement, the light, the life of the island that had shaped both of them. The complex poetic vitality of the passage is an index to the complex nature of an emotion which may have been irrational and subjective but was remote from empty fancy or casual sexual desire.

If I had to summarize the Hardyesque views that I have been trying to analyse, it would be in something like the following terms. However confused and deceiving its origins, however uncertain its subsequent course, love can irradiate, can quicken and heighten and poetically cross-relate our responses to everything around us. In illustrating the process so feelingly in his work Hardy enforces his point by conveying the very tang of enhanced vitality. To read his accounts of love literally and censoriously, with a 'mean unglamoured eye', is scarcely to read them at all.

Notes

1. Quotations from *Desperate Remedies, The Hand of Ethelberta* and *A Group of Noble Dames* are taken from Macmillan's New Wessex Edition (London: Macmillan, 1974–7). Quotations from Hardy's other novels and short stories come from The World's Classics Edition (Oxford: Oxford University Press, 1985–93). Chapter references for quotations are given in parentheses in the text.

2. See, for example, Chapter Six.

3. 'I was a child till I was 16, a youth till I was 25; a young man till I was 40 or 50.' Thomas Hardy, *The Life and Work of Thomas Hardy*, ed. Michael Millgate (London: Macmillan Press, 1984) p. 408.

DOUGLAS DUNN

Thomas Hardy's Narrative Art:
The Poems and Short Stories

Hardy was such a productive writer that I can hardly hope to do full
and proper justice to my subject. *The Complete Stories*,[1] in Professor Page's
edition, runs to some 839 pages of text, or about 50 tales, and I don't need
to emphasise Hardy's plurality of poems. It's best summed up for me by
Christopher Ricks in his essay 'A Note on Hardy's "A Spellbound Palace"',
where he writes that, 'A friend of mine, when I recently presented him with
"A Spellbound Palace", said, with simple truth, "There's *always* another
Hardy poem"'.[2] There may even be a note of irritation in this constant
discovery of '*another* Hardy poem'. However, for those of us who can't get
enough of Hardy's poetry, the bottomlessness of *The Complete Poems* is a
delight and fascination rather than an annoyance. It's when you find yourself
having to write about them that the astonishing numerousness of his poems
becomes—not irritating, but humbling, and perhaps even baffling.

Although not the first of his published stories, 'The Three Strangers'[3]
is especially interesting in that it contains a poem, or, rather, a song, '*As sung
by* MR CHARLES CHARRINGTON *in the play of "The Three Wayfarers"*',
indicated beneath the title of 'The Stranger's Song' in *The Complete Poems*.[4] So,
this is a work that appeared in three ways. First, it was published as a tale in
Longman's Magazine in March 1883, and reprinted in *Wessex Tales* (1888). At
the suggestion of J. M. Barrie it was made into a one-act play and performed

From *The Achievement of Thomas Hardy*, edited by Phillip Mallett, pp. 137–54. © 2000 by
Macmillan Press Limited.

for a brief period at the Terry Theatre in London in 1893. Then the lyric parts of an otherwise balladic prose narrative appeared in *Wessex Poems*. While the presence of the song is in itself effective as a narrative device—through it Hardy reveals the second stranger at the Fennels' christening party as a hangman—its impact and effectiveness are increased by the delays in its distribution of episodes and revelations. Hardy was too traditional a storyteller, too much in tune with the people about whom and for whom he was writing, to permit the song to be sung all at once. Instead, the narrative insists on purposeful postponements and surprises. Here, though, is the song.

THE STRANGER'S SONG

(As sung by MR CHARLES CHARRINGTON in the play of 'The Three Wayfarers')

O my trade it is the rarest one,
   Simple shepherds all—
  My trade it is a sight to see;
For my customers I tie, and take 'em up on high,
  And waft 'em to a far countree!

My tools are but the common ones,
   Simple shepherds all—
  My tools are no sight to see:
A little hempen string, and a post whereon to swing
  Are implements enough for me!

Tomorrow is my working day,
   Simple shepherds all—
  Tomorrow is a working day for me:
For the farmer's sheep is slain, and the lad who did it ta'en,
  And on his soul may God ha' mer-cy!

It is artfully contrived as entirely appropriate for the mouth of who sings it in the story, and for the inhabitants of a remote and rural farm who listen to it; all the cleverness in the world would fail to achieve that naturalness without there being present in the writer a familiarity and loyalty to place and community so confirmed as to function at the level of instinct. And that's what I mean when I claim that Hardy was a traditional storyteller. In his essay 'The Storyteller', first published in 1936 as an introduction to a collection of the Russian writer, Leskov, Walter Benjamin found it possible to say: 'Familiar though his name may be to us, the storyteller in his living immediacy is by no means a present force. He has already become something remote from us and something that is getting even more distant.' A few pages later he becomes more pessimistic. 'The art of storytelling', he writes, 'is reaching its end because the epic side of truth, wisdom, is dying out.' And he continues:

> This, however, is a process that has been going on for a long time. And nothing would be more fatuous than to want to see in it merely a 'symptom of decay', let alone a 'modern' symptom. It is, rather, only a concomitant symptom of the secular productive forces of history, a concomitant that has quite gradually removed narrative from the realm of living speech and at the same time is making it possible to see a new beauty in what is vanishing.[5]

It seems to me that in his earlier stories Hardy is very aware of 'the realm of living speech', and of 'the epic side of truth, wisdom'. He asserts his authority as a storyteller of that place, although looking backwards in time, through the use of dialect, but especially through the kind of narrative he is writing. It has the symmetry and inevitability of ballad—three strangers, three knockings on the door, the discovery that the second arrival is the hangman, the false assumption that the third is an escaped prisoner, and the surprise that it is the first stranger who is the escaped prisoner awaiting execution in Casterbridge jail and that the third stranger is, in fact, the brother of the first. The crime was sheep-stealing, so the story also carries, although lightly, a burden of social comment. Much of that authority is conveyed by phrasemaking and descriptive touches in the writing. But while it is 'living speech' in the sense that it is closely in touch with the community it evokes, Hardy's prose outside of dialogue is more written than spoken, or to use terms coined apparently by critics of African-American writing, more writerly than speakerly. Consider this extract, for example, where the first stranger is introduced, but some time before he enters Higher Crowstairs, so that the reader sees him before the Fennels and their friends:

> It was nearly the time of the full moon, and on this account, though the sky was lined with a uniform sheet of dripping cloud, ordinary objects out of doors were readily visible. The sad wan light revealed the lonely pedestrian to be a man of supple frame; his gait suggested that he had somewhat passed the period of perfect and instinctive agility, though not so far as to be otherwise than rapid of motion when occasion required. At a rough guess he might have been about

forty years of age. He appeared tall, but a recruiting sergeant, or
other person accustomed to the judging of men's heights by the eye,
would have discerned that this was chiefly owing to his gauntness,
and that he was not more than five-feet-eight or nine.

Notwithstanding the regularity of his tread there was caution
in it, as in that of one who mentally feels his way; and despite the
fact that it was not a black coat nor a dark garment of any sort that
he wore, there was something about him which suggested that he
naturally belonged to the black-coated tribes of men. His clothes
were of fustian, and his boots hobnailed, yet in his progress he
showed not the mud-accustomed bearing of hobnailed and fustian peasantry.[6]

Hardy's prose here is wonderfully measured, and although we haven't yet met
the hangman, the one who turns out to be the escaped prisoner is described
as if *he* were the executioner. At the same time Hardy comes close to giving the game away. If the reader remembers that passage I've just quoted,
then, along with other clues—he's a pipe-smoker, but doesn't have a pipe or
tobacco, for example—as soon as the mead-swilling hangman reveals who
he is, a slightly confused or agitated atmosphere of suspicion surely arises.

But the skill of that passage, and the story's date (late 1870s, early 1880s)
should remind us that Hardy had been a professional novelist for around
ten years, even if *The Mayor of Casterbridge, Jude the Obscure* and *Tess of the
d'Urbervilles* were still to come. My point is that for Hardy the short story
was not the site of apprentice work as it has been for many more modern
writers (or as it was for R. L. Stevenson, for example, in Hardy's younger lifetime). Indeed, unless you take seriously such antics as sound poetry, concrete
poetry, cyberpoetry, and so on, then the literary short story is the newest of
literary forms. Sir Walter Scott's 'The Two Drovers' is credited with being
the first, but that forgets Pushkin, although Pushkin was much influenced by
Scott's narrative poems and novels. The form had been in existence for only
60 or so years when Hardy wrote 'The Three Strangers'. Its development in
Europe and America was of course stimulated by the demands of a market
in the form of the magazines from which writers like R. L. Stevenson and
Hardy made much of their livelihood. Even more important, though, is that
the short story in a sense had *always* existed except that it was expressed
in verse, the chief medium of literature until the mid-to-late seventeenth
century. I know of eighteenth-century chapbooks by Dugald Graham, the
'Skellit Bellman' of Glasgow—the Glasgow town-crier—and they are short
prose tales, crudely written, but interesting enough for all that. There must be
lots more from other parts of the island, waiting for a brass-bowelled scholar

immune to book-dust to sift through and make a claim for the earlier, non-literary origins of the prose tale as a written form designed to be appropriated by the purchaser probably for spoken performance and adaptation.

Hardy came to the short story after considerable experience as a novelist and as a poet. This may not strike us as in any way remarkable, but there is at least one sense in which it is. 'What differentiates the novel from all other forms of prose literature', Walter Benjamin wrote in the essay from which I have already quoted,

> —the fairy tale, the legend, even the novella—is that it neither comes from oral tradition nor goes into it. This distinguishes it from storytelling in particular. The storyteller takes what he tells from experience—his own or that reported by others. And he in turn makes it the experience of those who are listening to his tale. The novelist has isolated himself. The birthplace of the novel is the solitary individual, who is no longer able to express himself by giving examples of his most important concerns, is himself uncounseled, and cannot counsel others.[7]

'Oral tradition' is quite clearly foregrounded in many of Hardy's stories. For example, the very last sentence of 'The Three Strangers' reads: 'But the arrival of the three strangers at the shepherd's that night, and the details connected therewith, is a story as well known as ever in the country about Higher Crowstairs.' And I feel convinced that Hardy really enjoyed the resonance of that sentence. Above all, he enjoyed forging that link, whether through invention or re-telling, with 'a story as well known as ever'. Indeed, one of the most fascinating aspects of Hardy's writing as a whole is his status as a 'tradition-carrier', as they say of traditional singers and storytellers in Scotland and Ireland, especially in Gaelic culture and the balladists of the travellers. Written literature, the expression of High Culture, has much room for tradition-carriers too, for chroniclers of place and community. Similarly, at the end of 'The Melancholy Hussar of the German Legion',[8] Hardy concludes with a nod to 'the epic side of truth, wisdom', to the invaluableness of communal epic, when he writes: 'The older villagers, however, who know of the episode from their parents, still recollect the place where the soldiers lie. Phyllis lies near.'[9] Also, it is Phyllis, cruelly thwarted in love, who has told the story to the narrator, presumably when she was very old and the narrator very young, a feature of Hardy's earlier tales shared by J. M. Barrie's of the 1880s which were founded on stories told to him by his mother. But the short story has always been much involved with memory. Part of its business has been the chronicles of the tribe, from Scott's 'The Two Drovers',

James Hogg's and John Galt's stories, Hawthorne's, Turgenev's, Chekhov's, or Sherwood Anderson's *Winesburg, Ohio*, William Faulkner's stories, Dylan Thomas's early stories of the Jarvis Valley (and also *Portrait of the Artist as a Young Dog*), and through to some more recent writers.

John Bayley once described poems by Hardy—he mentions 'The Frozen Greenhouse'—as 'sung short stories'. (Incidentally, I've quoted his delightful phrase so often that it's high time I sent Professor Bayley an acknowledgement.) While it can apply to a great many of Hardy's poems, though far from all, it makes especial sense when thinking about such poems as 'A Trampwoman's Tragedy', which like his poems of Wessex traditions and memories from far back, stems from the same source as his stories and fiction in general.

As storytelling, 'A Trampwoman's Tragedy' is masterly in its unfolding of one of Hardy's habitual concerns—mistakes in love and their consequences. There would seem to be little more to be said. Reading Hardy's notes to the poem (dated April 1902) suggests that it could be an example of his archaeological imagination playing over recollections of local materials and family memories. Blue Jimmy in the tenth stanza is said to have stolen a horse belonging to a neighbour of Hardy's grandfather. Any memory at all can result in a poem, but this particular memory seems a bit unimportant, although perhaps not to a writer like Hardy with his fascination for memories and for hangings. It's a haunted poem, with a haunting in it. Strangely, too, it permits Hardy to use balladic speech to an extent that he could never quite get into the narrative parts of his stories. He had too much prose experience for that to be entirely possible in his tales where his best touches are literary and outside the linguistic scope of the oral tradition from which his stories emerged. In 'The Withered Arm',[10] for example, he writes of Mrs Lodge's face being as pale as Rhoda Brook's seen against 'the sad dun shades of the upland's garniture'. A little later we're told that 'a story was whispered about the many-dairied lowland that winter'. Diction and phrasings of that kind would have been inappropriate to the tramp-woman. But Hardy's notes also add to the poem. In its final sentence, for example, the location of Ilchester jail is said to be 'now an innocent-looking green meadow'. It adds considerably to the poem's effect. For one thing, it returns the reader to the present. As a result 'A Trampwoman's Tragedy', as well as being spoken by an underdog, one of those marginalised beings which the short story especially seems drawn to represent, leaves the reader—or this reader—with the sense of a curiously farsighted glimpse of that rugged, wilder past which Hardy was determined should not be forgotten. Even in the movement of the verse he seems doggedly obedient to what was current long before and which he seems to be asserting as tuneful and authentic. But his meaning is a contemporary one—the power of jealousy, and the reckoning that will have to be paid when its passion overwhelms reason.

If 'A Trampwoman's Tragedy' is a bold and brave poem in its encounter with the past, then the same can be said of 'The Withered Arm'. Unlike Stevenson, whose fondness for the supernatural was overdone, Hardy's tale hinges more on the impact of thoughts on another person, the intuitive transfer of hurt or disfigurement inflicted against the conscious wishes of the inflicter. It suggests dream as an active intermediary in human affairs. Rhoda Brook's vision of a withered arm materialises in Gertrude Lodge, who has just married the father of Rhoda's illegitimate son. There is something uncanny about Hardy's storytelling skill. 'Yes, mother,' said the boy. 'Is father married then?' In contemporary short fiction it is extremely difficult to get away with a sentence like this: 'Half a dozen years passed away, and Mr and Mrs Lodge's married experience sank into prosiness, and worse.' That is 'telling', not 'showing', and very unfashionable. However, the tale in Victorian times enjoyed a greater spaciousness of timescale than is nowadays preferred, just as a 'short' story then could be a great deal longer than is now the case, due to the generosity of page-space granted by magazines in response to what readers desired and expected. But even with such spaciousness at his command, there are some tricky moments in the narrative of 'The Withered Arm', where Hardy must have felt obliged to be both delicate and brief. After Rhoda and her son have left, due to the unbearable disclosure by Conjuror Trendle that Gertrude's withered arm has been inflicted by the power of an enemy, namely Rhoda, although it is not intentional, the childless Lodges are given this exchange followed by Hardy's necessary explanation. (And if there's one thing that story-writers detest, it's being obliged to explain.)

> 'Damned if you won't poison yourself with these apothecary messes and witch mixtures some time or other,' said her husband, when his eyes chanced to fall upon the multitudinous array.
>
> She did not reply, but turned her sad, soft glance upon him in such heart-swollen reproach that he looked sorry for his words, and added, 'I only meant it for your good, you know, Gertrude.'
>
> 'I'll clear out the whole lot, and destroy them,' she said huskily, 'and try such remedies no more!'
>
> 'You want somebody to cheer you,' he observed. 'I once thought of adopting a boy; but he is too old now. And he is gone away I don't know where.'

And this is the moment which Hardy must have found obligatory, for although the reader knows, the reader also has to be told how Gertrude Lodge knows.

She guessed to whom he alluded; for Rhoda Brook's story had in
the course of years become known to her; though not a word had
ever passed between her husband and herself on the subject. Neither
had she ever spoken to him of her visit to Conjuror Trendle, and
of what was revealed to her, or she thought was revealed to her, by
that solitary heathman.[11]

Conjuror Trendle offers a cure. It is to touch the neck of a prisoner freshly cut
down from the scaffold. 'It will turn the blood and change the constitution.'
And you're dead right: it most certainly would. But during her conversation
with the hangman the alert reader guesses who the unfortunate prisoner is—
aged 18 and condemned to hang for burning a hayrick. It's Rhoda's son. Of
course it is. High drama, of the kind in which Hardy revelled, is the result:

> Gertrude shrieked: 'the turn o' the blood', predicted by the conjuror,
> had taken place. But at that moment a second shriek rent the air of
> the enclosure: it was not Gertrude's, and its effect upon her was to
> make her start round.[12]

Quite probably, the reader won't be taken by surprise; but the reader will
certainly be engrossed, with hair raised, by the sheer curiosity of the episode, the dead youth's neck already having been described as having on it 'a
line the colour of an unripe blackberry', which Gertrude touches with her
wasted arm.

> Immediately behind her stood Rhoda Brook, her face drawn, and
> her eyes red with weeping. Behind Rhoda stood Gertrude's own
> husband; his countenance lined, his eyes dim, but without a tear.
>   'D—n you! what are you doing here?' he said hoarsely.
>   'Hussy—to come between us and our child now!' cried Rhoda.
> 'This is the meaning of what Satan showed me in the vision! You
> are like her at last!' And clutching the bare arm of the younger
> woman, she pulled her unresistingly back against the wall.
> Immediately Brook had loosened her hold the fragile young Ger-
> trude slid down against the feet of her husband. When he lifted
> her up she was unconscious.
>   The mere sight of the twain had been enough to suggest to her
> that the dead young man was Rhoda's son.[13]

No, they don't write them like that any more. They don't even try to. But
Hardy was right in engaging so much with stories set in the past, before he

was born, but whose survivors lived on into his own earlier days. It enabled him to write freely about enormous and destructive passions. Gertrude dies three days later and Lodge sells his farms, dying after two years of lonely life in lodgings elsewhere, and leaving his money to a reformatory for boys 'subject to the payment of a small annuity to Rhoda Brook, if she could be found to claim it'. Most writers would end there, but Hardy adds a final paragraph which discreetly and perhaps for Hardy necessarily connects the story to the oral tradition and history from which it grew:

> For some time she could not be found; but eventually she reappeared in her old parish,—absolutely refusing, however, to have anything to do with the provision made for her. Her monotonous milking at the dairy was resumed, and followed for many long years, till her form became bent, and her once abundant dark hair white and worn away at the forehead—perhaps by long pressure against the cows. Here, sometimes, those who knew her experiences would stand and observe her, and wonder what sombre thoughts were beating inside that impassive, wrinkled brow, to the rhythm of the alternating milk-streams.[14]

'The Withered Arm' is a better title, but it could as easily have been called 'The Milkmaid's Tragedy'. Hardy's poem, 'The Milkmaid', from *Poems of the Past and Present*, while serious, is also more light-hearted.

> The maid breathes words—to vent,
> It seems, her sense of Nature's scenery,
>   Of whose life, sentiment,
> And essence, very part itself is she.

We can take that as the serious aspect of the poem, that association of the milk-maid with the landscape of a remote place. However, the poem continues,

> She bends a glance of pain,
> And, at a moment, lets escape a tear;
>   Is it that passing train,
> Whose alien whirr offends her country ear?—

> Nay! Phyllis does not dwell
> On visual and familiar things like these;
>   What moves her is the spell
> Of inner themes and inner poetries: . . .

—which fairly sets up the reader's expectations, as if anticipating a Wordsworthian flourish. But it finishes with:

> Could but by Sunday morn
> Her gay new gown come, meads might dry to dun,
>   Trains shriek till ears were torn,
> If Fred would not prefer that Other One.

The seeds of tragedy are there, perhaps, as in any love story; but Hardy chooses to observe with worldly amusement. But he must have his story, too.

Particularly successful as a short-story poem is 'At the Railway Station, Upway', from *Late Lyrics and Earlier*.

> 'There is not much that I can do,
>   For I've no money that's quite my own!'
>   Spoke up the pitying child—
> A little boy with a violin
> At the station before the train came in,—
>   'But I can play my fiddle to you,
> And a nice one 'tis, and good in tone!'
>
>   The man in the handcuffs smiled;
> The constable looked, and he smiled, too,
>   As the fiddle began to twang;
> And the man in the handcuffs suddenly sang
>   With grimful glee:
>   'This life so free
>   Is the thing for me!'
> And the constable smiled, and said no word,
> As if unconscious of what he heard;
> And so they went on till the train came in—
> The convict, and boy with the violin.

In telling the story of this encounter on a station platform, Hardy or his narrator is a perceiving presence (as in 'The Milkmaid'), and protected by an unannounced or absent first-person singular. Convict, boy and constable, are more than ciphers or unnamed strangers, though. They're untold stories. I agree with Tom Paulin, in his book *Thomas Hardy: the Poetry of Perception* (1975)[15] when he claims that when Hardy is at his most perceptive and observational the result is a quality of seeing that becomes what Paulin calls 'visionary'. What I would add to that is this: Hardy's observational/visionary dynamic is the direct result, not just of uncannily perceptive powers—and is there a finer poet at sheer *naming* than Hardy?—playing through 'inner themes and inner poetries', but of highly developed narrative, storytelling skills. A fine example is another railway poem, 'Midnight on the Great Western', from *Moments of Vision*—but where do you draw the line?—there's always another poem by Hardy. Note, though, the directness of the two titles—'At the Railway Station, Upway' and 'Midnight on the Great Western'. Each title asserts a fact of place and encounter. It is against the challenge of such a simplicity of statement that Hardy's tuneful skills are obliged to contest the real with the visionary. Note, too, the plainness of the opening lines of both poems. 'At the Railway Station, Upway', starts with the 'pitying child's' declaration of pennilessness, for which he compensates by playing his fiddle for the convict (and with innocent wisdom, for it leads the convict to break into ironic song: 'This life so free/Is the thing for me!'). 'Midnight on the Great Western' opens with plain statement: 'In the third class seat sat the journeying boy.' We could suppose that the phrase 'the journeying boy' (repeated four times in the poem) is poetic, but it could hardly be described as remarkable. What's peculiar about it is its timelessness: 'the journeying boy' could be from any place and age, and the fact that he's on a train is neither here nor there. Similarly, the descriptive purpose of the remaining lines of the first stanza seems to reach for a higher poetic level than the first line achieves (although I doubt if Hardy meant his first line to be in any way 'powerful'):

> And the roof-lamp's oily flame
> Played down on his listless form and face,
> Bewrapt past knowing to what he was going,
>   Or whence he came.

So much of what is poetic in Hardy's poetry is a matter of narrative heightened by the vigour and delicacy of the tunes given to him by his venturesome, robust versification, flexible to the point of elasticity. The second stanza continues with a close-up, one of Hardy's best and most intuitive touches in his poetry. Readers at this point ought to be entranced by the commonplaceness of the objects evoked—the ticket, the key to the boy's box on a piece of string—and then the near-visionary leap of the play of light on the key. As a poem about vulnerable innocence then the key is surely significant, perhaps almost symbolic, but in too demotic, too real a manner for the concept of symbolism to be critically apt. (And this is a dimension of Hardy's poetry which I adore: the way he makes the commonplace proud of being what it is.)

> In the band of his hat the journeying boy
>   Had a ticket stuck; and a string
> Around his neck bore the key of his box,
> That twinkled gleams of the lamp's sad beams
>   Like a living thing.

Clearly, a poem by the author of 'Old Furniture'. But this, too, is a poem in which the story is that of an encounter. The story of 'the journeying boy' is untold, and if Hardy, poignantly, tries to guess, his speculation never gets beyond a question.

> What past can be yours, O journeying boy
>   Towards a world unknown,
> Who calmly, as if incurious quite
> On all at stake, can undertake
>   This plunge alone?

Strangely plain, and yet strangely soaring also, Hardy's question is primary to the narrative art of this poem. It invites the reader to make up the boy's story and yet because Hardy has himself refused to do so it also lays down the limits beyond which such guessing would be sentimental and condescending.

> Knows your soul a sphere, O journeying boy,
>   Our rude realms far above,
> Whence with spacious vision you mark and mete
> This region of sin that you find you in,
>   But are not of?

Presumably, 'region of sin' indicates that the train is approaching London, and for a reader of the present time the image evoked is of those runaway children of the North who somehow fetch up on the predatory concourses of King's Cross Station. 'But are not of' enforces the boy's innocence, perhaps with the rueful implication that it will not last for long in the Great Wen, or that his Dorsetshire origins (presumably) will help see him through. It could also suggest Hardy's conviction in the virtue of the district of the south-west of England from which the boy has come. But the boy has a box and round his neck on a piece of string the key to it. So someone has prepared him for his journey. Perhaps he's an orphan being sent to live with an aunt or other relative. Perhaps, perhaps. . . . Inevitably, the reader tries to make up a story, and Hardy encourages it while at the same time he forbids it. Indeed, it is not a story, but a lyrical anecdote that could become a story were more known by fact or provided by imagination. Or if it is a story then it is one of the poet's perception, the drama of compassion and speculation picked out on a verse melody from Hardy's immense and constantly plundered repertoire.

A poet's 'narrative art', especially that of a poet like Hardy, who excelled in the novel and shone in the short story, by itself introduces a constant possibility of fiction. Real persons and real events may well be changed to a lesser or greater extent by the poet's psychological momentum—'inner themes and inner poetries'—and by a need to re-experience the lived, which may be, according to the fact, imperfectly re-created (from the point of view of the prosaic), but which turns into perfect poetry. For example, was Hardy an habitual railway passenger in the third class? I doubt it. Who *was* the boy? Was it Hardy himself re-observed in adulthood? Is it a poem about ambition and cutting loose from the ties of livelihood and trade? Was the boy one whom Hardy sat opposite on the train? Was it an encounter he experienced or one that was told to him by another? Did he make it up? Does it matter?

There are clues in Hardy's poetry which can help us to define his 'psychological momentum' as I've called it. Essentially, it has to do with the status of time. In a sonnet either of April 1887 or written then, when he was in Italy, 'Rome: On the Palatine', he concludes:

> When lo, swift hands, on strings nigh overhead,
> Began to melodize a waltz by Strauss:
> It stirred me as I stood, in Caesar's house,
> Raised the old routs Imperial lyres had led,
> And blended pulsing life with lives long done,
> Till Time seemed fiction, Past and Present one.

'Till Time seemed fiction, Past and Present one'—it is a remarkable declaration of principle, and, of course, Hardy did not need to visit Rome to find it. His work is pervaded by it. The past in the present, the present in the past, time as fact and history, and time as stuff and substance of fiction and of art and poetry—such themes are everywhere in his work as a kind of pulse, and inform his versification, his obstinately creative exercising of the possibilities of timeless song offered by the English language with a local or (in a good sense) provincial root. Hardy is the least deracinated and, next to Chaucer, Shakespeare, Wordsworth, Crabbe, and, more recently, Geoffrey Grigson, Ted Hughes and Philip Larkin, the most English of poets—and maybe it takes a disinterested Scot to see this exhilarating phenomenon.

When Hardy came to write his celebrated 'Poems of 1912–13', his poems recollecting Emma Hardy, and other poems after these dates on the same subject, he was already more than well-rehearsed in haunting and being haunted. This time, though, the haunting was even more real than those which had happened before. And the haunting was not fictitious, although the potency of fictitious hauntings is not one which I would care to dismiss. A poet's 'narrative art' is just as likely to be as powerful, and probably more so, when speaking in *persona propria* as in poems where the first-person singular is absent or observational merely. In Hardy's case, the result was a melismatic and elegiac complicatedness, for reasons which we all know about. It led to such a complex line as the last of 'Your Last Drive'—'You are past love, praise, indifference, blame', perhaps the best earned and truest of all his lines. The poem is full of minute give-aways, to such an extent that I would claim that a poet's 'narrative art' is not so very different from that of a novelist or a short-story writer (although, as has often been said, the short story is closer to the lyric poem than to the novel; and as a writer of both I find myself increasingly doubtful of this critical commonplace). Outside of his poems of first-person, haunted predicament, Hardy's work, it seems to me, is pretty well all of a piece, but it's his first-person poems, no matter their possible fictitiousness, that strike me as his masterpieces. 'Your Last Drive', though, is a risky poem to the extent that it introduces dialogue from his dead wife. In terms of fiction, an ethical hazard is undertaken in that it reports speech the actuality of which can only be asserted by the poet. Is it real? Did she say it? And then, once again, does it matter?

But more important, perhaps, is the question of how an accomplished versification can dulcify or change a real experience or set of emotions. Could the verse skills and narrative or storytelling skills of a writer like Hardy modify lived experience to a point where the result could be a kind of misrepresentation, or even mendacity? I think the answer is 'Of course, but does it matter, if the poet is also being honest to what we know of the biographical record?' And that's the case with these poems, especially when you consider the harshness of 'Without Ceremony', the last line of which is 'Good-bye is not worth while!', meaning what it did when Emma was alive and taking off without telling Hardy, and that her haunting of him would be permanent, and a reckoning which he would have to continue to meet until the day he died. Here, though, is 'Your Last Drive':

> Here by the moorway you returned,
> And saw the borough lights ahead
> That lit your face—all undiscerned
> To be in a week the face of the dead,

And you told of the charm of that haloed view
That never again would beam on you.

And on your left you passed the spot
Where eight days later you were to lie,
And be spoken of as one who was not;
Beholding it with a heedless eye
As alien from you, though under its tree
You soon would halt everlastingly.

I drove not with you . . .

Already a reader's eyebrows may have risen in a tic of interior puzzlement or questioning at 'You told of the charm of that haloed view / That never again would beam on you' after a reading of 'The Going', which precedes 'Your Last Drive', and which expresses the surprise of Emma's death. Also, 'I drove not with you . . . ', followed as it is by three dramatic dots . . . well, the three dots are themselves an expression of remorse—punctuation as gasp, as breath withheld. Hardy, however, doesn't persevere with his absence but, instead, imagines his presence:

Yet had I sat
At your side that eve I should not have seen
That the countenance I was glancing at
Had a last-time look in the flickering sheen,
Nor have read the writing upon your face,
'I go hence soon to my resting-place;'

'You may miss me then.'

'You may miss me then'—is that not Hardy mounting a terrible indictment upon himself through speech directed at him from the wife whom he may have neglected and who could have been difficult and awkward towards him? From the biographical evidence, we think we know about this, but it's too easy to be prurient or decisive. Hardy's poem picks up the story—and it is a story, Hardy's own story, the story of his marriage, but as told by Hardy, even if part of it is told riskily and fictitiously through the words of his wife, Emma:

'But I shall not know
How many times you visit me there,
Or what your thoughts are, or if you go

There never at all. And I shall not care.
Should you censure me I shall take no heed,
And even your praises no more shall need.'

Clearly, there's something rueful there—'I shall not care/Should you censure me' ... and 'even your praises no more shall need.' Death, then, is a sort of release from the demands of her husband, Thomas Hardy. It's honest of Hardy not to say so, precisely, but to implicate himself in the truth of the matter. However, it's Hardy who, inevitably, has the last word:

True, you'll never know. And you will not mind.
But shall I then slight you because of such?
Dear ghost, in the past did you ever find
The thought 'What profit,' move me much?
Yet abides the fact, indeed, the same,—
You are past love, praise, indifference, blame.

To be perfectly blunt about the matter, a poet's narrative art is the dynamic of thought, disclosure, description, and so on, that leads up to the conclusion of a poem, especially the last line. Much the same design can be experienced in Hardy's short or shorter fiction, or in his novels—the distribution of time, or events, or of thoughts. But it is when we read a poem like 'During Wind and Rain' that we really find ourselves faced with Hardy's 'narrative art' in verse and poetry at its most powerful, when his passion, versification and tunefulness meet the invisible but communicative and moving story he has to tell. Never mind that it is one of Hardy's greatest poems, it is one of the great poems of the world.

They sing their dearest songs—
He, she, all of them—yea,
Treble and tenor and bass,
And one to play;
With the candles mooning each face ...
Ah, no; the years O!
How the sick leaves reel down in throngs!

They clear the creeping moss—
Elders and juniors—aye,
Making the pathways neat
And the garden gay;
And they build a shady seat ...

> Ah, no; the years, the years;
> See, the white storm-birds wing across!
>
> They are blithely breakfasting all—
> Men and maidens—yea,
> Under the summer tree,
>   With a glimpse of the bay,
> While pet fowl come to the knee . . .
>   Ah, no; the years O!
> And the rotten rose is ript from the wall.
>
> They change to a high new house,
> He, she, all of them—aye,
> Clocks and carpets and chairs
>   On the lawn all day,
> And brightest things that are theirs. . . .
>   Ah, no; the years, the years;
> Down their carved names the rain-drop ploughs.

Notes

1. *Thomas Hardy: the Complete Stories*, ed. Norman Page (London, 1996).

2. Christopher Ricks, 'A Note on Hardy's "A Spellbound Palace"', in *Essays in Appreciation* (Oxford, 1998), p. 239.

3. *Complete Stories*, p. 7.

4. This is number 22 in *The Complete Poems*. Subsequent references are to this edition.

5. Walter Benjamin, *Illuminations*, ed. Hannah Arendt (London, 1970), pp. 83, 87.

6. *Complete Stories*, p. 10

7. Walter Benjamin, *Illuminations*, p. 87.

8. *Complete Stories*, pp. 32–47.

9. *Complete Stories*, p. 47.

10. *Complete Stories*, pp. 48–51.

11. *Complete Stories*, p. 61.

12. *Complete Stories*, p. 70.

13. *Complete Stories*, p. 70.

14. *Complete Stories*, p. 71.

15. Tom Paulin, *The Poetry of Perception* (London, 1975), p. 11 and passim.

WILLIAM KERRIGAN

Eight Great Hardys

A paradigm ago, before the theorists turned literary value into an affair of political self-interest, some of our best critics wrote troubled essays on the poetry of Thomas Hardy in which the word "great," the citadel of standards, got used in a stingy way, as if this author had not quite or just barely earned it.

R. P. Blackmur saw in Hardy "a great art beaten down, much of it quite smothered to death, by the intellectual machinery by means of which Hardy expected it to run and breathe free." The "intellectual machinery" here is the philosophy Hardy cobbled together, without benefit of university training, from Darwin, Spencer, Huxley, and Schopenhauer. This defiant, godless pessimism was much complained of in the days of the New Criticism, I think because it was assumed that a poet should be judged on the basis of his farthest-reaching ideas; that Darwinian speculations were Hardy's farthest-reaching ideas; and therefore that the poems expounding those ideas had to hold a central position in assessments of his work. Under those assumptions, liking Hardy meant finding a way of enjoying "Nature's Questioning" or "Hap." As a result these inferior poems expounding rough-hewn ideas still make their dour appearances in modern selections of Hardy. He never needed them, having written a number of better ones.

From *Raritan* 21, no. 3 (Winter 2002): 76–99. © 2002 by *Raritan*.

But there were other things to worry about. Preeminently, not everyone felt that he had written a whole lot of better ones. James Gibson's variorum edition contains 947 poems and runs to over 950 pages. That's a bulky harvest for a poet who devoted only half his career, around thirty years, to the continuous writing of verse. Much of it, some critics felt, was embarrassingly feeble stuff. John Crowe Ransom wanted to be an exception, and seemed on the right track in declaring that "The poems of Hardy number close to a thousand, and all by themselves constitute a literature of irony which is solid perhaps beyond any parallel." Yet a few pages later we find him "recording in advance my consent to the charge that Hardy was an uneven poet, and capable of marring fine poems by awkward and tasteless passages; and even of writing whole poems that now are too harsh, and again too merely pedestrian." The double urge to praise and denigrate then issues in the usual turbulent passage about greatness: "He is a special poet, a great minor poet if the phrase is intelligible, and a poor major poet. He should rate well among English poets since Wordsworth, but that would be because in that span the greatest poets have had very disagreeable imperfections."

Being fair to Hardy was obviously a way of demonstrating that one knew what the word "great" really meant in the sphere of poetry. Allen Tate, for example, belabored a point about "Nature's Questioning" in his essay on Hardy, and did not feel that an apology was in order: "Great passages of poetry are rare." Enough said, at least in ordinary circumstances. But this is an essay on Hardy: "Great passages of poetry are rare; because they are exceptionally rare in Hardy we must exert ourselves to the utmost to understand their value." There were, apparently, numerous occasions to belabor a point into fine precision when opining about T. S. Eliot. You didn't get many chances to show your mettle when writing about Hardy.

It stands to reason that F. R. Leavis would be the most reluctant of all the praisers of Hardy, for he of course considered himself to have the highest standards for the use of the word "great." Eliot had declared in his famous essay on Andrew Marvell that Hardy had no wit. He would later, in *After Strange Gods*, deplore the fact that Hardy had indeed forged an emotional bond with a large popular audience; since "the majority is capable neither of strong emotion nor of strong resistance, it always inclines to admire passion for its own sake" as "the surest evidence of vitality." That the emotional Hardy was popular did not, in this sense, speak well for the current state of civilization. Leavis, clearing the ground in *New Bearings in English Poetry* for Pound, Eliot, and, it must be said, for a couple of other poets, William Empson and Ronald Bottrall, who did not in the end amount to much, predictably dismissed Hardy as "a naive poet of simple attitudes and outlook."

People like that can be neither witty—which as Eliot declared involves "a recognition, implicit in the expression of every experience, of other kinds of experience which are possible"—nor ambiguous, which is another name for witty. Hardy was not experimental either, at least not in the right way. He had no interest in vers libre. His father was a country fiddler of some renown, and Hardy himself performed successfully on the same instrument as a young man. When an old poet, his heart brimmed with embarrassing old songs. Leavis found the tunes intolerable: "And, often to the lilt of popular airs, with a gaucherie compounded of the literary, the colloquial, the baldly prosaic, the conventionally poetical, the pedantic and the rustic, he industriously turns out his despondent anecdotes, his 'life's little ironies,' and his meditations upon a deterministic universe and the cruel accident of sentience." One can only imagine the rigorous programs of self-improvement necessary to protect poets and critics from the gaucherie of popular airs and undisciplined diction.

Hardy was given to uninspiring aesthetic pronouncements such as "All we can do is to write on the old themes in the old styles, but try to do a little better than those who went before us." Although this seems to me excellent advice, Leavis was anticipating modernist successes on a grand scale. The peculiar venom of his attack issues in the most personal of the uneasy uses of "great" in Hardy criticism: "It is all in keeping with this precritical innocence that his great poems should be only a very small proportion of his abundant output." How small? Six poems only. The other 941 poems were sunk in "precritical innocence"—an innocence of serious literary criticism, of Richards and Eliot and no doubt Leavis himself. Leavis was not one to mince words: what was not written in an awareness of such criticism would be dismissed by such criticism. Hardy belonged to an earlier paradigm. Like Housman, he thought poetry was "emotion put into measure." "The ultimate aim of the poet," Hardy believed, "should be to teach our hearts by showing his own, and not to exhibit his learning, or his fine taste, or his skill in mimicking the notes of his predecessors." The twentieth-century poets Leavis admired were no longer addressing hearts. Suspicious of mass culture and deliberately turned away from a popular audience by its cultivation of learned difficulty, the new modernist poetry was addressed to the new modernist criticism. No one else had the learning and the patience to expound it. A wider audience, if one could be found, would in the first place have to be taught it. In this atmosphere, Hardy was history.

One might suppose that, as modernism secured its place in English and American universities, the uneasiness over Hardy would tend to wane. And it has, to some extent. Dennis Taylor has written three wonderfully energetic books on Hardy in which many overlooked poems come to life. But the old gestures have proved tenacious. Donald Davie, in *Thomas Hardy and English Poetry*, worked up an elaborately backhanded praise for Hardy's technique. In the end his very expertise becomes a symptom of being too much at home in the modern secular world. Hardy lowered the bar by failing to offer a visionary alternative to this world. He never advanced beyond quotidian reality; he glossed it. He did not displace common sense; he spoke it. Hardy "sold the vocation short, tacitly surrendering the proudest claims traditionally made for the act of poetic imagination." Samuel Hynes, the editor of the Oxford *Complete Poetical Works*, has spent his entire professional life studying Hardy's verse, and has never ceased to worry the time-honored question of which sort of Hardy poem must be dismissed as "not just relatively unsuccessful, but awful." His book *The Pattern of Hardy's Poetry* begins carping at the poet in its very first sentence, and is still at it in its next-to-last, where the author concludes that "Hardy left a larger body of unsuccessful verse than any other major poet of the English language."

Bestowing a painstakingly qualified greatness on Hardy still matters, I think, because Hardy in his vast precritical innocence was not simply outside the modernist paradigm. He was the obvious alternative to it, the greatest nonmodernist English poet of the twentieth century. No other author (with the exception of Robert Frost) could have threatened the modernist critics and poet-critics as seriously as Hardy, and they responded by doing their level best to make him unreadable—selecting him poorly, pretending to be unmoved by all but a handful of his lyrics, praising him forbiddingly. Hardy's emotional directness, his formal excellence, his ability again and again to come to a conclusion, stand as a magnificent rebuke to what Yvor Winters called the "Laforguian snicker" of early Eliot and some of Wallace Stevens: "it seems to me the business of a poet is to arrive at an attitude that he can offer without apology, and I find something definitely sloppy in poetry that establishes a slightly facile attitude only to laugh it down." Once one escapes from the orthodoxies of modernist poetry and criticism, the tortured restrictions on Hardy's greatness fall away, and the great poems are there before us, one after another, in abundance.

Philip Larkin showed the way:

> I'd always rather assumed with Lytton Strachey that "the gloom was not relieved even by a little elegance of diction." But when I was about twenty-five, I suppose, I was in some digs which faced east and the sun used to wake me very early in the morning—you know, about six. It seemed too early to get up, so I used to read, and it happened that I had Hardy's own selection of his poems,

and I began to read them and was immediately struck by them. I was struck by their tunefulness and their feeling, and the sense that here was somebody writing about things I was beginning to feel myself. . . . Curiously enough, what I like about Hardy is what most people dislike. I like him because he wrote so much. I love the great *Collected Hardy* which runs for something like 800 pages. One can read him for years and years and still be surprised, and I think that's a marvellous thing to find in any poet.

We have no need for a typology of Hardy's badness: all that project ever came to was an affirmation by negation of modernism's goodness. More to the point just now is to appreciate Hardy on his own terms, wandering through those hundreds of pages with a capacity for surprise.

That, at any rate, is what I have been trying to do. When I first encountered the Larkin passage, around five years ago, I went to the library and checked out the very same volume of Hardy's own selections from his verse. An early riser myself, I spent several months of mornings with the poetry. It was the beginning of an ongoing entrancement; before long I graduated, again like Larkin, to the mammoth *Complete Poems*. Many surprises do indeed await patient readers of this great book.

The following are discussions of eight of Hardy's pieces. Some of my choices may seem eccentric, but I expect that most of those with a taste for Hardy will agree with over half of my selections. The proudly short list of F. R. Leavis included "Neutral Tones," "A Broken Appointment," "The Self-Unseeing," "The Voice," "After a Journey," and "During Wind and Rain." I would place "A Broken Appointment" somewhere near the bottom of Hardy's top fifty. The grim "Neutral Tones," so far as I'm concerned, can go on the slag heap with "Hap" and "Nature's Questioning." Of the remaining four, all of them superb, I will write about two.

It is a matter of some regret that I could not find places for "The Temporary the All," "Thoughts of Phena," "A Sign-Seeker," "Song of Hope," "A Spot." "His Immortality," "In Tenebris I," "The Darkling Thrush," "Shut Out That Moon," "The Convergence of the Twain," "To Meet, or Otherwise," "'My Spirit Will Not Haunt the Mound,'" "The Going," "The Haunter," "After a Journey," "Places," "A Poet," "The Oxen," "The Last Signal," "The Sunshade," "The Shadow on the Stone," "Snow in the Suburbs," "Weathers," "'If It's Ever Spring Again,'" "An Autumn Rain-Scene," "Waiting Both," "This Summer and Last," "Proud Songsters," "He Never Expected Much," "I Am the One," "The Mound," "Voices from Things Growing in a Churchyard," "An Ancient to Ancients," and many others. I have arranged the poems in what I believe to be their ascending order of value.

#8: "The Self-Unseeing"

It sometimes seems as if Shakespeare anticipated all the important English poets. Where in Shakespeare do we find Hardy's great originals? I think first of Feste's song at the end of *Twelfth Night*, where the stanzas, each of them containing a refrain both literal and symbolic about wind and rain, move chronologically from childhood to maturity through a lifetime of disillusionments; a lot of Hardy lies coiled in that song. "Under the greenwood tree" in *As You Like It*, where the upbeat mood is crossed by Jaques's mocking stanza, seems also to foreshadow him.

A passage in Duke Vincentio's "Be absolute for death" from *Measure for Measure* may be added to this list. Scholars have shown that all of this life-denying speech is conventional save for a few lines on youth and age, which appear to contain an observation original to Shakespeare:

Thou hast nor youth, nor age,
But as it were an after-dinners sleepe
Dreaming on both, for all thy blessed youth
Becomes as aged, and doth beg the alms
Of palsied eld: and when thou art old and rich,
Thou hast neither heat, affection, limb, nor beauty
To make thy riches pleasant.

These words inspired one of Samuel Johnson's best annotations: "This is exquisitely imagined. When we are young we busy ourselves in forming schemes for succeeding time, and miss the gratifications that are before us; when we are old we amuse the languour of age with the recollection of youthful pleasures or performances; so that our life, of which no part is filled with the business of the present time, resembles our dreams after dinner, when the events of the morning are mingled with the designs of the evening." When young, we dream about having the riches and privileges of the elderly; when old, we dream about having the health and vigor of the young. Here Shakespeare happens onto one of those disillusioning truths Hardy called "life's little ironies."

Hardy worked his own version of this little irony in "The Self-Unseeing":

Here is the ancient floor,
Footworn and hollowed and thin,
Here was the former door
Where the dead feet walked in.

She sat here in her chair,
Smiling into the fire;

He who played stood there,
Bowing it higher and higher.

Childlike, I danced in a dream;
Blessings emblazoned that day;
Everything glowed with a gleam;
Yet we were looking away!

The poet walks through the ruined cottage, remembering. *Here* is the floor, *here* the former door, *here* the place she sat, *there* the place he played. Until the last stanza Hardy hues strictly to the facts, attaching memory to place, then to now. The reader is left to make connections. The "dead feet" are those of the man and woman, perhaps also of the people who came, on that day in the past, to dance. The woman smiled into the fire, clearly in a state of reverie brought on by the man's music. He was probably playing the songs of their courtship. The couple are, it seems likely, Hardy's own parents.

As in Shakespeare, age stares back at youth. But the rather crass irony of *Measure for Measure*—that the elderly dream enviously of the young— becomes in Hardy the idea that as we age we increasingly inhabit memories of our youth, lived in worlds that no longer exist. Gone, too, is the acquisitive envy of youth for age. The "dream" of Hardy and the other youthful dancers in the final stanza seems no more than self-absorption in their pleasure and their anticipation of future pleasure.

The hammer blow of revelation comes in the final line. It is only now, the cottage having fallen into ruin, the young dancer having aged, that he realizes the great blessings of that day, everyone here, and alive, and happy. How ironic that the young dreaming Hardy staring ahead at the future Hardy did not see this Hardy, the revisitor of the cottage, staring back at him. How ironic, perhaps not in a little way, that the consciousness of blessings and the consciousness of loss have to arrive together. "We live forward," Hardy once wrote in a notebook, copying out a passage from William James, "we understand backward."

"It is too late to call back yesterday." "Age and experience teach wisdom." "If the young man would, and the old man could, there would be nothing undone." "What youth is used to, age remembers." These are venerable English proverbs. Hardy not only spoke common sense. He improved it, lending it new precision and charging it with fresh emotion. On this occasion, he also improved on his origins in Shakespeare.

#7: "Lying Awake"
Can it really be considered a limitation if it were true that Hardy never left quotidian reality? Every segment of the day has its poem. No previous

writer, to my knowledge, had found a poem in lying awake in bed in the
morning, the first segment of the day:

> You, Morningtide Star, now are steady-eyed, over the east,
>> I know it as if I saw you;
> You, Beeches, engrave on the sky your thin twigs, even the least;
>> Had I paper and pencil I'd draw you.
>
> You, Meadow, are white with your counterpane cover of dew,
>> I see it as if I were there;
> You, Churchyard, are lightening faint from the shade of the yew,
>> The names creeping out everywhere.

This is one of several quiet masterpieces in Hardy's final and posthumous
collection, *Winter Words* (1928).

Long anapestic pentameters alternate with long trimeters, each of which
(save the last, which I scan with two dactyls) has at least one anapest. In the
first stanza and the first half of the second stanza Hardy establishes a clear
pattern. The five-beat lines describe "You," and "You" refers to things in dawning nature—the Morningtide Star, the Beeches, the Meadow. The three-beat
lines contain the response of "I" to "You," and that response is always in the
subjunctive. He knows the morning star *as if* he saw it, which he does not; *had*
he paper and pencil, which he does not, he would draw the beeches in all their
detail; he sees the meadow *as if* he were there, which he is not. The subjunctive lines project a Hardy who is up and about, outside, doing and sketching
and observing. Instead he is lying awake, the world in his mind rather than
at hand. There is in fact a pride in the accuracy with which his mind can
represent the world. Line 4 neatly doubles the pride, since he could draw the
beeches, not by direct representation, but by reference to his mental image of
them. "I hardly need to get up," the pattern implies, "so self-sufficient is my
mind." He can greet the dawning world as a fully realized idea.

There are two worlds coming to light, then, a dawn and a mental dawn.
They correspond perfectly. It gradually dawns on the reader that there is a third
world, the word-world of this lucid poem. Just as the world has been copied in
the speaker's mind, so the poem's dawn and mental dawn have been copied in the
reader's mind. That becomes part and parcel of the poem's pattern. The reader sees
the morning star and mental morning star, the beeches and the mental beeches,
the meadow and the mental meadow, as if he were there, which he is not. How
did this happen? The speaker had to get up and write the poem. In order for that
to happen, the speaker had to overcome his sense of prideful self-sufficiency—
and seize the day. The lyric is a variation on the ancient carpe diem theme.

Hardy repeatedly designed poems so that a pattern would be broken or significantly varied or fully realized by the final line or stanza. One might call it a simple strategy: work toward a powerful finish; put the punch at the end. But novice poets would do well to study the many ways in which Hardy made this technique work. Here the last "You," the Churchyard, shatters the expectation formed by the previous six lines by belonging to culture rather than nature, as Hardy seems to remind us by placing the homonym "yew" at the end of line 7. The next line does not return to "I," but continues the mental image of the "lightening faint" from the prior line, "The names creeping out everywhere." The names are of course the names of the dead engraved on the tombstones in the churchyard. They are the last things to come to light, the last things to be named, and they seem to break out in sudden profusion, ubiquitous, "everywhere."

The broken pattern in the final line completes the poem because if Hardy were to have kept to the pattern, he would have written as a final line something like "I read them as if I were there." When we realize that, we understand that the early morning spell of proud self-sufficiency has come to an end in the recognition of forthcoming death. For the poet will indeed be there, and not in the subjunctive mood, but as a name among those many graven names. Hardy was a haunted poet. The churchyard was not just his destiny, but his poetic turf. The churchyard names creep out like ghosts, calling him to his own vocation of naming. "Come old man, time to go to work, to make the poem." And he did, as we know from the very fact that we are reading it.

#6: "On the Departure Platform"

Journeys end in lovers' meetings. Lovers' meetings end in journeys. This poem opens with the meticulous reconstruction of a memory, from the absolute togetherness of "We kissed" to the absolute separation of "vanished quite":

> We kissed at the barrier; and passing through
> She left me, and moment by moment got
> Smaller and smaller, until to my view
>   She was but a spot;
>
> A wee white spot of muslin fluff
> That down the diminishing platform bore
> Through hustling crowds of gentle and rough
>   To the carriage door.
> Under the lamplight's fitful glowers,
> Behind dark groups from far and near,
> Whose interests were apart from ours,
>   She would disappear,

Then show again, till I ceased to see
That flexible form, that nebulous white:
And she who was more than my life to me
    Had vanished quite. . . .

A kiss seals their parting. Hardy remains at the barrier. The woman, mingling with "dark groups" of fellow passengers, walks down the departure platform, which seems from his fixed perspective to be "diminishing" or narrowing the farther away she gets, to board the railway carriage. His intense fixation on her visual image seems on the one hand a symbolic attempt to prolong the kiss; seeing her is at least contact of a sort, keeping her in the present. But this intense regard can only end as it does, in her vanishing, and that, too, seems part of Hardy's fascination: to watch her slip into the past, becoming inaccessible, a memory only.

This double feeling of prolonging and ending will be familiar to most people. I have seen it a hundred times. Lovers being separated by a departing train became central to the iconography of cinematic romance in films such as *Since You Went Away, Brief Encounter, The Clock, The Earrings of Madame de . . .* , and *My Foolish Heart*. Often the journeying lover is reluctant to break an embrace and board the train. But he or she does, consenting to fate, and, as the train pulls out, the reluctance is played out again in their desperate but hopeless attempt to maintain eye contact. It is a testament to Hardy that his image is graphic enough to equal, if not exceed, the mnemonic power of the movies. Part of the secret lies in saving the meaning of the disappearing woman, "she who was more than my life to me," till the very last, to serve as the subject of "had vanished quite." As in "The Self-Unseeing," the meaning of presence arrives with the fact of absence.

In the final two stanzas, the poet assesses his loss:

We have penned new plans since that fair fond day,
And in season she will appear again—
Perhaps in the same soft white array—
    But never as then!

—"And why, young man, must eternally fly
A joy you'll repeat, if you love her well?"
—O friend, nought happens twice thus; why,
    I cannot tell!

She will appear again, perhaps in the same white muslin dress, "but never as then!" Is this simply to say that the past cannot be relived? Or has his love for her diminished? Is she no longer "more than my life to me"? The exclamation point insists that the loss is no ordinary one, and the friend's voice in the next stanza, requesting an explanation, a "why," suggests that there is something extreme in this bereavement. He too wonders if Hardy's love for the woman is still intact.

William Pritchard maintains that Hardy's "truest response" to a memory "is to insist on its uniqueness and the impossibility of repeating it":

> The exclamation mark is a wonderfully expressive device with which to make this insistence, since along with the regret, the pang of loss when the past moment is viewed in memory's landscape, there is also a present exhilaration of not merely recalling the moment but of asserting its forever-lostness: "nought happens twice thus," and so "never as then."

Yes, there is indeed something willful and exhilarating about "never as then!" It repeats the rupture of the lovers on the departure platform. The intervention of the friend sets the stage for yet another repetition of that departure. If joy cannot be repeated, the loss of joy surely can. Hardy the watcher of her disappearance ultimately triumphs over Hardy the prolonger of her kiss.

But the tag line from Heraclitus, "nought happens twice thus," seems relatively halfhearted, and the poem trails off into puzzlement: "why, / I cannot tell!" The loss of that "fair fond day" may have as much to do with Hardy's character, his ability to nourish ideals in the past that he cannot sustain in the present, as with the character of time. In the end these alternatives yield the same result. The ideal day will not return, except as lost, in memory. Time is what it is. Hardy is what he is.

#5: "Logs on the Hearth"

The poem finds Hardy in his customary posture, turned away from the reader, intent on something in the world or in his mind. This time it is both, for like the mother in "The Self-Unseeing," he is staring at a hearth in a state of reverie:

> The fire advances along the log
>   Of the tree we felled,
> Which bloomed and bore striped apples by the peck
>   Till its last hour of bearing knelled.
>
> The fork that first my hand would reach
>   And then my foot,

In climbings upward inch by inch, lies now
    Sawn, sapless, darkening with soot.

Where the bark chars is where, one year,
    It was pruned, and bled—
Then overgrew the wound. But now, at last,
    Its growings all have stagnated.

Those of us who buy cords of wood for the pile in the backyard, or more shamefully, buy logs in plastic-covered bundles at the hardware store, cannot but be struck by the poet's organic relationship to his fire. These are logs "we felled." He knows the tree, remembers its blooms and its pecks of apples, remembers climbing it as a child, remembers the dark spot where once the tree was pruned. As the fire advances anapestically along the log, Hardy recalls the role of the tree in his life. If the poem has any other motive, it is to bid a lingering farewell to this "Sawn, sapless," and "stagnated" apple tree. A few of my students have wanted to bring Eden into it. But there's no Eden here, no supernumerary mythological growth. This is just one particular tree.

    Thus lulled, we feel much as Hardy does the unexpected bloom of memory in the final stanza:

My fellow-climber rises dim
    From her chilly grave—
Just as she was, her foot near mine on the bending limb,
    Laughing, her young brown hand awave.

The poem was written about a month after the death of Mary, Hardy's favorite sister, in 1915. The last service of the good apple tree is to release the memory of her childhood self from the chilly grave of unconsciousness—and there she is, "Just as she was," "her young brown hand awave." Goodbye.

#4: "Afterwards"

The first line of this "autoelegy," as Joseph Brodsky termed it, is controversial:

When the Present has latched its postern behind my tremulous stay,
    And the May month flaps its glad green leaves like wings,
Delicate-filmed as new-spun silk, will the neighbors say,
"He was a man who used to notice such things"?

C. Day Lewis thought the opening line "an intolerably over-written variant of 'When I am dead.'" Brodsky noted that death is one of the busiest mothers of circumlocution, but Dennis Taylor is surely right to concentrate on the details of Hardy's brief allegory. A "postern" is a gate. The Present, Taylor explains, "is Hardy's host who latches the postern behind Hardy's 'stay.' Presumably the Present is saying goodbye, but the grammar is such that the Present could be saying hello. Is Hardy going or staying?" I feel sure that the grammatical ambiguity, if there is one, was not intended. Hardy is going.

I think he had in mind the closing passage of Coleridge's "Youth and Age," a poem mentioned in his literary notebooks:

> Where no hope is, life's a warning
> That only serves to make us grieve,
> 		When we are old:
>
> That only serves to make us grieve
> With oft and tedious taking-leave,
>
> Like some poor nigh-related guest,
> That may not rudely be dismist;
> Yet hath outstay'd his welcome while,
> And tells the jest without the smile.

Hardy is the Present's guest. The postern shuts on his stay, which is over. "Afterwards" opens with the logical climax, the afterwards, of Coleridge's metaphor.

But Hardy's is a quiet passing away. He is not Coleridge's grumbling, irritating guest. The poet is fixed on the world, as usual, but in a peculiarly indirect and complex way. He wonders if neighbors will notice the details of the season at the time of his death, as he himself, when alive, used to notice the details. The stanzas of the poem move through possible times of death, noticing them in the sensory detail of the verse, and asking if this power of noticing will be noticed as his primary way of being.

Hardy was indeed a great noticer. Winters put it well:

> The simplest and most obvious thing that one can say about Hardy
> is that he had the best eye for natural detail in all British poetry.
> Wordsworth is supposed to have been a nature-poet, among other
> things, but his language is almost always stereotyped and the detail

is blurred. Hardy, like Charles Darwin in his *Journal of Researches*, had the seeing eye, and he seldom let any literary nonsense get between the eye and the object.

By "seeing eye" Winters does not mean a solely visual crispness, but rather a receptivity to sensory experience in its entirety. Hardy had, as Winters wrote to Allen Tate, the ability to "lay the complete world naked at a stroke."

The gift can be illustrated almost at random. Take the breakers in "The Wind's Prophecy":

> The waves outside where breakers are
> Huzza like a mad multitude.

"Huzza" sometimes means "buzz," but when said of a crowd, as it is here, means "to shout, to hurrah." Beyond the breakers a whole sea of heaving swells huzzas the waves that one by one shatter themselves against the cliffs. Take the bats of "The Musical Box":

> At whiles would flit
> Swart bats, whose wings, be-webbed and tanned,
> Whirred like the wheels of ancient clocks.

The sequence of "whiles," "would," "Swart," "whose," "wings," and "webbed" builds up an almost unnoticed onomatopoeic alliteration that springs to the surface in "Whirred like the wheels." No other English poet in the Romantic line worked so close to the world. The seeing eye was a particular way of using language, merging it in precise ways with the objects under description. To quote Winters again: "A large part of Hardy's genius lies in his masterly understanding of the history (I mean the artistic and human history, not the philological) of every word he touches." Had Winters had the benefit of reading Taylor's *Hardy's Literary Language and Victorian Philology*, he would have happily conceded that the understanding was philological as well as artistic and human.

In the second stanza of "Afterwards" Hardy provides a masterful example of his power to notice. The word "it" refers to the time of his death:

> If it be in the dusk when, like an eyelid's soundless blink,
> The dewfall-hawk comes crossing the shades to alight
> Upon the wind-warped upland thorn, a gazer may think,
> "To him this must have been a familiar sight."

Robert Mezey is moved to imprudence: "As for comparing the approach of the hawk to an eyelid's soundless blink, is there a better simile in English poetry?" I wouldn't know, but this one is awfully fine. As with a blink, something dark and vague and soundless comes down rapidly from the top of the visual field. You are not sure whether or not you actually saw it, but there, alighted on the thorn, is a hawk that was not in the picture a moment back. The term "dewfall" seems another hidden simile. One does not see the dew fall: in the dawn, it is all of a sudden there, like the meadow's counterpane in "Lying Awake." But the hawk and the two fine similes about its almost imperceptible descent belong also to an implicit simile for the quick descent and sudden overness of life's last moment. Blink: the postern is latched.

#3: "The Pedigree"

Hardy spent a lot of time researching his ancestry and making up charts. One of them, drawn in his own hand, is labeled "The Hardy Pedigree."

The poem itself opens "in the deep of night," with Hardy in his study, bent over his family pedigree. Clouds pass across the moon. Hardy senses a spectral presence, "Like a drifting dolphin's eye seen through a lapping wave"—something alien but conscious staring back at him. He returns to his family tree, but it soon develops a disturbing personality of its own:

> So, scanning my sire-sown tree,
> And the hieroglyphs of this spouse tied to that,
> With offspring mapped below in lineage,
>   Till the tangles troubled me,
> The branches seemed to twist into a seared and cynic face
> Which winked and tokened towards the window like a Mage
>   Enchanting me to gaze again thereat.

The window is now a mirror in which he sees "a long perspective" of his "begetters," "Generation and generation of my mien, and build, and brow." What he sees in this mirror spells an end to illusions of unique selfhood:

> And then did I divine
> That every heave and coil and move I made
> Within my brain, and in my mood and speech,
>   Was in the glass portrayed
> As long forestalled by their so making it;

The first of them, the primest fuglemen of my line,
Being fogged in far antiqueness past surmise and reason's reach.

"Forestalled" means "anticipated, acted before." He has neither privacy nor specialness. The earliest Hardys might have had those privileges. They were "the primest fuglemen," a fugleman being a soldier who teaches other soldiers the drill.

The poem ends with what is seemingly the only authentic move left:

Said I then, sunk in tone,
"I am merest mimicker and counterfeit!—
Though thinking, I am I,
And what I do I do myself alone."
—The cynic twist of the page thereat unknit
Back to its normal figure, having wrought its purport wry,
The Mage's mirror left the window-square,
And the stained moon and drift retook their places there.

We have to make some guesses. The sardonic Mage, I suggest, is the first Hardy, the primal fugleman, who alone was free to invent Hardyness. His cynical purpose is to induce the thought Hardy utters at the beginning of this stanza, and, "having wrought its purport wry," the Mage departs, lifting the spell. But what is "wry" about this mission?

Let's suppose that this is loosely speaking an allegory, and the truth delivered by the cynical Mage stands in some fashion as everyman's truth. Heredity is indeed a supreme determinism, one to which Emerson paid due tribute in "Fate": "How shall a man escape from his ancestors, or draw off from his veins the black drop which he drew from his father's or mother's life?" Such is true for all. But Hardys have to know that it is true. They have to have the revelation, and it is the wry, timeless duty of the primal Hardy to put the final stamp of certification on all subsequent members of the pedigree. Now, having learned that he is a counterfeit who merely thinks "*I am I, / And what I do I do myself alone.*" Hardy is a Hardy, and completely himself.

#2: "Life Laughs Onward"

When Time laughs in Thomas Hardy, it is usually a laughter of cruel mockery, and he himself is the butt of the joke. The death of Emma Lavinia Hardy inspired the "Poems of 1912–13," in which his love for her, dormant for years in a soured marriage, rose mysteriously to its original pitch. What could be more futile? "Time's derision," he called it in "After the Journey." But even before Emma's death, in "Shut Out That Moon," he defined the time of youthful courtship as "When living seemed a laugh," and the laugh, in the end, was on him:

> Too fragrant was Life's early bloom,
>   Too tart the fruit it brought!

The poem was published in a volume entitled *Time's Laughingstocks and Other Verses* (1909).

"Life Laughs Onward" looks to be another bout of derision:

> Rambling I looked for an old abode
> Where, years back, one had lived I knew;
> Its site a dwelling duly showed,
>   But it was new.

> I went where, not so long ago,
> The sod had riven two breasts asunder;
> Daisies throve gaily there, as though
>   No grave were under.

> I walked along a terrace where
> Loud children gambolled in the sun;
> The figure that had once sat there
>   Was missed by none.

Three times the poet visits a place where something once present is now missing. No one notices but him. Life buries the past and his memory is its grave. A reader who knows his poet prepares for the mockery of the final stanza. But this time Hardy himself laughs onward:

> Life laughed and moved on unsubdued,
> I saw that Old succumbed to Young:
> 'Twas well. My too regretful mood
>   Died on my tongue.

Life does not mourn. It laughs. Life does not commemorate. It replaces. "'Twas well." Learning from this brutal indifference to the old, Hardy corrects himself, and a too regretful mood dies on his tongue.

At the end of the poem we find a fourth and final example of a scene where something familiarly present is now missing: a Thomas Hardy poem without too much regret.

#1: "During Wind and Rain"

We have near unanimity here. This was Yvor Winters's favorite Hardy poem: "The management of stanza, meter, and rhythm is that of a master." In 1987 Harold Bloom declared it "as good a poem as our century has given us." In "During Wind and Rain," Norman Page writes, "Feeling and form, emotion and 'measure,' are perfectly married." The lyric holds a place on Leavis's precious list of six. Even the hard-to-please Samuel Hynes thinks it "one of Hardy's finest lyrics." Many a book and essay on Hardy accords this work a central position.

Even by Hardy's standards, the poem displays a remarkable degree of structural precision:

> They sing their dearest songs—
> He, she, all of them—yea,
> Treble and tenor and bass,
>   And one to play;
> With the candles mooning each face....
>   Ah, no; the years O!
> How the sick leaves reel down in throngs!
>
> They clear the creeping moss—
> Elders and juniors—aye,
> Making the pathways neat
>   And the garden gay;
> And they build a shady seat....
>   Ah, no; the years, the years;
> See, the white storm-birds wing across!
>
> They are blithely breakfasting all—
> Men and maidens—yea,
> Under the summer tree,
>   With a glimpse of the bay,
> While pet fowl come to the knee....
>   Ah, no; the years O!
> And the rotten rose is ript from the wall.
>
> They change to a high new house,
> He, she, all of them—aye,
> Clocks and carpets and chairs
>   On the lawn all day,

And brightest things that are theirs. . . .
   Ah, no; the years, the years;
Down their carved names the rain-drop ploughs.

There are four stanzas with two refrains, appearing alternately. The refrains are unrhymed. The first word of every stanza is "They." "He, she, all of them—yea," in the first stanza reappears as "He, she, all of them—aye" in the last: the middle stanzas have, in the same position, the pairs "Elders and juniors," "Men and maidens." The end-word in the second line of each stanza alternates between "yea" and "aye," which rhyme. The fifth line in each stanza falls off into elision. These unwinding repetitions make the poem seem enclosed on itself, like a verse clock intent on its own internal music.

There are two present tenses. In one of them the story of a family unfolds stanza by stanza in chronological order. Things in this domestic world are precious, loved. "Dearest songs" are performed. Pathways are "neat," the garden "gay." They breakfast "blithely," happy and carefree. Possessions on the lawn all day during their move are the "brightest things that are theirs." A second present tense opens in the concluding tetrameters. Here, as the title leads us to infer, a storm is building. Though we suppose the descriptions of the oncoming storm to be chronological, there is no narrative frame, no immediate sense of where or when this second present is located. As Norman Page nicely observes, "each stanza ends with a highly charged line in which another, very different visual image—so powerful in its compression of statement as to be almost an Imagist poem in itself—overlays the earlier one."

Taylor postulates, reasonably enough, that the speaker of the poem is in a reverie. Four times, once per stanza, his memories of the family are interrupted by present perceptions of the oncoming storm. Associations born of each storm-perception then reappear in the domestic memories of the subsequent stanza. Thronging leaves prompt a memory about clearing pathways. Storm-birds come back, domesticated, in the "pet fowl." After the rose is ripped from the wall, the speaker remembers a "high new house." Not until the final line of the poem do we realize that the remembering poet is in a churchyard, standing before the family's graves. Regret cannot be defeated this time. They have moved to their final residence, a low new house. And the storm has broken: "Down their carved names the rain-drop ploughs." The line, initiated by the downturn of a trochee, and continued with a spondee, an iamb, and another near spondee, progresses slowly and emphatically toward its rough verb.

Between the two presents come the ballad refrains. "Ah no," they both begin. The refrains' resistance to moving from memory to perception contrasts with the "yea" and the "aye," the narrative-welcoming yes words, found in the happy reveries. One refrain proceeds with "the years O!" Here the vocative "O," rhyming internally with "no," manifests the emotional pain implicit in that word. The second form of the refrain, "the years, the years," by doubling the time between memory and present perception again expresses the dizzying horror of transversing this gap. But the motive for this horror does not become clear until the final line, where for the first time "They," the people remembered in each stanza, also pass through the gap of years in the form of "their names." It was that transfer, we can now recognize, the speaker was resisting in the refrains.

Hardy has designed a poem in which everything converges on the multiple revelations of the final line. The storm breaks. The dislocated speaker is placed in a churchyard. "They" bursts through the gap of years as "their names," clarifying the heretofore mysterious relationship of the two present tenses. The resistance in the refrains at last makes sense. Where in English literature, outside of Shakespearean tragedy, can we find a comparable merging of understanding and desolation? "During Wind and Rain" is only twenty-eight lines long. A small clock, but what power when it strikes!

Chronology

1840	Born on June 2 in Higher Bockhampton in England, the son of Thomas Hardy, a stone mason, and Jemima Hand Hardy.
1855	Begins teaching at the Stinsford Church Sunday School.
1856	Accepted at the office of architect John Hicks as pupil.
1862	After settling in London, goes to work for architect and church restorer Arthur Blomfield.
1867	Returns to Dorset and resumes working for John Hicks.
1870	Travels to Cornwall, where he meets Emma Lavinia Gifford, his future wife. Publisher William Tinsley agrees to produce *Desperate Remedies* at the author's expense.
1871	*Desperate Remedies* is published.
1872	*Under the Greenwood Tree* is published. *A Pair of Blue Eyes* appears in serial form.
1873	Hardy is invited by Leslie Stephen to contribute to *Cornhill*; Hardy then begins the serialized version of *Far from the Madding Crowd. A Pair of Blue Eyes* is published.
1874	*Far from the Madding Crowd* is published. Marries Emma Lavinia Gifford.
1878	*The Return of the Native* is published.

1880	*The Trumpet-Major* is published. Meets the poet laureate, Alfred, Lord Tennyson.
1881	*A Laodicean* is published.
1882	*Two on a Tower* is published.
1883	Hardy moves to Dorchester, where he begins building his home, Max Gate.
1886	*The Mayor of Casterbridge* is published.
1887	*The Woodlanders* is published. Hardy visits Italy.
1888	*The Wessex Tales*, a collection of short stories, is published.
1891	Both *Tess of the d'Urbervilles* and *A Group of Noble Dames* are published.
1892	Father dies. First version of *The Well-Beloved* is serialized. Relations with his wife begin to deteriorate and worsen over the next two years.
1893	Travels to Dublin and Oxford, where he visits Florence Henniker, with whom he writes a short story, and, it is believed, falls in love.
1894	*Life's Little Ironies*, a collection of poems, is published.
1895	*Jude the Obscure* is published and receives primarily outraged reviews. As a result, Hardy decides to discontinue novel writing and from then on produces only poetry.
1897	*The Well-Beloved* is published.
1898	Publishes *The Wessex Poems*.
1901	Publishes *Poems of the Past and the Present*.
1904	*The Dynasts*, part 1, is published. Hardy's mother dies.
1906	*The Dynasts*, part 2, is published.
1908	*The Dynasts*, part 3, is published.
1909	Publishes *Time's Laughingstocks*.
1912	Wife dies on November 27.
1913	*A Changed Man* is published.
1914	Marries Florence Emily Dugdale. A collection of poems, *Satires of Circumstance*, is published.

1915	His sister Mary dies.
1917	*Moments of Vision*, a collection of poetry, is published.
1919	First *Collected Poems* is published.
1921	Publishes *Late Lyrics and Earlier*.
1923	*The Famous Tragedy of the Queen of* Cornwall, a drama, is published.
1925	*Human Shows*, poetry, is published.
1928	Dies on January 11; his ashes are buried at Westminster Abbey, and his heart is placed at his first wife's grave. *Winter Words*, poetry, published. Florence Emily Hardy publishes *The Early Life of Thomas Hardy*, believed to have been written largely by Hardy himself.
1930	*Collected Poems* published. Florence Emily Hardy publishes *The Later Years of Thomas Hardy*.

Contributors

HAROLD BLOOM is Sterling Professor of the Humanities at Yale University. He is the author of 30 books, including *Shelley's Mythmaking*, *The Visionary Company*, *Blake's Apocalypse*, *Yeats*, *A Map of Misreading*, *Kabbalah and Criticism*, *Agon: Toward a Theory of Revisionism*, *The American Religion*, *The Western Canon*, and *Omens of Millennium: The Gnosis of Angels, Dreams, and Resurrection*. *The Anxiety of Influence* sets forth Professor Bloom's provocative theory of the literary relationships between the great writers and their predecessors. His most recent books include *Shakespeare: The Invention of the Human*, a 1998 National Book Award finalist, *How to Read and Why*, *Genius: A Mosaic of One Hundred Exemplary Creative Minds*, *Hamlet: Poem Unlimited*, *Where Shall Wisdom Be Found?*, and *Jesus and Yahweh: The Names Divine*. In 1999, Professor Bloom received the prestigious American Academy of Arts and Letters Gold Medal for Criticism. He has also received the International Prize of Catalonia, the Alfonso Reyes Prize of Mexico, and the Hans Christian Andersen Bicentennial Prize of Denmark.

TREVOR JOHNSON is the former head of the Department of Language and Literature at Manchester College of Higher Education and has lectured at Manchester University. He has published several titles on Hardy. He authored *Thomas Hardy* and edited *Poems by Thomas Hardy*, among other titles.

SIMON GATRELL is a professor at the University of Georgia. He is coeditor of the Clarendon Press edition of *Tess of the d'Urbervilles*, general editor of the Oxford World Classics edition of Hardy's collected novels, and editor of *Tess of the d'Urbervilles*, *The Return of the Native*, and *Under the Green-*

181

wood Tree in the same series. He also is the author of *Thomas Hardy's Vision of Wessex, Hardy the Creator,* and other works on Hardy and other Victorian novelists and poets.

PETER WIDDOWSON was a professor of literary studies at the University of Gloucestershire. He was a research reader in English and general editor of the university's publishing imprint, the Cyder Press. Among his publications are a New Casebook on *Tess of the d'Urbervilles* and *Thomas Hardy: Selected Poetry and Nonfictional Prose.* He was also coeditor of *Thomas Hardy and Contemporary Literary Studies.*

ROBERT SCHWEIK is a professor emeritus of the State University of New York and an honorary vice president of the Thomas Hardy Society. He is editor of the Norton Critical Edition of *Far from the Madding Crowd* and author of other texts. Also, he has authored many essays on Hardy and on other authors and topics.

SAMUEL HYNES is a professor emeritus at Princeton University. He is the author of one of the first book-length studies of Hardy's verse, *The Pattern of Hardy's Poetry,* and has authored several other works as well. He also is the editor of *The Complete Poetical Works of Thomas Hardy* published by Clarendon Press. He is an honorary vice president of the Thomas Hardy Society.

MICHAEL IRWIN is a professor at the University of Kent. He authored *Reading Hardy's Landscapes,* a study of Fielding's novels, *and Picturing: Description and Illusion in the Nineteenth-Century Novel.* He is a reviewer of fiction and fiction writer himself and has translated numerous operas.

DOUGLAS DUNN is a professor at the University of St. Andrews and founded the school's master of letters in creative writing. He has published several volumes of poetry, two collections of stories, and four edited books. His work has been translated into multiple languages.

WILLIAM KERRIGAN was professor emeritus at the University of Massachusetts. He published several titles, including works of Shakespeare and Milton that he edited.

Bibliography

Adamson, Jane. "Who and What Is Henchard? Hardy, Character and Moral Inquiry." *Critical Review* 31 (1991): 47–74.

Armstrong, Tim. *Haunted Hardy: Poetry, History, Memory.* Houndmills, Basingstoke, Hampshire [England]; New York: Palgrave, 2000.

Banerjee, A., ed. *An Historical Evaluation of Thomas Hardy's Poetry.* Lewiston, N.Y.: E. Mellen Press, 2000.

Bloom, Harold, ed. *Edwardian and Georgian Fiction.* Philadelphia: Chelsea House Publishers, 2005.

Chapman, Raymond. *The Language of Thomas Hardy.* New York: St. Martin's Press, 1990.

Daleski, H. M. *Thomas Hardy and Paradoxes of Love.* Columbia: University of Missouri Press, 1997.

DeVine, Christine. *Class in Turn-of-the-Century Novels of Gissing, James, Hardy and Wells.* Aldershot, England; Burlington, Vt.: Ashgate, 2005.

Dolin, Tim, and Peter Widdowson, ed. *Thomas Hardy and Contemporary Literary Studies.* Houndmills, Basingstoke, Hampshire; New York: Palgrave Macmillan, 2004.

Fisher, Joe. *The Hidden Hardy.* New York: St. Martin's Press, 1992.

Gatrell, Simon. *Thomas Hardy's Vision of Wessex.* Houndmills, Basingstoke, Hampshire; New York: Palgrave Macmillan, 2003.

Gilmartin, Sophie, and Rod Mengham. *Thomas Hardy's Shorter Fiction: A Critical Study.* Edinburgh: Edinburgh University Press, 2007.

Green, Brian. *Hardy's Lyrics: Pearls of Pity.* New York: St. Martin's Press, 1996.

Hardy, Barbara. *Thomas Hardy: Imagining Imagination: Hardy's Poetry and Fiction*. London; New Brunswick, N.J.: Athlone Press; Somerset, N.J.: distributed in the U.S. by Transaction Publishers, 2000.

Harvey, Geoffrey. *The Complete Critical Guide to Thomas Hardy*. London; New York: Routledge, 2003.

Irwin, Michael. *Reading Hardy's Landscapes*. New York: St. Martin's Press, 2000.

Jann, Rosemary. "Hardy's Rustics and the Construction of Class." *Victorian Literature and Culture* 28, no. 2 (2000): 411–25.

Joh, Byunghwa. *Thomas Hardy's Poetry: A Jungian Perspective*. New York: Peter Lang, 2002.

Johnson, Trevor. "'A Unique Quality of Elegiac Feeling': Hardy's 'During Wind and Rain.'" *Thomas Hardy Yearbook* 33 (2002): 20–27.

Jurta, Roxanne. "'Not-So-New' Sue: The Myth of *Jude the Obscure* as a New Woman Novel." *Journal of the Eighteen Nineties Society* 26 (1999): 13–21.

Knowles, Ronald. "Thomas Hardy: Elements of the Tragic." *Thomas Hardy Journal* 22 (Autumn 2006): 223–34.

Lanzano, Ellen Anne. *Hardy: The Temporal Poetics*. New York: Peter Lang, 1999.

Mallett, Phillip, ed. *Palgrave Advances in Thomas Hardy Studies*. Houndmills, Basingstoke, Hampshire; New York: Palgrave Macmillan, 2004.

Mattisson, Jane. *Knowledge and Survival in the Novels of Thomas Hardy*. Lund: Lund University, 2002.

Matz, Aaron. "Terminal Satire and *Jude the Obscure*." *ELH* 73, no. 2 (Summer 2006): 519–47.

McEathron, Scott, ed. *Thomas Hardy's* Tess of the d'Urbervilles: *A Sourcebook*. London; New York: Routledge, 2005.

Miller, J. Hillis. *Thomas Hardy, Distance and Desire*. Cambridge, Mass.: Belknap Press of Harvard University Press, 1970.

Moore, Kevin Z. *The Descent of the Imagination: Postromantic Culture in the Later Novels of Thomas Hardy*. New York: New York University Press, 1990.

Musselwhite, David. *Social Transformations in Hardy's Tragic Novels: Megamachines and Phantasms*. New York: Palgrave Macmillan, 2003.

Mustafa, Jamil. "'A Good Horror Has Its Place in Art': Hardy's Gothic Strategy in *Tess of the d'Urbervilles*." *Studies in the Humanities* 32, no. 2 (December 2005): 93–115.

Neill, Edward. *The Secret Life of Thomas Hardy: "Retaliatory Fiction."* Aldershot, Hampshire, England; Burlington, Vt.: Ashgate, 2004.

Nicholson, Sarah. "The Woman Pays: Death and the Ambivalence of Providence in Hardy's Novels." *Literature & Theology* 16, no. 1 (March 2002): 27–39.

O'Malley, Patrick R. "Oxford's Ghosts: *Jude the Obscure* and the End of the Gothic." *Modern Fiction Studies* 46, no. 3 (Fall 2000): 646–71.

Page, Norman. *Thomas Hardy: The Novels*. Houndmills, Basingstoke, Hampshire; New York: Palgrave, 2001.

Persoon, James. *Hardy's Early Poetry: Romanticism through a "dark bilberry eye."* Lanham, Md.: Lexington Books, 2000.

Pettit, Charles P. C., ed. *Celebrating Thomas Hardy: Insights and Appreciations*. Houndmills MacMillan Press Limited: New York: St. Martin's Press, 1996.

———. *New Perspectives on Thomas Hardy*. New York: St. Martin's Press, 1994.

Plotz, John. *Going Local: Characters and Environments in Thomas Hardy's Wessex*. Princeton, N.J.: Princeton University Press, 2008.

Pritchard, William H. Hardy's Poetry of Old Age." *Literary Imagination: The Review of the Association of Literary Scholars and Critics* 6, no. 1 (Winter 2004): 78–93.

Radford, Andrew. "The Making of a Goddess: Hardy, Lawrence and Persephone." *Connotations: A Journal for Critical Debate* 12, nos. 2–3 (2002–2003): 202–32.

Ray, Martin. *Thomas Hardy: A Textual Study of the Short Stories*. Aldershot, Hants, England: Brookfield, Vt.: Ashgate, 1997.

Schoenfeld, Lois Bethe. *Dysfunctional Families in the Wessex Novels of Thomas Hardy*. Lanham, Md.: University Press of America, 2005.

Stave, Shirley A. *The Decline of the Goddess: Nature, Culture, and Women in Thomas Hardy's Fiction*. Westport, Conn.: Greenwood Press, 1995.

Sternlieb, Lisa. "'Three Leahs to Get One Rachel': Redundant Women in *Tess of the d'Urbervilles*." *Dickens Studies Annual: Essays on Victorian Fiction* 29 (2000): 351–65.

Sumner, Rosemary. *A Route to Modernism: Hardy, Lawrence, Woolf*. New York: St. Martin's Press, 2000.

Taylor, Dennis. *Hardy's Literary Language and Victorian Philology*. Oxford: Clarendon Press; New York: Oxford University Press, 1993.

Thomas, Jane. *Thomas Hardy, Femininity and Dissent: Reassessing the Minor Novels*. New York: St. Martin's Press, 1999.

Ward, John Powell. *Thomas Hardy's Poetry*. Buckingham; Philadelphia: Open University Press, 1993.

Widdowson, Peter. *Thomas Hardy: Late Essays and Earlier*. Houndmills, Basingstoke, Hampshire: Macmillan Press; New York: St. Martin's Press, 1998.

Wright, T. R. *Hardy and His Readers*. Houndmills, Basingstoke, Hampshire; New York: Palgrave Macmillan, 2003.

Zeitler, Michael A. *Representations of Culture: Thomas Hardy's Wessex & Victorian Anthropology*. New York: Peter Lang, 2007.

Acknowledgments

Trevor Johnson, "Hardy's Poetry: A General Survey." From *A Critical Introduction to the Poems of Thomas Hardy*. © 1991 by Henry Anthony Trevor Johnson. Published by Macmillan Education Ltd. and reproduced with permission of Palgrave Macmillan.

Simon Gatrell, "*The Mayor of Casterbridge*: The Fate of Michael Henchard's Character." From *Thomas Hardy and the Proper Study of Mankind*. © 1993 Simon Gatrell. Reproduced by permission of the University of Virginia Press.

Peter Widdowson, "'Moments of Vision': Postmodernising *Tess of the d'Urbervilles*; or, *Tess of the d'Urbervilles* Faithfully Presented by Peter Widdowson." From *New Perspectives on Thomas Hardy*, edited by Charles P. C. Pettit, published by St. Martin's Press. © 1994 by Peter Widdowson.

Robert Schweik, "The 'Modernity' of Hardy's *Jude the Obscure*." From *A Spacious Vision: Essays on Hardy*, edited by Phillip V. Mallett and Ronald P. Draper, published by the Patten Press. © 1994 by Robert Schweik.

Samuel Hynes, "How to Be an Old Poet: The Examples of Hardy and Yeats." From *Reading Thomas Hardy*, edited by Charles P. C. Pettit. © 1998 by Samuel Hynes. Reprinted by permission of SLL/Sterling Lord Literistic, Inc.

Michael Irwin, "From Fascination to Listlessness: Hardy's Depiction of Love." From *Reading Thomas Hardy*, edited by Charles P. C. Pettit, published by St. Martin's Press. © 1998 by Michael Irwin.

Douglas Dunn, "Thomas Hardy's Narrative Art: The Poems and Short Stories." From *The Achievement of Thomas Hardy*, edited by Phillip Mallett. © 2000 by Macmillan Press Ltd. Reproduced with permission of Palgrave Macmillan.

William Kerrigan, "Eight Great Hardys." From *Raritan* 21, no. 3 (Winter 2002): 76–99. © 2002 by Raritan.

Index

189